THE VALLEY OF HEART'S DELIGHT

A Silicon Valley Notebook
1963–2001

Michael S. Malone

John Wiley & Sons, Inc.

Published by John Wiley & Sons, Inc., New York.

Published simultaneously in Canada.

This publication is designed to provide accurate and authoritative information in regard to the subject matter covered. It is sold with the understanding that the publisher is not engaged in rendering professional services. If professional advice or other expert assistance is required, the services of a competent professional person should be sought.

ISBN: 0-471-20191-X

Printed in the United States of America.
10 9 8 7 6 5 4 3 2 1

To Carol
Who read my first writings, and
who will no doubt read my last.

FOREWORD

Silicon Valley is a young community with a rich history. It is only about fifty years old, dating from the mid-1950s, when William Shockley came home to Palo Alto with his Nobel Prize and set out to create a business empire.

His enterprise failed but the defection of Dr. Robert Noyce and seven other key employees to form Fairchild Semiconductor was the seminal event in the history of what is now known as Silicon Valley. Fairchild in time failed as well and to some extent for the same reason that Shockley failed: An inability to align its objectives with the hopes and dreams of a new generation of techno-entrepreneurs. Over the years, the talent that made Fairchild a star, was scattered all over Santa Clara Valley and the adjoining San Francisco peninsula . . . and Silicon Valley was born.

All of this is a well-known story; taught these days in schools around the world. With good reason: From that tiny (if volatile) start, Silicon Valley grew.

I am probably the only person still leading a business in our industry who saw this story unfold firsthand. I was one of those

v

"Fairchildren" who founded the Valley. I joined the company at the age of 24 in early 1961, rose through the management ranks at a heady pace, became worldwide director of sales and marketing at a shockingly young age and joined the Fairchild diaspora in 1968. I then—with luck and the grace of God, stubborn determination, and the help of many very bright and dedicated people—built one of the Valley's best-known companies, AMD. In 2000, AMD earned $1 billion on over $4.5 billion in sales. Today more than one of every five PCs produced in the world are powered by an AMD Athlon Family microprocessor (XP). The AMD Athlon XP is the highest performance PC processor in the world.

A lot of D.I. water has passed over a lot of wafers since the early days of Silicon Valley leading to today's fame and fortune. It wasn't a quest for fame and fortune that drove us in those early years of isolation and struggle. It was passion—a passion to develop, proliferate, and evangelize technology to empower people everywhere to lead more productive lives. We were trying to sell a revolution . . . and few people were listening.

One person who did listen was, of all people, a local kid, barely out of his teens, working in public relations at Hewlett-Packard Co. We first learned of him when the *San Jose Mercury News* business section suddenly, and more than belatedly, began to regularly cover the electronics industry in its own backyard. It wasn't long before we noticed the by-line: "Michael S. Malone."

Who was this kid? We'd certainly never seen his name in the trade magazines. He didn't seem to be a technologist, but he knew about technology. As his stories began to evolve from simple news stories to thoughtful features, it soon became apparent that this young reporter was less a business writer than a human interest reporter. Needless to say, such long-awaited attention was more than a little gratifying.

And then, he disappeared as suddenly as he had arrived. He simply walked out of the *Mercury-News* . . . to be replaced, over the years, by an army of reporters. The *Mercury-News* eventually became "the newspaper of Silicon Valley" and employed many fine high-tech journalists. But Malone was the first, and none since have ever gotten so deeply into our heads.

Within a few months, Mike Malone reappeared, now writing for a consortium of newspapers, including the *New York Times*. Then one day, he called, said he was writing his first book, and asked for an interview.

As you may know by my reputation, I am not afraid to talk with anyone. Nor have I ever passed up an opportunity to tell our story. Nevertheless, the call filled me with trepidation. Malone, writing what would become his history of Silicon Valley, *The Big Score*, didn't just want to talk to me about AMD's history, or our chip products, he wanted the story of my life.

It is a story with an unhappy beginning, one that I'd resisted discussing publicly until then. Now here came Malone with his tape recorder, his innocent round Irish face topped by a head full of boyish black curls. We had talked on several occasions before, mostly at my speeches or press conferences. But this was a private one-on-one; it would last three hours.

For the first time, I watched Malone close up, and experienced the technique he would use on hundreds of others (including me, fifteen years later) in magazine profiles and public television series. He had a casual, intimate style, like the neighborhood kid just back from college. And his interview technique was oddly oblique; the questions seemed to come in sideways, leaving blank spaces that induced one to keep talking long after you'd planned to stop. It was disarming—and in the end I gave Malone everything he asked for, telling him things I'd never told a journalist, even many of my friends, before.

When the chapter appeared, it sent out shockwaves—to my employees and to my peers in Silicon Valley, but most of all, to my family. Some of my relatives never forgave me.

Do I regret it? Sure, you always regret things that cause others pain and anguish. But I would do it again—and in fact, did do it again—with Mike Malone. The reason, I think, is that there is something deeply human, and humane, in everything he writes. Even when he was an ambitious young reporter on the run, trying to make his name with big stories and shocking language, there was always that other, warm-blooded core in his writing. As he's grown older, as the need to shock has fallen away, that other side has come to the fore, producing some of the most memorable writing of the digital age. It's a long ways from "Has Silicon Valley Gone Pussy?" to the celebrated *Big Issue* essays, from that nervous, curly-haired post-adolescent to the veteran author just beginning to gray that I see today, yet in all the important ways Mike Malone hasn't really changed.

Perhaps that is because he is also the most literary of technology writers. He is always telling the stories of the people behind the tech, from the assembly line workers, to the anxious young entrepreneurs, to even aging semiconductor company CEOs. He often writes about the Valleyite he knows best: himself. Because of this, because he hasn't had his head turned by the latest gadget in a long, long time, Malone has gained a unique perspective on Silicon Valley and the high-tech revolution. It's that perspective that often makes him, like all of us who have been up and down the long roller coaster ride of high tech, seem a skeptic during the good times and an optimist when times are bad.

It is that same perspective, almost unique among tech and business writers, that has always enabled Malone to step back and look at the larger historical, even philosophical, forces behind the crazy, hyperaccelerated world in which people like me work. His old employer, the *Mercury-News*, a few years ago called Malone "the Boswell of Silicon Valley." There's a lot of truth in that. Mike Malone has been less a reporter than our historian in real time. When the world today—and probably for generations to come—thinks of Silicon Valley and the Digital Age, it often uses Malone's imagery. So too with people: from near deities like Hewlett, Packard, Noyce, and Moore, to the tortured volatile Steve Jobs . . . even to the "flamboyant" Jerry Sanders, Malone has given us all a kind of immortality in words that may rival or surpass in longevity the great companies that we've built.

For that I am thankful, if a bit disconcerted. I still remind myself to be very, very careful of what I say when being interviewed by Mike Malone. Then after a few minutes of small talk and friendly conversation, I am ready once again to tell him nearly everything. Soon I almost don't even notice that the notebook is open and the recorder is running . . . almost.

JERRY SANDERS
Founder, Chairman, and CEO, AMD
and recipient of the
American Electronics Association
2001 Medal of Achievement Award

ACKNOWLEDGMENTS

For a book that covers a career's worth of work, acknowledging everyone who has ever helped you is an impossible task. There have been hundreds of editors, copyeditors, and fact checkers who have worked on my stories over the years. There has also been a long line of teachers, professional peers, and friends who have given me good advice on story ideas and style. I am thankful for each and every one of them, and I hope this book is a testament to your good works.

What I can do is identify those individuals whose contribution to my work was critical and decisive. I suppose for some people, the path to becoming a professional writer is straight and true, but in my case it has always been two steps forward and one step back. Every time I thought I knew what I was doing, some wiser, older veteran always stepped up to knock some sense back into me. Thank God.

Among my teachers, several stand above the rest. At the beginning, there was Mrs. Worth, who taught me to love knowledge and Mrs. Arwine, who taught me to pursue an artistic life. At the end of my schooling, Chris Leviestro supported my work even at its worst, and Jim Degnan prepared me, often painfully, for what the life of a professional writer would really be like.

As I entered my working life, I was privileged to be mentored by two remarkable groups: First, at Hewlett-Packard, the men and women in the corporate public relations department (notably David Kirby, Ross Snyder, Peter Nelson, and John Kane) did more than anyone, before or since, to teach me how to stop writing for myself and start writing for others. Then, at the *San Jose Mercury-News,* my editors, Jim Mitchell and Jack Sirard, forced me to write tight, on deadline, and to strip away everything superfluous. I only wish I'd learned their lessons better.

Beginning with my departure from the *Merc* in 1980, my career has largely been one of a freelancer, working for one editor after another at different publications. Several have been particularly influential in my career. Chief among them is Rich Karlgaard, who as editor of *Upside* and then *Forbes ASAP,* gave me almost carte blanche to write the most creative, controversial, and thoughtful pieces I could. It was Rich who supported me in the creation of the *ASAP Big Issue,* which enabled not only me, but dozens of far better writers, to produce some of the best essays of our careers. It was also Rich who recommended me to replace him as *ASAP* editor.

Among others who provided the opportunity to write at the limits of my abilities were Eric Nee and Richard Brandt, Karlgaard's successors at *Upside;* Karen Southwick, then also of *Upside,* the editor of my serialized novel in that magazine, and my superb lieutenant at *ASAP;* and Alan Webber and Bill Taylor, the founders of Fast Company. At the *Wall Street Journal,* Tim Ferguson and, more recently, Max Boot, have given me the opportunity to be the voice of Silicon Valley on the national stage. At the *Mercury-News' West Magazine,* first Jeffrey Klein and then Patrick Dillon, let me push the limits of local feature writing . . . and Pat, as my successor at *ASAP,* continues to give me brilliant advice and masterful editing. Finally, but far from least, Ed Clendaniel, the

Acknowledgments

Perspective section editor of the *Merc* (and now a compatriot at *ASAP*), allowed me to play with all of the conventions of editorial writing, taking a considerable career risk of his own in the process. I am not a good enough writer to express the depth of my gratitude to all of them.

I entered the world of book writing with the tag team help of three men: Valley icon Regis McKenna, novelist Niven Bush, and editor Luther Nichols. As elsewhere, my subsequent career as an author has been peripatetic, hopping from one publisher to the next; with each book forging deep relationships with individual editors, only to move on long before the book hit the remainder shelves. Three editors, though, were particularly influential: Adrian Zackheim, then of Doubleday, because we were both at the beginning of our careers; Alan Wylde, then of Springer-Verlag, because he was a friend and neighbor long before he became my editor; and Ed Burlingame, then of HarperCollins, because he was a consummate professional.

What has never changed in my book writing career is the presence of my agent, the legendary Don Congdon. Almost 20 years ago, he took on this neophyte author and with infinite patience and wonderful, instructional stories, has guided me now through 11 books. I only hope he thinks it was worth it.

Finally, in the end, no group of people has more influence on one's career than family, friends, and professional peers. In the Introduction, I list many of the great reporters with whom I've worked. Here I'll make mention of fellow writers whose work I've shared, who've set the standard for professionalism, or whose friendship I've cherished. They include Leigh Weimers, Bob Grove, Owen Edwards, Paul Gigot, Bill Davidow, Tom Hayes, Tom Siebel, Leif Edvinsson, Kathy Rebello, Brenna Bolger, and Adam Glenn. To them I add the only two men who have ever given me jobs in journalism, Larry Jenks and Tim Forbes; and the two extraordinary women, whose assistance has been more vital than any employer:

ACKNOWLEDGMENTS

Marge Martich at the beginning and Ann McAdam today. It was Ann, in fact, who compiled and edited this book, with the assistance of Mike Boland and Brandon Russell of *Forbes*, Gloria Emelson, and Sue Chenoweth from the *San Jose Mercury-News*.

No one can ever truly value the day-to-day support of one's own family. My parents swallowed hard when I chose this career, yet were unflinching in their support. With them behind me, I knew I couldn't fail. It was same with my sister Edie, my lifelong pal Craig Windmueller, and my adult buddy Paul Derania. By the same token, there is no way to fully thank my wife and children for the sacrifices they made to my career. For my wife Carol, I hope the nearby dedication begins that process.

CONTENTS

CONTENTS

PART III
Silicon Town

PART IV
Silicon World

PART V
Silicon Home

INTRODUCTION

A Silicon Neighborhood

A dozen years ago, when I was researching my first book, on the history of Silicon Valley, I received a phone call from my mother. She and my dad had been cleaning out the den and had come across an old binder full of school papers. Did I want them?

They proved to be a collection of one-page geography reports, written, it appeared, by a class of fourth graders. Interesting enough in a nostalgic way, but as I thumbed through the sheets I was struck that I didn't recognize the names. Obviously, it's easy to forget the names of your elementary school classmates, but these names had no ring of familiarity at all. Who were these kids?

Then I saw a name I knew: Steven Jobs.

I'd often written that Silicon Valley, for all its fame, was in fact a very large small town, and that if you lived there you would eventually meet, work for or against, or sleep with every one of your neighbors. But this was carrying things a little too far. It seemed that somehow, in about 1965, I'd picked up a stack of papers belonging to my best friend's younger brother. And now here was a memento of a young boy who would one day be among the most famous names of his generation.

It would be easy to say that I knew who Steve Jobs was back on the playground of Monta Loma School in Mountain View, but to a sixth grader, fourth graders were little more than vermin. We wouldn't formally meet for another 15 years.

By odd coincidence, just a few weeks later, I had dinner with Jobs at a Japanese restaurant in Cupertino, a half block from Apple Computer headquarters. The restaurant was across the street from the Donut Wheel where I (and a suspect Jobs, too) used to stop as a teenager at 3 A.M. on the way home from dates. Just for fun, I kicked off the interview by handing Steve his old geography report. He eyed me suspiciously, "Where did you get this?" For him, it was not a joke. Five months hence, at the now-legendary Macintosh introduction, Steve Jobs would burst in the world's consciousness as a unique and fully formed character—half hippie shaman, half tech savant. He was already busy constructing that persona that night . . . and the last thing he needed was a reporter who seemed to have a dossier on his entire life.

After Macintosh, as the world began to ask where this extraordinary figure had come from, I remembered that geography report and the neighborhood in which we grew up. The little suburban ranch houses, with their antagonistic populations of long-established blue collar workers and newly arrived professionals come West for jobs at NASA, Lockheed Martin, or Hewlett-Packard. It was the recipe for class tension, and much of it found its release, in escalating degrees of violence, at Monta Loma, Crittenden Middle School, and Mountain View High School. We all had our share of fights, usually lost, and we grew to dread going to school each day. In the end, in the internal migration that has always characterized Silicon Valley, we moved upscale to Sunnyvale. The Jobs's did too, to a house just down the street from mine. The difference was that Steve's family had moved on Steve's demand, an early lesson that did much to explain his confidence, bordering on monomania, to come.

In the early 1970s, I used to see Jobs, with his two friends: Bill Fernandez, son of my Sunday School teacher, and an older Steve Wozniak, who swam butterfly on the local swim team with several of my buddies. I knew Woz was some kind of technical genius because I'd seen a computer he'd built at a science fair. I'd also met some his hacker counterparts at one of the groups, an Explorer Post at NASA Ames Research Center that was a precursor of the Homebrew Computer Club. Now Woz, Jobs, and Fernandez were just three scruffy longhairs loitering in the back of Owen Whetzel's hobby shop in our neighborhood shopping center. We all thought they were buying alligator clips for smoking joints, not for building the Apple I computer and changing the course of civilization.

It was about this time that *Electronic News* reporter Don Hoeffler first gave Silicon Valley its name. But for most of us, it would remain Santa Clara Valley for at least another decade. I often passed the Fairchild building on my way out to Moffett Field; and one buddy's girlfriend had a father who was an executive at Intel, but these were just two of the many buildings popping up out of orchards all over the Valley. I scarcely noticed as some of my neighbors, continuing the upward Valley migration that began in Mountain View, took their brand new high-tech wealth and decamped from Sunnyvale to big houses in nearby hill towns of Saratoga, Los Altos, and Woodside. Meanwhile, I picked cherries and got shot at with rock salt trying to sneak through the orchard down the street. My girlfriend (who would one day be my wife) spent her summers cutting apricots at the Mariani's plant in Cupertino. She still has the scars. Out of college, imagining myself a great writer because I'd written an obscene column for the Santa Clara University newspaper, I took a job in public relations at Hewlett-Packard Co. (HP). Despite a disastrous job interview, I was nevertheless hired by HP's rising young star, the supernaturally self-assured Ed Mc-Cracken (later chairman of Silicon Graphics) and wrote an endless stream of press releases for executives like Bill Krause (later founder of 3Com) and HP clients like Sandra Kurtzig of Ask.

I was working on an MBA at Santa Clara University at the same time, but my real education was at Hewlett-Packard. The veteran writers who made up HP Corporate Public Relations (PR) were tough enough to show me I didn't know a damn thing about writing, and kind enough to apprentice me into doing it right. Almost everything I know today about reporting and writing comes from them. Meanwhile, working inside a big corporation gave me an understanding of the human side of business that wasn't in any of my grad school textbooks. And I had my first encounter with two great men: Bill Hewlett and David Packard, already billionaires, who nevertheless sat next to me on a bench in the HP lunchroom. In years to come, I would judge many a Valley executive by Bill's and Dave's impossibly high standards.

For the moment though, I turned out to be a very good PR man. It is a curse in this life to be talented at something you don't want to do. I knew within months that I didn't want to be a flack the rest of my life. It tore my guts to see some reporter for *Electronic News* steal my best lines and present them as his own. Public relations is about professional pride and literary humility. By comparison, I didn't care about either—I just wanted my own by-line. I was a newsy at heart. And so, at 26, I left the perfect job in the greatest company on the planet and went to work in the cruddy, unfriendly newsroom of a major American daily, the *San Jose Mercury-News*. I wanted to be a feature writer, but instead I was made into a business writer—in fact, the world's first daily high-tech reporter.

It was not a prestigious position in 1980. But it had its benefits, among them the opportunity to have long drunken lunches with Don Hoeffler, by then the most notorious newsletter writer in the business. It was in those pages where I first learned the names of the Valley's most famous leaders—Charlie Sporck, Marshall Cox, Jerry Sanders, Robert Noyce—men I would later know well.

Don Hoeffler taught me that Silicon Valley was more than just a story of technology and business, it was also a place of giant personalities, of epic feuds and heroic friendships. It was a people story even more than a technological story. Most of all, that if you could understand the personalities and interrelationships of these people, you would have an unmatched understanding of how the Valley worked, why firms failed and why they succeeded.

It was at one of these lunches that Hoeffler offered me his newsletter. He would own it, I would write it. It was an enormous honor, even though Don's reputation had been diminished by too many inaccurate one-source stories and too much booze (the first would destroy him, the second would kill him). The job would have meant instant fame, at least in high tech, and the power that comes with fear. But I turned it down, because I was too young, too inexperienced and mostly too scared to take on such a business by myself. Nevertheless, I came away from the experience with an unquenchable desire to tell the real story of Silicon Valley, the way Hoeffler did at his best. And I knew I wasn't going to get there writing sales-and-earnings stories for the business section. So I buried myself in the dark side of Valley life, trying to dig up the hidden truths that everyone whispered about but no one had ever verified. I was lucky to partner with two great reporters who made up for my lack of skills. With the late Susan Yoachum (later the political editor of the *San Francisco Chronicle*), a Texas girl no older than me, we broke a four-part series that first exposed the rampant use—and abuse—of toxic chemicals in Silicon Valley. Nothing I have done since has had as much impact on the daily life of my community. It cost local companies an estimated $200 million in pollution control equipment . . . but the Valley, as it always does with its townies, forgave me my sins.

Next I had the honor to work with Peter Carey, now a shared Pulitzer Prize winner and, one of the best reporters in the country. Carey gave me only a glimpse of the skills he would later use to help pull down Ferdinand Edralin Marcos, but that was enough. Together, we spent two years taking on every taboo subject we could find. Drugs, gold thievery, sweatshops, and espionage. We ran stings, interviewed criminals and junkies, chased revolutionary groups and spies, and generally made Silicon Valley—having grown complacent in its image as America's cleanest and safest industry—squirm. I had the time of my life. There were moments when I felt like I understood Silicon Valley better than anyone alive.

Looking back, I realize that this was a phase in my growing-up as a writer and as a citizen of Silicon Valley. It was my career adolescence. I felt betrayed by my town, and now I was intent on showing the Naked Silicon Valley, to strip away the veil of hypocrisy I saw around me—and to earn a little respect of my own in the process. My father, who'd been a spy, warned me about the dangers of "cops disease," but I dismissed the idea. I would never grow cynical or take seriously my acquaintance with the rich and famous, or flex my new power. And of course I did all of those things. I grew contemptuous of Silicon Valley, while at the same time flaunting my influence in it.

And yet, after everything, there were still the stories. I was lucky enough to be living in, and recording, one of the most extraordinary eras in human history. Those businessmen and scientists, my neighbors, were seeing their wildest dreams come true. They and their companies were becoming the stuff of legends. People I had known or worked with were now cover stories in *Fortune* and *Business Week*. I was talking on a daily basis to men and women whose names would be taught to schoolchildren a hundred years hence. It had happened so unexpectedly. Every community thinks it is the center of the world. But here it came true. When *Newsweek* devoted a cover to America's new billionaires, I realized to my shock that I knew half of them. And at a 1980 conference in New Orleans, I sat next to a mousy young man who would one day be the richest man in the world.

As Silicon Valley grew more famous, so too did it become the object of more attention by the press. By the time I left the *San Jose Mercury-News* in 1983, there were already dozens of computer and high-tech business magazines. Ten years later there were hundreds.

Each had staked out a little corner of the business as its reporting territory. And because they were dependent on a few big advertisers, most were, if not in the pocket of one or two companies, than of an entire industry. And the stories they carried were almost always about technology, not people.

In Silicon Valley, by the 1980s, those who weren't inventing new products were making a living writing about them. But I had already lost interest in the novelty of technology after all those daily articles for the *San Jose Mercury-News* business pages. I'd done more than my share of announcing with great fanfare new technologies that never went anywhere, and hot new products nobody wanted. I'd also been fooled one too many times by an interesting new company with an exciting product and a charismatic management that disintegrated within weeks after my writing a laudatory article about it.

Meanwhile, I looked right at some of the greatest products of the era, and walked down the hallways of some of the most famous companies-to-be . . . and utterly missed their future importance.

Luckily, I wasn't alone.

I would continue to write about these technologies and products and business—I continue to this day—but it would never again be enough. The real story—at least the real story for me—was the inner workings of daily life in my hometown, in the souls of my neighbors. What was it about this community that had made it Ground Zero of the electronics revolution? What made a person into an entrepreneur? What possessed people to commit their entire lives to a single project or company or leader? And perhaps most important of all, how long could this miracle last?

But I had no idea of how to tell this story. Even if I did, I no longer had a job or even an outlet for such writing. I was living with my wife-to-be in a converted chicken coop in the foothills of Monte Vista. The electronics revolution was beginning to explode around me, and I seemed to be sliding backwards. My annual income at age 30 was half what it was at 23. I was searching for a career that I could run by myself. Without planning it, like a true child of Silicon Valley, I had become an entrepreneur. The career I did create for myself over the next decade was as much to the credit of some adventurous editors as to any talent of my own. It was they who took the greatest risk, publishing eccentric, often controversial articles, usually written in a form they'd never published before. They put their careers and reputations on the line. By comparison, I had nothing to lose.

My search for the soul of Silicon Valley took me in many strange directions, and into the unlikeliest literary forms: saloon reviews, obituaries, poetry exegeses, rants, satires, even fiction. I set up my own newspaper syndicate, writing stories on my Apple III and transmitting them at 2400 baud to *the Boston Globe, Dallas Morning News,* and the *International Herald-Tribune.* It was Jeffrey Klein, editor of the *Mercury-News West* magazine (later editor of *Mother Jones*) who took the first and biggest risk. Jeffrey allowed me to try literary saloon reviews, epic obituaries, and most importantly, a satirical deconstruction of the Valley's power brokers. He suffered for it, but never flinched. The "100 Most Powerful" article in turn served as a model for a cheeky new magazine, *Upside,* being created by two crazy young publishing entrepreneurs named Rich Karlgaard and Tony Perkins. Rich and Tony set me loose to write anything I wanted. The result was the stories (for good and bad) that are most associated with my name. After five remarkable years, Rich left to run *Forbes ASAP,* the distinguished magazine for which

I've perhaps done the best writing of my career, and Tony founded the wildly successful *Red Herring*. Meanwhile, I continued writing for *Upside*. Through a succession of editors—Eric Nee, Karen Southwick, Richard Brandt, *Upside* remained the one publication that consistently allowed me to try anything, from hard reporting, to outrageously opinionated essays . . . even to serializing a novel. It was the creative playground every writer dreams of.

Others took great chances with me as well. Ed Clendaniel, editor of the Sunday Perspective section of the *San Jose Mercury-News*, let me use a Sunday op-ed section as a platform for everything from jeremiads about the state of historic preservation in the Valley to essays linking seventeenth-century metaphysical poetry with modern high-tech Life.

Even the Gray Lady herself had a fling with me. In 1984, John Lee, then business editor of the *New York Times*, came out to California on a visit. I'd been freelancing to the *Times* for a few years, and now he approached me about taking a job. I reluctantly turned him down because of the paper's requirement of five year's work in New York (how could you cover Silicon Valley from Manhattan?); but before he left, Lee did give me the title of my first book. It was a nice parting gift. A decade later, the *Times* called again, this time to ask if I'd be a writer of its Executive Life column. I was happy to accept, and spent a couple years describing the odd and compelling lifestyles of the Valley's rich and powerful. And every time I talked to the curt, overworked, and terrified editors back in New York, I secretly thanked God that I'd made the right decision years before.

As I write this, I am on the eve of turning 48 years old, about the age Don Hoeffler was when he renamed my town. In many other professions, I would still be a young punk, but here I am among the old timers. I've been on hand to see the transition of my town from orchards to semiconductor chips to computers to the World Wide Web. After all these years, I've reluctantly learned that

Silicon Valley is in fact just a handful of stories told over and over with slight variations. And yet, I still find every one of those stories compelling. Each time I return from someplace in the world where I've been asked to describe the miracle of Silicon Valley, I still look down out the plane window and thrill at the miracle of the place, the little collection of suburban towns that changed history. And I feel infinitely lucky to have called his place my hometown—a place so dynamic, so protean, and so maddeningly complex that I will never grow tired of it. I am not alone. Regis McKenna once famously said that Silicon Valley is "a state of mind." It sounded good, but I knew better. That's because Regis has been my neighbor since he was a young PR executive at National Semiconductor and I was a troublesome eighth grader. At 20 I ran the publicity for Dianne McKenna's first campaign for office in Sunnyvale. It was a joint ticket with a guy I worked with at Hewlett-Packard, Dave Barram. Diane won, ultimately becoming a County Supervisor. Dave lost, ultimately becoming U.S. Under-Secretary of Commerce, then director of the General Services Administration. Thus, even as he was describing the Valley as an intellectual construct, Regis McKenna was planting roots into its soil. Proof of that came with the big money—when the McKennas chose not to leave Sunnyvale for one of the wealthy enclaves in the surrounding hills, but merely moved to a bigger, older house down the street. They were home. And so am I. I'm still a neighbor of the McKennas, having bought my own historic home, the survivor of another California Gold Rush, now incongruously nestled within miles of tract houses. There my wife and I are raising our sons, trying to prepare them for an almost unimaginable future. It isn't easy. The cost of living grows by the month, the traffic is worse than ever, and every square inch of the old Santa Clara Valley, the Valley of Heart's Delight, is buried under the asphalt and concrete of Silicon Valley.

And yet, the heart can delight in this new Valley, too. In its rhythms, in the entrepreneurial vitality that fills the air the way the fragrance of fruit blossoms once did, and most of all in the thrill of being in the cockpit of one of the greatest technological and social transformations in human history. When will it end? I knowingly predicted Silicon Valley's imminent demise in 1980, 1985, 1989, and 1994. Eventually, I learned my lesson. The rest of the media world obviously has not—regularly indulging in yet another paroxysm of features about how the Valley is losing its crown to Austin, Orange County, Bangalore, even Boise).

Perhaps. All I know is just months after the last time I predicted the Valley's end, I found myself regularly having lunch in a Chinese restaurant in Campbell with two young entrepreneurs.

At the end of the meal, we would all dig in our pockets to come up with the 20 bucks for the bill. The company they were building was called eBay.

Now, once again, as the papers cover the last heartbeats of the dot.com boom, I am again meeting brilliant young entrepreneurs busily creating the next generation of great companies. After almost 40 years in Silicon Valley, I still see miracles occurring on a regular basis. What follows is a history of Silicon Valley told—in news stories, columns, editorials, magazine features, even fiction —as it occurred. The chapters were chosen not for their completeness—that awaits some future history—but for their ability to capture the tenor of their times. As with any "first drafts of history," there are errors of fact, of prediction, and, I'm afraid to say, weak reporting and bad writing. I've chosen to leave them intact, not only for the sake of truthfulness, but because they too capture something of the era.

The stories are also arrayed chronologically—not by the date they were written, but by the date of the subject. As a result, an article I wrote covering an immediate event in 1983 may appear in the book after an article written a decade later about Silicon Valley's early history.

This is not just a collection of reporting about an important socioeconomic phenomenon at the end of the twentieth century. Rather, it is a diary of one local boy desperate to understand the truth about his neighbors. Together, these essays, and stories and scraps of fiction, tell the story of the most amazing neighborhood in the world at the end of the twentieth century. I am proud to be a hometown boy.

MICHAEL S. MALONE

Sunnyvale, California

PART

I

SANTA CLARA VALLEY

1

SNOW TRACKS

In March 1936, an unusual confluence of forces occurred in Santa Clara County.

A long cold winter delayed the blossoming of the millions of cherry, apricot, peach, and prune plum trees covering hundreds of square miles of the Valley floor. Then, unlike many years, the rains that followed were light and too early to knock the blossoms from their branches.

Instead, by the billions, they all burst open at once. Seemingly overnight, the ocean of green that was the Valley turned into a low, soft, dizzyingly perfumed cloud of pink and white. Uncounted bees and yellow jackets, newly born, raced out of their hives and holes, overwhelmed by this impossible banquet.

Then came the wind.

It roared off the Pacific Ocean, through the nearly uninhabited passes of the Santa Cruz Mountains and then, flattening out, poured down into the great alluvial plains of the Valley. A tidal bore of warm air, it tore along the columns of trees, ripped the blossoms apart and carried them off in a fluttering flood of petals like foam rolling up a beach.

This perfumed blizzard hit Stevens Creek Boulevard, a two-lane road with a streetcar line down its center, that was the main road in the West Valley. It froze traffic, as drivers found themselves lost in a soft, muted whiteout. Only the streetcar, its path predetermined, passed on. . . .

I am haunted by this image of the little trolley soldiering its way through a fruit flower blizzard, its riders cocooned. One reason, I think, is that it presents something profoundly strange and unexpected about the hometown I know so well. Another is that it will never happen again. By the time the same combination of events occurred, the orchards were gone and the wind blew emptily through the parking lots of the emerging Silicon Valley. It is an experience lost forever.

But the biggest reason is that the past—or more precisely, some moment that contrasts neatly with today—is always a happier place. Agrarian people dream wistfully of the life of the hunter; democrats envy the sophistication of the aristocracy. Americans forever relive the bandstand and barbershop quartet world of 1910. And I console myself with images of the petal-bound trolley as I drive the treeless, six-lane arterial that is the modern Stevens Creek Boulevard, home of a hundred auto dealerships.

But the past is a lie, a trick of the mind. It is a fraud because our imaginations are too small to encompass even a single moment of it. Our Music Man vision of 1910 doesn't include diphtheria, the black Pullman porter in the background, or the Jacob Riis tenement scene on the other side of town. Our awe at the great British country houses doesn't also carry the knowledge that they were paid for on the backs of Haitian slaves.

Even my sweet little streetcar, bathed in petals, is more complex than my reveries will allow. It doesn't include the smeared goo on the windshield wipers, or the sour sweat unhappiness of the seasonal workers on board as they watch half of their annual income blow by. Most of all, my dream doesn't include the fact that a common itinerary for travelers on this trolley was to leave downtown San Jose, stop at Vic's Curve Inn and its 112-foot bar ("longest between LA and Frisco!") for a quick shot of courage before riding to the Cupertino terminus of the line, home of the Hoo Hoo House, the Valley's best bordello.

I know all these things, yet they don't intrude on my warm little trolley fantasy. They offer too much complexity and contradiction. The present is a movie, but the past is a photograph. And that is just how we like it. We never have to look to the next frame or pan the camera. We just choose the single image that holds us in its warm glow and ignore the messy rest. It may be a lie, but it is a welcome one. Unfortunately, it also means that we can never really go back. We can never answer the question: Was any time in the past really happier than now? As nice as it would be to know the answer, we would never trade that knowledge for the greater happiness that nostalgia provides.

But if the past offers only false comfort, then the only escape from the dreary quotidian present is into the future. Here on Stevens Creek Boulevard, in the heart of Silicon Valley, we have grown very adept at flinging ourselves forward in time. In the silicon gate, we have found a way to accelerate time. In digitizing ever more of the world, we have put vast territories of nature under a metronome set at presto.

Not only has the world grown faster, but so, we like to think, has our ability to look into the future. After all, if we know the beat, then we need only count the steps ahead to picture where the dance will take us.

But in fact, all we really see is a masquerade: ourselves and our world dressed up in strange clothes and operating even stranger technology. Just as our imaginations cannot encompass the past, neither can they imagine a future that is the consequence of a trillion random events and odd trajectories occurring between now and then. Most of all, we cannot imagine—or simply don't care— about a future without *us*.

Yet, though it too is a lie, the future offers one thing the past cannot. We can actually inhabit it. If the present is inhospitable, then we will race to the future . . . and if not there, then the future of that future. And if not there—and God knows, it probably won't be—then still further, until we are hurdling into the future atop our tools and powered by our technologies.

This is Nostalgia for the Future. It is Silicon Valley's greatest contribution to the age; an invention born in traffic jams on roads like Stevens Creek Boulevard. There is, of course, great irony—and perhaps even greater tragedy—in the idea of going faster and faster in order to stop. Yet, despite all of our doubts and fears, we will try it. We will take the risk because somewhere down that long rail, somewhere on our path between the saloon and the whorehouse, all of us weary and lonely riders may look up to find ourselves, if just for a brief moment, in a place where everything fades to silence and time appears to stop. A place where it rains flower petals.

Written in 2001. Previously unpublished

2

THE MISSION BELL'S TOLL

In the frenetic world of Silicon Valley, where the daily obsession is to shave a microsecond from every transmission, revision, and decision, a vital lesson about time lies unnoticed. As we spend billions struggling to glimpse just one product generation ahead, a prophecy about our future lies with two Ohlone Indian skulls buried to the eyeballs, cranium down, in a box of rice.

At the very heart of Silicon Valley sits Santa Clara University, an oasis of adobe buildings and gardens surrounded by a sea of industrial parks and suburban housing developments. And at the university's heart, literally and emotionally, is Mission Santa Clara, founded by the Franciscan order in 1777.

Around the mission lie rose gardens, wisteria walks, and one old adobe wall. Each tells a story. But the story told by the rose garden is the most terrible. There, beneath the thorns, and yellow and salmon and red petals, trapped within the deep and gnarled roots, are the skeletons of an untold number of Ohlone Indians, young and old, victims of smallpox and chicken pox, mumps and measles . . . but most of all, victims of the passage from one era to the next. They are the first valleyites to be sacrificed to the unforgiving passage of time.

The Ohlones ruled the valley for several thousand years. Yet now all that remains of them is a few dusty fragments tucked away in Tupperware bins in the abandoned football team locker room. There, in the remotest building on campus, archaeologist Russell Skowronek manages a staff of two assistants and five student volunteers as they race to save the artifacts from the oblivion of asphalt parking lots and poured concrete foundations. What they have found and cataloged is the detritus of America's manufacturing history, a rag-and-bone shop of early California culture: a poker chip, slate pencil, crockery toy marble, shriveled peach pits, the lower half of a glass mustard container, and other shattered and yellowed objects pulled from university grounds and the remains of a privy from a forgotten Santa Clara tannery. And, shockingly, the pair of Ohlone skulls in the desiccant. Sitting in the university's faculty club, Skowronek anxiously stirs his coffee. An energetic man with a long mustache, he speaks quickly, like a man used to not being heard.

"We're sitting right now on ground zero of the modern computer age," he says. "You already knew that. But what you didn't know is that it started 220 years ago."

Skowronek smiles. "Let me explain. Before 1777 the Ohlone Indians lived in a cyclical world. It hadn't changed in 10,000 years, not since the last Ice Age. There was really no sense of time being linear, only circular. The seasons came and went. You hunted or you planted. It was not a time-based world. In fact, despite our arrogance about how much better our lives are today, we estimate that it took only one adult Ohlone just 20 hours per week to feed and shelter his or her family."

It was not a long life, Skowronek continues, nor an especially complex one. The Ohlone lived in clans that rarely interacted—

except for the occasional fight or marriage—with neighboring clans just a half mile away. With little east-west trade, clans that lived just a mile from San Francisco Bay might never eat a fish or a clam but instead subsisted largely on deer and on acorns pounded into meal. The early European explorers of the region were frustrated when the guide from one clan would lead them only as far as the next stream and then refuse to go on in fear of losing his life.

"It all ended in January 1777, with the founding of the mission," says Skowronek. "Suddenly, the Ohlone found themselves in time—Western European time. Life at the mission was run by the bell. You got up, ate, prayed, worked, and signed off the day at midnight with the bell. And from the moment the mission bell rang for the first time, the clocks of Santa Clara Valley began—and they kept going faster every year."

It wasn't just the priests who were trapped in this time but the Ohlone as well. Having lived millennia without time, they had no resistance to the temporal march ringing each day from the mission tower.

Mission Santa Clara soon became the locus for all activity in the valley. Suddenly, clans that hadn't moved more than five miles in 500 years were crossing ancient boundaries and making regular visits to the mission to trade. Many chose to stay and live near the mission grounds. Stunted for generations, trade soon flourished, as did communications between clans. For the first time the Ohlone became a distinct tribe but in the process gave up the 50 subdialects and unique styles of family artisanship that had long distinguished them. Their arts and languages hybridized into single, common forms. In listening to the time bell, the Ohlone had embarked on a path from which there was no going back.

The Ohlone's vulnerability to the bell was emblematic of a lack of resistance to many things Western, most horribly contagion. In the first three decades of the mission's existence, hundreds of Ohlone died from epidemics of childhood diseases to which they had no immunity. Those baptized were buried in what is now the rose garden. But many others died from less obvious causes that nevertheless were tied to the Western European pattern of time: diet, overwork, industrial accidents, medicine, and the stress of living in a timed world.

"This new world not only changed the pace of the valley but even its look," says Skowronek. "The daily demands of commerce, faith, and schooling meant you had to build more and more buildings and homes. That meant roof tiles and adobe bricks, and that in turn meant kilns. And kilns meant charcoal, and that meant oak trees. And that deforested the valley floor, which meant no more acorns for the Ohlone. From now on they had no choice but to eat a Western diet and live a Western life."

By 1827 and the end of the valley's first modern era, Santa Clara Mission was home to 1,462 people. Spanish was now the lingua franca.

Tens of thousands of cattle roamed the valley floor, and the first vineyards were planted near the mission. Alta California, because of its unique location on the Pacific Rim, also rapidly became a center for trade in a global economy: The priests wore silk vestments from China, and mission residents regularly bought items imported from Acapulco and Mexico City, the Philippines, Spain, and even England.

The second revolution in valley life, which occurred in the decade after 1845, was as profound as the first, and it teaches the same lessons. One is that technological change not only produces wholly new types of products but it also forces the reorganization of the society around it. Furthermore, this reorganization is not just structural but temporal. Its participants physically and culturally restructure the world and society, and inhabit an irrevocably new timescape with its own unique rhythms and cycles.

The third lesson is the most disturbing: When a society encounters such a point of inflection, it divides into two groups. One group, usually the majority, which cannot or will not cross over to the new world, is lost. The other, the minority that does cross over, to be joined by the next generation and new arrivals, establishes a new identity so complete as to erase all traces of the people they were before.

"You see it at the mission during the first half of the nineteenth century," says Skowronek. "You start out with 50 clans, and almost overnight they become Ohlone Indians. Then come the Catalonian Spanish priests and the mestizo soldiers. Before long, they are Californians. Then, in the 1840s, the Anglos arrive. They are squatters—at least until the Bear Flag Revolt and the gold rush. Then they become 'pioneers.' It would be easy to say these are merely changes in nomenclature, mixed with some public relations. But in fact, these name changes represent a fundamental transformation. These before-and-after groups, even when they include the same people, inhabit very different worlds."

No group felt this change more than the Ohlone. The few who had survived the first revolution in time had, within a few years, stopped being Indians and became, in an odd metamorphosis, Mexicans. "Then," says Skowronek, "after U.S. statehood, they became, basically, nothing.

"They were disenfranchised, dehumanized. And in response they simply disappeared. They hid as best they could in the ethnic population, losing their Ohlone identity. Their descendants wouldn't emerge again until it was safe, in our time."

Meanwhile, the Spanish/Californians, too, became Mexicans and were largely marginalized as the valley filled with new immigrants—Irish, Italian, Yugoslavian (Americans)—who easily adapted to the new pace of life.

One of these was a German, Jacob Eberhard, who bought a tannery, itself the descendant of a tanning works that was as old as the mission, from his father-in-law. Lasting nearly 170 years until finally closing its doors after the Second World War, the tannery was the most enduring business in valley history. Eberhard brought the latest inventions and consumer products to the factory and his own home. By 1880, his home featured a privy and new Edison lights, and the tannery had become a giant complex of a dozen buildings beneath a towering, belching smokestack. The tannery was a foul-smelling, unpleasant place to work—and wasn't very popular at the new college campus across the street when the wind shifted. Nevertheless, it was on the cutting edge of American technology in the years after the Civil War. Leather was the plastic, the silicon, of the nineteenth century, and nobody made it better than Eberhard.

At its peak, the factory shipped 900,000 pounds of cow, calf, and sheep hides throughout the world, most notably to the shoe factories of Lowell, Massachusetts. But Eberhard wasn't just a mass producer of rendered flesh; he produced some of the best saddle leather on the planet, the finest of which became part of a bejeweled, silvered, and gilded $10,000 saddle ordered by the 101 Wild West Show. It was, according to contemporary accounts, "the most beautiful and high-priced saddle in the United States."

The world of the Eberhard Tannery in the 1880s was one of alarm clocks and pocket watches, factory whistles and train schedules. This was the new timescape, and those who could adapt to its regime survived.

Those with a gift for it thrived. Once again, the new time transformed the landscape. An added level of complexity had been bolted to the manufacturing process.

Now there was a hierarchy of order processing, from customer to retailer to distributor to manufacturer to supplier (like Eberhard) and back again. This system demanded the rapid transfer of information and material, and soon the valley was crisscrossed with telegraph wires and railroad tracks. And where they and the cattle ranches met, towns appeared. The mission faded in importance to the commercial centers of the valley. Increasingly, the mission became an object of nostalgia for the past, not a part of the active present.

The valley floor itself was now one vast cattle ranch, with the last of the great oak trees felled or killed by grazing.

Living in hovels, the surviving ancient Ohlones died out. Meanwhile, in 1881 Martin Murphy Jr., founder of what is now Sunnyvale and owner of most of the ranch land in the valley—indeed, the largest private landowner in the world—celebrated his Golden Wedding Anniversary by inviting the entire state to a party. An arrogant man, he celebrated not just his own wealth and power but also the victory of the industrial world. Trains were chartered from around the state; hundreds of cattle were slaughtered. Eberhard was there, as were all of the successful businessmen of Santa Clara Valley. This was their moment, the high watermark of their era.

Yet even as they were celebrating, that era was coming to an end.

Within a decade, the cattle ranches would almost be gone, replaced by miles of fruit trees. Technology had once again sped up the clock.

Thanks to artesian wells and water pumps, mass production, marketing, and reliable railroads and highways, Santa Clara Valley was now the Valley of Heart's Delight, with the most prosperous orchards in the nation. The valley moved on corporate time, the punch clock, and the Taylor Method: In the vast new Del Monte and Libby canneries, workers were shown time-motion films on how to cut apricots and boil cherries and pit prunes.

The flats of goods were wrapped in colorful promotional labels, sold according to Chicago Board of Options Exchange prices, and shipped by rail to markets in Minneapolis and Manhattan.

The children of the deceased Martin Murphy and Jacob Eberhard now lived in turreted gingerbread homes in downtown San Jose and sent their well-dressed sons to Santa Clara University and their daughters to the College of Notre Dame. The local towns swelled with the new cannery workers from Portugal and Eastern Europe, who deposited their wages at the new Bank of Italy (soon to be Bank of America).

Mansions now lined the Alameda from the old mission to San Jose, the very path once taken by the Franciscans.

And in the spring, the streets would whiteout from a blizzard of blowing fruit blossoms. Busy drivers, rushing to work in the new corporate time, complained about the nuisance to city magistrates.

Once again, as time accelerated and the valley floor was transformed, and as the production process grew more subtle and complex, the people again changed. The aging pioneers, now distinguished but anachronistic, were trotted out at museum openings and interviewed by the local paper about how it was in the old days. And thanks to a new generation of writers like Jack London and local publications like *Sunset* magazine, a cult of nostalgia sprang up, creating an enduring myth of graciousness out of the hard life of the mission era. By the 1920s, houses in a growing number of new valley developments featured walls painted in adobe hue, tile roofs, and even little ersatz bell towers—along with a garage to house that most representative object of the new timescape.

Yet even as the Valley of Heart's Delight was celebrating its newfound luxury, two young men, Bill Hewlett and David Packard, were turning on the switch of their new audio oscillator, in whose high-frequency waves could be heard the squeal of the valley's next era. Then, in 1955, two years after a feeble Eberhard Tannery finally shut its doors, William Shockley, armed with a team of brilliant young men and a Nobel Prize for creating the transistor, returned to his old hometown to reset the clock and, in doing so, annihilate the valley of his childhood. It is a curious fact, long known to biologists, that every animal—from the torpid giant tortoise to the frantic housefly—is given as its birthright about one billion heartbeats. Even that cynosure of the ephemeral, the mayfly, gets its 10^9 as a larva before its brief fling at flight.

Why a billion—two at most—and not more? The answer seems to lie in some kind of clock within the cells. It is as if the Almighty, with uncharacteristic democracy, ordained that every species would have its same threescore and ten, the same span of experiences, no matter how quickly or slowly it was forced to live them. Clotho may change the content of each life's thread, but Lachesis always draws out the same length for Atropos to cut. And all of our vast and costly struggles—medicine, nutrition, safety, genetic engineering—to extend this deadly timer will, it seems, at most improve our fateful number of heartbeats by a factor of two.

But in the digital, solid-state world that is the new metronome of valley life, it is a different story. The modern integrated circuit chip will soon be able to perform approximately one billion operations per second. One gigahertz. A billion electronic heartbeats: the equivalent of a lifetime in a single second. And, of course, at the end of those billion beats, there won't be a tiny electronic death but another billion-beat second, and another. And, since silicon is incredibly stable and invulnerable to almost everything but cosmic rays, there will be a billion more of these digital lifetimes for each chip—more than all the generations of life on earth—before it goes dark.

This is the new clock, our clock, the timepiece of the valley's digital era. This is the mission bell that tolls quicker than the synapses can arc across our brains, that counts out an eternity of silicon days in the time it takes to blink your eye. And thanks to Moore's Law—that defining rule of our lives and augury of our future superfluity—this new silicon clock will grow faster and faster, doubling in speed every few years, until it too produces whole cosmologies of change that are beyond human comprehension. And what then? What happens when the next clock resets the time once again? Who gets through the next time, and what do they become?

Look at any newspaper, magazine, or television show; surf the Net; shop at the local department store; listen to the words you use in daily speech: Silicon Valley is now the center of the world, the greatest creator of new wealth and employment in human history, the dynamo of innovation transforming the modern world, the creator of a new paradigm that is redefining the way we speak, live our daily lives, even how we see the world. And in this digital universe, Silicon Valley is the new Greenwich: We build the clocks and set the pace; the world revolves around our time. We are *sui generis,* we are unique in all the world and all of history, we are without precedent, and without end. The 1990s have been our golden age—this has been our great party, and we have invited the whole world to attend. We speak knowingly of long booms and perpetual prosperity as if God himself has blessed our good works with immortality.

Yet the lesson of the past is that none of this is new, only the magnitude. In fact, in the 220 years of modern Santa Clara Valley history, there have been three other such eras. Each of them was kicked off by a technological revolution, each of them operated to a different and faster clock, each of them was global in scope, each of them transformed the nature of the valley itself and the self-image of its residents, and each effectively erased all real memory of what came before. And at the moment of each era's greatest arrogance and self-assurance, each was within a decade or two of coming to an end. The clock shifted again and they were as effectively erased as Minos or Carthage. Their children lived in a different world, spoke different words, and bore different names. If the cycles of the past hold, the end of Silicon Valley and of the digital revolution as we know it lies sometime in the years just beyond 2010.

And then? The clocks reset themselves once more, this time perhaps to the speed of nucleotides forming and re-forming a trillion times each second in biological computers, or quantum dots, or perhaps one vast global computer, humming away in 100 billion interconnected computers and chips, bearing all the world's knowledge in a new kind of silicon consciousness.

But whatever the clock, the pace will be unimaginably fast. And under such a blazing discipline, who among us will be able to cross over to the other side? A few will, perhaps our children and our children's children who have spent their entire lives as navigators of cyberspace.

But it is also not hard to imagine that no one, at least no one human, will enter this new world, or the next one that arrives in the final decades of the twenty-first century.

Who, or more accurately what, will this new era, this new timescape, belong to? Intuitively, we already know: the machines themselves. Chips can live a lifetime in a second, then live a billion lifetimes more. For them the pace of this new clock is almost pastoral. Eventually, anthropomorphic software agents will be our surrogates into this world . . . until they need us no more. They will in time take over cyberspace as their own universe—real ghosts in the machine. Unlike us, they will be able to change their identities and their roles in microseconds and, thanks to Moore's Law, will grow ever smarter and faster and more capable of dealing with this hyperaccelerated timescape.

Then the tool will become the toolmaker, and perhaps the toolmaker the tool. And the numerous objects of our lives will become the broken relics in some future cyberarchive.

We have entered into a kind of Faustian bargain with time: Just join the world of the clock, and we'll give you progress, we'll give you hope. And medicine. A longer life span. Libraries of knowledge. The ability to reach around the world. And fly to the moon. Just listen for the bell and attend to its call . . .

We have listened, and we have been rewarded in extraordinary ways.

But it has come at an enormous cost—perhaps none greater than the one that lies ahead. Time is about to speed up again. Soon the pace will leave us behind.

And then, as for the Ohlone, the mission bell may signal the end of our day.

From *Forbes ASAP* Magazine © Forbes Inc., "The Big Issue," November 30, 1998. Reprinted by permission.

3

THE SOUL OF THE "HP WAY"

The most momentous meeting of the modern world was scarcely noticed by its two participants.

It took place in the late summer of 1930 on a football field at Stanford University. It was classic freshman football tryouts: dozens of young men standing around the sidelines, appraising one another, determining who their competition would be for a slot on the team.

On this day, two of those young men who nervously eyed one another were destined to become lifelong friends—and that friendship would determine the form of the Digital Age. One, handsome and extremely tall, came from Pueblo, Colorado, the son of a lawyer struggling to make ends meet in the Depression. The other, short and chunky, was an indifferent student from San Francisco. His father, a doctor, had died when he was 12—only the man's reputation had gotten the boy into Stanford.

The tall one, David Packard, would make the team. The short one, William Hewlett, would be cut a few days later. Over the next couple of years, the two would occasionally run into each other on campus or in engineering class. But it wasn't until their junior year that, through a mutual friend, they discovered a common love of the outdoors and a shared admiration for their electronics professor, Fred Terman. They became fast friends.

After graduation, the two went in different directions. But Terman soon drew them back to Palo Alto and convinced them to start their own company. The Packard garage, where the company was founded, would become the most famous such structure in the world. But it was Hewlett who found that house for the newlywed Packards, and it was Hewlett's design—for Terman—of an audio oscillator that would be the source of Hewlett-Packard and Company's first real product.

With the death last week, at 87, of Bill Hewlett, the most enduring of all Silicon Valley legends finally concludes—and with it, the first generation of high-tech pioneers. Having put his name at the front of the most celebrated of all electronics companies, Hewlett achieved a form of business immortality, yet has little of the glitter or glory of his old partner.

That is unjust, but it is also appropriate. Silicon Valley is two overlapping cultures, one of entrepreneurs, the other of engineers. Entrepreneurs operate in the outside world of markets and customers and brands. When they succeed, their fame comes from the same direction. Engineers, by comparison, are insiders, tucked into labs, their work appreciated mostly by their peers. The latter is the fate of Bill Hewlett. Future generations will know little of him, but he will always be the founding father of engineering in the Valley. A direct lineage runs from him through the Fairchild (traitorous) Eight to crazy genius Bob Widlar at National Semiconductor, to Steve Wozniak, to the thousands of code writers and designers that toil today in labs around the world.

For Hewlett, that is probably enough—that, and the enduring engineering monument of HP itself. A gruff, plainspoken man with a warm heart, Hewlett was the CEO of a billion-dollar corporation, the recipient of endless awards, and a legendary philanthropist. Yet he seemed most happy standing at a lab table during one of his periodic competitions against other senior HP executives to see who could build fastest the latest HP product from a pile of components. More often than not, Bill would gleefully beat the youngsters—showing that the old man still had his engineering chops—and just as important, that HP was, after everything, still an engineering company. How many of his successors today would dare attempt the same competition?

If history is just, it should remember Hewlett for three things. The first is the "HP Way," that enlightened model of doing business built on trust. Maybe the best thing about the modern corporate world is that it echoes, if often only feebly, the Way. If Dave was the philosopher of the HP Way, Bill was its soul—and the man who implemented it every day.

The second is excellence. Hewlett was a great engineer who built great products for other engineers. That sense of excellence defined HP in its prime, extending from the company's products to its management to its rank and file. And that's why the company triumphed.

And finally, there is friendship. We shouldn't forget that a man like David Packard trusted Bill Hewlett with his reputation, his fortune, and his life. Over the course of nearly 70 years, there is no record of the two of them ever fighting. Because they trusted each other completely, they could trust their employees, their customers, even their competitors. Out of that grew a great company, and an even greater business philosophy.

The last important public appearance of Hewlett was five years ago at Packard's memorial. Debilitated by a stroke, he sat in a wheelchair in the front of the Stanford Chapel, just a mile from Hewlett-Packard world headquarters, a few blocks from the Fred

Terman Engineering Center he and Dave donated to the university, and just yards from the football field where he and Dave first met. That day, he said goodbye not only to his old friend, but to all of us.

But he's still with us. In Silicon Valley, more than ever, if you want to see William Hewlett's legacy, you need only look out the window.

From the *Wall Street Journal:* January 16, 2001. Eastern Edition [staff produced copy only] by Michael S. Malone. Copyright 2001 by Dow Jones & Co. Inc. Reproduced with permission of Dow Jones & Co. Inc. in the format Other Book via Copyright Clearance Center.

SILICON VALLEY

4

THE MICROPROCESSOR

The First 25 Years

The modern microprocessor was conceived a quarter century ago in a fateful meeting between an obscure start-up, Intel Corp., and a Japanese calculator company. What proved to be the invention of the century has not only spawned the PC industry but is becoming embedded in just about every aspect of our lives. And the five "principles" that have governed the microprocessor industry's development also offer a blueprint for the future.

It is a year for anniversaries: D-Day, the moon landing, Woodstock. But there is one more historical turning point to celebrate, an event that went unnoticed at the time but in the end proved to be as momentous as all the others.

It was 25 years ago this month, at a meeting in Santa Clara, California, that Intel Corp. made a proposal that changed the world and led to the most important invention of the century. Across the table were representatives of Busicom, a Japanese company struggling to find a competitive edge in the hard-fought electronic desktop calculator industry. But Busicom was lucky in one respect. It had a technologist, Masatoshi Shima, who—rare enough in Japanese industry—had the soul of an entrepreneur. Busicom was in desperate need of a breakthrough, and Shima was point man in the search.

At the time, a debate was raging in the decade-old semiconductor industry over how to best tap into the riches being offered by the calculator makers. One camp held that the solution was to create custom circuits for each calculator model. A second, less influential, camp said no, the best answer was to imitate at the chip level the architecture of computers—that is, general-purpose chips that would then be programmed for the specific application.

This second group drew few adherents because creating such a general-purpose device would require a greater level of integration than heretofore known. Every theorist in the industry knew it would soon be possible to put all of the functions of a calculator on a single chip—Rockwell International Corp., Pittsburgh, had even constructed a primitive processor. And most realized that the new MOS technology, invented by Federico Faggin at Fairchild Semiconductor, would be the process with which to do it. But such an attempt would be fraught with risk. After spending many months and millions of dollars on your quest, you might end up with nothing but a burned-out prototype.

Busicom knew that, which is why the specifications it put out for contract on its new calculator took the safe route and called for 10 custom circuits. One of the companies looking at those specifications was a year-old start-up called Intel. It had been founded by two industry pioneers, Robert Noyce and Gordon Moore, who had broken away from Fairchild—which they had also helped start—to pursue their own entrepreneurial dreams of building MOS memory chips. Ted Hoff, a Stanford University graduate who was employee number 12 at Intel, had been assigned to respond to the Busicom specs. He faced a dilemma: Intel needed such a contract, but the company had almost no expertise in custom chip design. So instead, he ignored Busicom's instructions and took a flier on an alternative proposal: an integrated design that would function like the new Digital Equipment Corp. computer with which he'd been doing circuit design.

As Hoff recalls, "I made some proposals to the Japanese engineers to do something along these lines—and they were not the least bit interested. They said they recognized that their design was too complicated but they were working on the simplification and they were out to design calculators and nothing else." Frustrated, but still convinced he was onto something, Hoff turned to Noyce and Moore. The two founders were as knowledgeable about solid-state electronics as anybody on earth—Noyce, after all, was co-inventor of the planar process that created the modern integrated circuit. They told Hoff to ignore Busicom and keep working on his idea.

Then an unexpected thing happened. Busicom did a complete about-face. Hoff remembers "it finally came to a point in October 1969. We held a meeting in which the managers of the Japanese company came over here for a presentation by their engineering group and by a group representing our firm. At that time, we presented our idea—that our new approach went well beyond calculators and that it had many other possible applications. They went for that."

Unknown even to the men gathered in that room, the Age of the Microprocessor had begun.

The Mature Microprocessor

It has been a quarter century now since the Busicom-Intel meeting. The landmark 8080 microprocessor, which history may recognize as the single most important product of the twentieth century, has now reached adulthood. The intervening years have been so chaotic and eventful that they seem like a blur. Once 386 IBM-compatibles were the hottest machines around, but that was in October 1986. Since then, there have been two more generations of the X86-architecture microprocessors, and another is just around the corner, hurried along by cloners such as Advanced Micro Devices Inc. and Cyrix Corp. and by the mighty team of Motorola Inc., Apple Computer Inc., and IBM Corp.

In the interim, the microprocessor has pervaded society faster than any invention in human history. We barely notice in the photograph of a Masai cattle rancher that he is wearing a digital watch or that the New Guinea villagers in the TV documentary listen to a solid-state short-wave radio. We are surprised to learn that BMW 3 series cars contain 100 microprocessors and controllers, while we forget that just about every car built in the last 20 years has contained a half-dozen or more such devices.

Recently, this author needed to know the total installed base of processors in the world. Some of the pioneers of the industry estimated 300 to 400 million installed units—a gigantic number when you consider that that's about as many television sets as there are in the world. Finally, needing a precise figure, this author checked with the Semiconductor Industry Association (SIA), San Jose. The SIA's industry watcher, Doug Andrey, said that the actual figure was about 200 million microprocessors—per year. And that's nothing, he said. The total number of microcontrollers (many of them older-model microprocessors) sold in a typical year is more than two billion. Even if you throw out the roughly one-third that have been scrapped over the years, that still puts the world's total installed base of microprocessors and microcontrollers at more than 10 billion units. That's two for every living soul on earth. With the exception perhaps of nails and Coca-Cola bottles, has any other manufactured good been as ubiquitous as the microprocessor?

Now, add to this the fact that the microprocessor is also the most complicated mass-produced item ever built—each one with as many architectural features as a medium-sized city and the product of programs as complicated as the Manhattan Project— and you get a sense of the miracle that takes place millions of times each day in fab plants as far apart as Seoul, Korea; Phoenix, Arizona; and Greenock, Scotland. Just why we're undergoing major cultural upheavals suddenly becomes apparent. You can't change the technological heart of a society this fast—the equivalent of the Industrial Revolution every couple of years—without affecting every corner of the culture.

It's not that we've forgotten all of this; rather, there just hasn't been much time to notice. Amnesia is implicit in microprocessors. When the PowerPC 601 or Pentium is announced, we instantly forget the previous generation and scan the freshly printed specifications to see what exciting new applications await us. The past is never a lesson but a burden—even an embarrassment—when you temporarily lag behind the digital Zeitgeist. More than any other technology business, the semiconductor industry has never been much for looking back. When you are hurtling down the highway faster than you can steer, there isn't much time to look over your shoulder to see where you've been. When you do, it's usually sparked by a momentous event—a pothole in the highway of history so jarring that you stop for an instant, if only to get your head clear.

One of those moments was Noyce's death in June 1990, when Silicon Valley realized that it was mortal. Another was the Fairchild goodbye party shortly before, where feuds that had festered in solitude for a generation suddenly healed as graying men and women realized they had shared a great adventure.

The microprocessor's silver anniversary presents a similar opportunity, if we choose to take it. The disadvantage of being blind to hindsight is that there are few opportunities to gain wisdom.

Knowledge, yes. Every day, the semiconductor industry gains a little more competence—it learns how to improve its designs and increase yield rates and streamline fabrication and stoke the desire of customers and consumers for its latest product offerings.

But in terms of understanding the larger patterns, the themes running through the microprocessor story, we are nearly as ignorant of what is happening as the leaders of Busicom and Intel were 25 years ago. How do we make sense of an industry that has encompassed personalities and events as diverse as Andy Grove, Jerry Sanders, Intel Inside, Al Stein, Michael Slater, the Z80, IBM, Gilbert Hyatt, Charlie Sporck, Six Sigma, doctored Intel documents, chip thief John Henry "One-Eyed" Jackson, Art Rock, the KGB, Hiroe Osafune, and Operation Crush?

The first step must be to look back through the filter of experience.

A Difficult Birth

The delivery of the microprocessor was both painful and protracted. The critical figure was Faggin, who arrived at Intel from Fairchild in April 1970 and was placed in charge of developing the new calculator chip set. The four components in that set (designated the 4000 family) had already been outlined by Hoff, Shima, and another Intel scientist, Stan Mazor: a 4-bit logic CPU, a 2,048-bit ROM, a 320-bit RAM, and a 10-bit I/O shift register.

Up till now, history has always given Faggin short shrift in the story of the microprocessor's beginnings, instead awarding the invention to Hoff. Muddling the story still further was the fact that Intel did much of the early stumping for the microprocessor—and was much more interested in promoting one of its own fellows (Hoff) than one of its biggest rivals (Faggin, who later left to form Zilog Inc., Campbell, California). In reality, while Hoff was the inventor of the microprocessor—the man who not only had the vision but also sold it to both customer and employer—Faggin could certainly be called the microprocessor's creator.

The project Faggin inherited that April was in crisis. Contrary to his expectations, the architecture and logic design was incomplete. To make matters worse, Shima arrived soon after. Recalls Faggin: "Shima expected to review the logic design, confirming that Busicom could indeed produce its calculator, and then return to Japan. He was furious when he found out that no work had been done since his visit approximately six months earlier. He kept on saying, in his broken English, 'I came here to check. There is nothing to check. This is just idea.' The schedule that was agreed on for his calculator had already been irreparably compromised."

With Hoff gone on a business trip, Faggin set about solving one problem after another. First came the architecture. Next, the logic and circuit design. Finally, the layout of the four chips. It was not without a hitch, however. For one thing, Faggin had to develop a new methodology for random-logic design with silicon-gate technology. Then, when the design proved power inefficient, Faggin had to invent a way to bootstrap the gate on the transistor—something thought to be impossible.

By July, Faggin had the 4000 family design completed. Prototyping began in October. First up was the ROM chip. Perfect. In November, the RAM and the register. Also very good. Finally, in the last week of 1970, the model 4004 logic chip. Disaster. Not only did the 4004 fail as a whole, it failed in every part as well. Frantic, Faggin tried to figure out what he'd done wrong. Then he found it: An entire deposition layer had been omitted during fabrication. At least it isn't the design, he told himself.

The next run came in the second week of January 1971. It was late at night in Intel's Middlefield Road lab. Taking the 2-inch wafer, Faggin placed it in the probe station. He was alone and, he admits, his hands were shaking and he was praying—not that it would work, but that there wouldn't be too many bugs to handle. By 3 A.M., exhausted and exhilarated, Faggin knew he had succeeded. In February 1971, the 4004 went into production. In mid-March, the first of the 4000 family of chip sets were shipped to Busicom.

Skepticism Abounds

Busicom wasn't that excited about this silicon miracle. The calculator market was overheating, prices were plummeting, and what Intel had originally proposed as a competitive breakthrough was now, in Busicom's eyes, not only a year late but outrageously overpriced. The Japanese company demanded a renegotiation of the price. But Hoff, Mazor, and Faggin, if no one else, knew what Intel had. They begged the marketing department to restructure the deal to remove Busicom's exclusivity. "[We] said, 'Get the right to sell to other people!' " Hoff recalls.

Intel resisted. After all, it was a MOS memory company, and just three years old, with $4 million in sales and a handful of products. It was facing the dislocation and expense of moving to its new Santa Clara location, planning to introduce a whole new technology (EPROMs) in September and expecting to go public in October. It didn't need to be pursuing brand new markets that were highly speculative.

So the trio went to the great man himself, Bob Noyce. Noyce was an excellent technologist. He was also a romantic. It is interesting to speculate on whether the microprocessor would have gotten a green light if it had come from any other company or if someone else (such as Andy Grove) had been running Intel at the time. But the new technology fired Noyce's imagination, as it did Gordon Moore's. In the end, what objections marketing and sales had were overridden and the new technology was justified, according to

Intel's then-publicist Regis McKenna, not for its intrinsic value but because "it would sell a lot of memory." By May, Busicom had signed away the 4000 family for everything but calculators; by the end of the year, it had given up all exclusivity.

Then the bomb hit. In an *Electronics* advertisement in late summer 1971, Texas Instruments Inc. (TI), Dallas, announced full MOS large-scale integration fabrication capabilities. No big surprise there. But the photograph in the ad was something else. It showed a chip (nearly a quarter-inch square) above a caption that read: "CPU on a Chip."

Intel reeled. Especially when it turned out that TI was building the processor for Computer Terminal Corp. (now Datapoint Corp., San Antonio, Texas)—something Intel was doing as well. CTC had contracted with Intel at about the same time as Busicom did, in late 1969. In CTC's case, the task was even more complex than the Busicom calculator chip set: Intel was to use MOS technology to reduce the nearly 100 bipolar-type logic chips in the CTC model 2200 computer terminal to a handful of MOS chips, and to cut both size and production costs.

It was Hoff who had looked at the CTC design and realized that with Faggin's silicon-gate MOS it would be possible to put all of the 100 bipolar logic chips on a single MOS circuit. It was an extraordinary claim, but Hoff convinced CTC to try it. Intel designated this new processor chip the 1201. Work began concurrently with the 4000 family and under the direction of another Intel engineer, Hal Feeney. But after a few months, a new memory chip was deemed higher priority and Intel management shifted Feeney off the 1201 project. For the next several months, the 1201 languished.

As the 4000 family was proving itself in prototype at the end of 1970, Faggin was asked to reanimate the 1201. With Feeney reassigned to him, the two spent the winter and spring translating what had been learned with the 4000 family, especially the 4004, to the

1201's 8-bit architecture. It all went smoothly until TI's advertisement. Suddenly, the Intel team, which for a year had believed it was opening a brand new technological world, realized that it was no more than an also-ran.

That was only the first shock. A month later, CTC announced that, given the recession then raging, the cost of logic chips had fallen so low it was no longer cost-effective to develop a new processor chip. CTC wanted out of the contract. Intel, having just learned that Japanese watchmaker Seiko Corp. was interested in the 1201 project, decided to go ahead with the program anyway and let CTC out of the deal without charging it for the work to date. CTC in turn handed over commercial rights of the 1201 to Intel.

That summer was a low point in Intel's history. It now had two apparently revolutionary products but no customers for them and a good chance that TI's new technology had already made Intel's products obsolete. Hoff hit the road to visit technical conferences and trade shows, trying to drum up interest—maybe even a customer—for the new processors. It wasn't easy. After all, this was a technology for which there was little precedent. Most audience members would fixate on the notion of a "computer on a chip" and then complain that the microprocessor would be difficult to repair. Hoff's reply—that you would just throw the chip away and replace it—only left audiences confused. Nobody ever threw computers away; they were too expensive.

Then, unexpected blessings. Word came that TI's "CPU on a chip" was dead on arrival. Ed Gelbach, recruited from TI (of all places), took over as Intel's new marketing director. Gelbach instantly saw the value of the 4000 family, now called the MCS-4. By November 1971, Gelbach's team hit the marketplace with what was, for the era, a major publicity campaign. In the meantime, Faggin, Feeney, and their team were finishing up the 1201. With CTC out of the picture, the product was renamed the 8008 to keep it consistent with the 4004. In August 1972, the 8008 was introduced. Intel had not only invented the microprocessor, but also managed the feat of leaping a generation in just six months.

Hoff, McKenna, and Gelbach were beginning to enjoy a sea change in the marketplace. The trade press was full of stories about the microprocessor, though many were vaporware announcements from Intel's frightened competitors. Requests were pouring in for Intel's microprocessor design tools and testing boards—suggesting, accurately, a burst of orders just ahead. And on the road, Hoff and Noyce were bewildered to find that audiences not only understood the implications of this new technology but were annoyed that it couldn't do more.

Faggin had heard similar complaints during a seminar series in Europe. And, he had to admit, some were valid. That's why he wanted to build a better 8-bit processor by increasing pin count, enhancing I/O speeds, adding additional instructions and switching to n-channel from the 8008's less efficient p-channel construction. But Intel wasn't ready. The wait was frustrating, and may have played a part in Faggin's later decision to leave Intel and found Zilog.

Finally, Faggin got the go-ahead. He made his planned corrections in the design. The first test of the new microprocessor took place in December 1973, four years after the fateful meeting with Busicom. It was formally introduced to the public in June 1974. Called the 8080, it was the first true microprocessor. As Faggin has written, "The 8080 really created the microprocessor market. The 4004 and 8008 suggested it, but the 8080 made it real."

Dickensian Roots

Perhaps more real than we imagine. One way to gain some perspective on the microprocessor is not to see it as a semiconductor but as a famous and powerful individual, one who has become a fixture in our lives for a quarter century. When we do that, it reads like a story right out of Dreiser or Dickens:

Born of uncertain parentage, it had an unwelcome birth, was reared in poverty and, at first, was resented as yet one more hungry mouth to feed. But through pluck, ability, and the patronage of some famous people, it soon was seen as a golden child.

As is often the case, however, early success led to a wayward youth. At the mercy of promoters, hucksters, fools, and kindly but misguided supporters, it lost its way. It began to believe its own newspaper clippings, it threw money away; it risked its reputation.

Then tragedy struck. It lost nearly everything and was left struggling just to survive. But though the experience left scars, it also brought a new determination to succeed. Though it took great sacrifices and years of hard work—fighting off challengers and naysayers at every turn—our hero not only regained all it had lost, but reached new heights of glory. Its name was on every lip, its presence felt in every home.

Now, in its maturity, battered and wary but stronger than ever, our hero rules a vast empire. It has had many great adventures and is likely to have many more. The glory won't last forever, but for now, at the pinnacle, it can look down from the heights in amazement at how far it has come.

Seen from this perspective, away from the glitz of MIPS and money, we can study the life story of the microprocessor and see some underlying truths that have been hidden. Consider these:

Marketing Rules.   The single most important event in the microprocessor story had nothing to do with products; on the contrary, it had everything to do with the lack of products. It was Intel's Operation Crush in 1980. Most people in the industry have heard of Crush, and two of its participants, Bill Davidow and Regis McKenna, have written at length about it. But the real, metaphysical, meaning of Crush has remained elusive. Simply put, in 1979 Intel found itself third in a three-company technological race. It knew its products were inferior to those of both Zilog and Motorola. As Davidow has written, "We decided what we needed was a new product that better fitted the needs of our customer base. We would have to invent one."

Obviously, Intel did not have time to design and fabricate a whole new architecture. That would take years. Instead, the Crush team essentially wove a new product out of thin air. In particular, it identified Intel's remaining advantages—a more extensive catalog, better customer support, more complete solutions—and set about through product positioning, new systems-level benchmarks, advertising, sales training, and the like to redefine the very definition of microprocessor. It was no longer a device but a system; not a component but a solution. The strategy worked. Zilog and Motorola fell behind and wouldn't catch up for years, which was too late for Zilog; had it not been for automotive electronics, it would have been too late for Motorola as well. By the end of 1980, Intel had 2,500 design wins. Best of all, it was ready to land the one that counted: IBM.

The echoes of Crush continue to this day. You can see it in the brilliant and innovative Intel Inside program, by which Intel has successfully fought the commoditization of its products by reaching through the distribution channel and convincing the end user to accept the dubious notion that Intel alone can be trusted to make quality X86 microprocessors. You can also see Crush in the carefully orchestrated Sturm and Drang of the PowerPC introduction. Motorola learned its lesson and is now copying the teacher.

Says Tim Bajarin, president of San Jose's Creative Strategies Inc., "It has never been the microprocessor itself that drove markets, but the solution that was wrapped around that microprocessor. Intel succeeded because it went back to Marketing 101, not

Technology 101. And when you start from the marketing point of view, you end up seeing the device not as a semiconductor, but as a new kind of computer, and not as a microprocessor but the embodiment of what a microprocessor can do."

Crush is the ultimate reminder that, despite the omnipresent emphasis upon technology, success in the microprocessor industry has always gone to the better marketer. Sure, you have to keep up with the competition performancewise, but you don't have to lead. Over the last 25 years, superior marketing has beaten superior technology almost every time. It still does. And if you don't believe that, how's that new DEC Alpha AXP personal computer of yours working?

PCs Are a Two-Edged Sword.   Time may show that the personal computer was not only the best thing that ever happened to microprocessors but also the worst. Sure, the PC and the Mac galvanized the semiconductor industry, established standards, cranked out big profits to fund future product generations and set the market on a treadmill of insatiable demand. But the PC also narrowed the options of the microprocessor industry, pulling its key players down narrow channels of compromise. IBM's decision to purchase the 8088, for instance, effectively brought the curtain down on the entrepreneurial era of the microprocessor for a decade, forcing other companies, some with better designs, to the margins. Though most of these other designs survived, they would never again be at the forefront of innovation. Imagine where we might be in the microprocessor story were there still a couple of dozen Motorolas and Intels out there, all racing to create eighth-generation processors.

Even the apparent winners compromised. Consider Intel, the biggest winner of them all. As impressive as Pentium and the impending P6 may be, they are still, in their heart of hearts, 8086s— a 15-year-old design. Intel doesn't have much choice: To bring its customer base along, its new chips have to be upwardly software compatible with its wildly popular early designs. The same is true, to a lesser degree, for every other well-known architecture, from the SPARC chip and Mips families to National Semiconductor Corp.'s CG peripheral processor engine.

Standardization is, of course, inevitable. In fact, the story of the microprocessor can be seen to recapitulate that of the mainframe computer industry 30 years earlier. In the 1950s and early 1960s, mainframes enjoyed a period of entrepreneurial fervor and innovation. But by the mid-1960s, a clear winner had emerged: IBM. With that company's introduction of the legendary 360 family, the race was essentially over. But the mind-boggling success of the 360 brought with it a host of unexpected new challenges. The same customer base that made IBM rich with the 360 became a drag chute when IBM began planning the 370—and a ball and chain thereafter. The demand for upward compatibility slowly hamstrung IBM's large computer business, turning it, by the mid-1980s, into a weakened giant, fearful of taking a step lest it crush some of its customers. The door was now open for attacks from above (Cray Research Inc.), from below (workstations, super-micros, PC networks, client-server systems, and so on) and within (cloners such as Amdahl Corp.). Together, these attacks accomplished the one thing IBM could not endure: They rendered Big Blue superfluous.

When we look at the microprocessor industry, the resemblance is uncanny. Here, too, we have a dominant firm—Intel—dragging along the steel trap of an aging architecture, hounded by packs of attackers coming from every direction. Whether it can find a way out remains to be seen. But sometimes the bear wins. Whatever the outcome, we still have to ask: In the long run, wouldn't both the industry and end users have been better served if the two key contracts—IBM/Intel and Apple/Motorola—had come five years later? Or never?

Grove's Law Trumps Moore's Law. We all know Moore's Law, or at least some crude version of it. It begins with the myth: In the early 1970s, Intel cofounder Gordon Moore was preparing for an industry speech when he decided to plot out the performance of Intel's processors introduced to date, as well as models still on the drawing board. He used logarithmic graph paper; to his surprise, the products plotted along a straight line. Twenty years later, they more or less still do: Transistor count (or processing power or, inversely, die size or price) doubles every 18 months or so. Moore had captured something profound about the nature of creativity and competition in the digital age. In doing so, he had given Intel and its competitors a telescope through which they could make out the mileposts into the future. But many companies have known of and appreciated the metronome pace and inevitability of Moore's Law—and still failed to meet its demands. Knowing the future doesn't always mean you'll get there.

By comparison, no semiconductor company that has followed Grove's Law has ever failed at the task, which is why, for all of its celebrity, Moore's Law takes a back seat to its lesser-known counterpart. What is Grove's Law? "Only the paranoid survive."

The more you look at Intel's story, the more obvious it becomes that its success has not come because it has never stumbled—in fact, Intel has probably stumbled more often than any of its major competitors—but because it has never fallen. Every time Intel's knees have been about to hit the ground—the 1974 recession, the ill-fated 432 project, the Motorola/Zilog challenge, the Japanese threat, the 80286—Grove has whipped the company back on to its feet. Some of the moves, such as Crush and the dividing of forces that created the 8086, have been breathtaking; others, cold-blooded (remember the doctored document in the AMD trial?). Grove has followed his own dictum; he has always run Intel as though unseen forces were gathering to destroy it.

And history has proven Grove right. If Intel didn't have reason to be paranoid 10 years ago, it sure does now. Perhaps the only way to succeed in the microprocessor industry is to be brilliant, paranoid and ruthless—to take no prisoners and expect your opponents to do the same. Keep product development punching forward, even during a recession, even if it breaks your staff. Keep your employees in a state of perpetual, frenzied war mobilization. Noyce couldn't have done that, nor could Bob Galvin, John Young, Ken Olsen, Jerry Sanders, or Faggin. That's why, even if you hate or fear him, Andy Grove is the most important figure in the microprocessor's first 25 years.

The Microprocessor Eats Its Young. It makes a nice story: How the microprocessor, by putting computer intelligence into a tiny, low-cost, low-power package, has revitalized many existing industries, from computers to consumer products to test and measurement instruments. But the truth is that for many of these businesses, to join the microprocessor revolution is to make a pact with the devil. In the short term, the gains can be thrilling, but over time, the microprocessor will likely eat your business alive.

Call it the Body Snatcher principle. Like the B-movies of the 1950s, the microprocessor slowly hollows out, kills, and replaces every business it enters. It may still look like a video game, but now it's not in an arcade but on your personal computer. Your TV is about to be there, too. Your telephone, modem, phone recorder? Ditto. Stereo? Same. The microprocessor is taking over the appliances in your kitchen and the items on your desk at work. "Everything analog will eventually go digital," says Bajarin. And with sufficient processing power at your fingertips, almost every physical product dissolves into software.

Here in the 1990s, many system vendors are finding themselves in the predicament of the poor farmer in Stephen Vincent

Benet's "The Devil and Daniel Webster": They signed the contract and got the gold, believing the Day of Reckoning would never arrive. Now it's seven years later and Old Scratch is at the door demanding their souls.

All of this suggests that computers might be the one safe place to be. After all, that's where everything else seems to be heading. Ah, but don't forget, microprocessors transformed computers first—and regularly, thanks to Moore's Law. The computer makers, especially in the PC business, have been at the mercy of Intel and Motorola for years. Beginning with the minicomputer, the microprocessor has also become the agent of a new process, categorical annihilation. Not only does the Pentium erase the 486 and the PowerPC 601 eviscerate the 68040 (or at least send them off into microcontrollerland), but now the microprocessor begins to send whole markets down the memory hole. The minicomputer dominated the world's electronics industry when the Intel-Busicom meeting occurred. Now the minicomputer is gone, thanks to microprocessor-powered workstations. The mainframe business is nearly gone, too.

All of this has been good news for customers, reminds Robert Tholemeier, program director at the Meta Research Group in Westport, Connecticut, because it leads to better products at lower prices. But it is often an ugly surprise to system houses. "[Microprocessor companies] don't care about the margins of the companies below them [in the distribution channel]," says Tholemeier. "Ultimately, they are focused on forcing commoditization on those firms to increase their own volumes." And that scenario is occurring anew: Tholemeier predicts that the P6 will so reduce the cost of midrange servers that they will crash into the top-end PC market, turning this currently mighty industry into another commodity business.

So don't look now, but at this very moment, Mr. Scratch may be waiting for you in the lobby with an exciting offer.

Good Ideas Never Die. In terms of units sold, what is the single most popular microprocessor/controller model ever built? It is probably the Zilog Z80, which was introduced in 1974 and which, as a microcontroller for items such as microwave ovens, still sells in the millions each year. In fact, last summer Zilog introduced a 32-bit version of the venerable design. The second most popular model? It's probably a tie between two other 8-bit microcontrollers, the Intel 8051 and the Motorola 6805—both designs that are more than 15 years old. And somewhere high on the list is the 6502, the heart of the Apple II and the Commodore 64. Its design has been passed around from MOS Technology to Synertek to Rockwell, and is now being produced by the 10-employee Western Design Center of Mesa, Arizona.

We don't hear about the Z80 and the 6502 because they don't fit into the standard March of the Microprocessor history. The Z80 was supposedly defeated by Intel when the latter's 8088 won the IBM PC contract. The 6502 fell off the radar screen when Commodore bought MOS Tech and Apple chose the Motorola 68000 for the Macintosh. History moved on to faster, more powerful circuits and newer, more exciting applications. And yet, these also-rans survived. Priced for pocket change, they have been stripped of much of their profitability. Once the heart of the most sophisticated new machines, they now reside in wall switches and watches.

Says Bajarin, "We always think about how the microprocessor industry is going forward, and we forget that it also marches backwards as well. An older processor like the 386 isn't in my computer anymore, but it might be in my PDA. And eventually it may be in my car or the blender in my kitchen."

What does the survival of these older chips teach us? For one thing, that the use of the microprocessor is far wider and deeper than we know; that 25 years from now we may look back and realize that we were so dazzled by the flashy high-end models that we missed the more important story—the sewing of the microprocessor into the fabric of everyday life, Bajarin's "backward march"—and that some may also have missed a great business opportunity.

There is another lesson as well. The history of the microprocessor is one of compromises accepted, promising pathways abandoned for reasons that had more to do with balance sheets than performance. And though those other trails have grown cold, they still exist. They can be revisited; their strengths and weaknesses reappraised. Perhaps buried within their transistors is the solution to a problem that didn't even exist when these devices were first designed.

The Next 25 Years

If understanding is our goal, what can we learn from the truths of the first 25 years of the microprocessor? First, that in the mid-1960s, Pat Haggerty, TI president and then-chairman, was right in his belief that, at the component level, the general-purpose product ultimately triumphs over the specialized, and sometimes even over customers and the entire distribution channel. That was the message Gelbach brought from TI to Intel at just the right moment.

Another bit of wisdom is that, while it is easy to be dazzled by technological innovation, electronics is ultimately a business, and success comes to those who do superior marketing, service, and all the other prosaic details of daily business life. Good inventions are nearly immortal; the trick is to tether them down and not let them float away. The only sure way to succeed in high tech is to act as though each new product generation was the first, to stay in perpetual terror of losing everything overnight and to be always fearful of unseen forces at work against you.

But with all this talk about the microprocessor being a business first, the most important business question remains unanswered. Where does the microprocessor go from here? Is there any truth to the predictions of wishful-thinking pessimists that the microprocessor won't survive the century? Can you build your business on the belief that the microprocessor will be around?

Two years ago, in Michael Slater's "Microprocessor Report," Don Lindsay of Carnegie-Mellon University looked at the limits of chip technology to see if there was an insurmountable technical wall out there that the microprocessor was destined to hit. And he found one, at least for microprocessors the way they are constructed now, at a Chip Performance Index between 1016 and 1019, or about three to six orders of magnitude from where we are now. That's a billion-chip transistor sometime soon after 2000. After that, the physics start to collapse.

But Lindsay also found a number of technical options of where to go from there. Gallium arsenide, microstrip interconnection, tiny cryogenic pumps, silicon carbide, diamond-film technology—enough options to convince him that one or more would pan out. Packaging, too, is moving forward to multichip modules and cubelets with thousands of interconnects. And that's just hardware. People like Faggin, who helped start it all, are hard at work on neural networks and other architectural designs that may enormously expand the microprocessor's overall system performance and applicability.

Those findings suggest a last truth:

The Microprocessor Will Outlive Us All.   The most important invention of the twentieth century may well be the most influential one of the twenty-first. Older, perhaps a little wiser and certainly with a lot more stories to tell, the microprocessor will undoubtedly be around for its golden anniversary in 2019; as the wizened veteran of the Electronics Age, it should even be at the table for its diamond anniversary in 2044.

From *Upside Magazine,* October 1994.

5

IPO DAY

Silicon Valley, California, 2:00 A.M. PST

Bob Miller didn't dream.

And when his eyes opened at two o'clock on Thursday morning, he was instantly awake—and knew why he was.

He padded down the hall to the kitchen on the thick legs of an old college lineman and made himself a cup of coffee. On the intercom, he could hear the rhythmic breathing of his baby daughter. This would be the most important day of her life and she wouldn't even know it. Pondering this, Miller decided to write a letter about this day she could read years hence.

That is, if this really was the day . . .

Sipping his coffee, there at the center island in the big kitchen of his French provincial estate in the foothill town of Woodside, California, Miller went over and over the sequence of events that had led up to this early morning awakening. There were still so many things that could go wrong. He began to write down all the possible things that could go wrong. He began to write down all the possible disasters that could yet occur and what could be done

47

about them. What if the SEC didn't accept the revisions? What if Latta got delayed getting to Washington, or if they kept him cooling his heels in the lobby? What if the *Wall Street Journal* or *New York Times* picked up the Dow wire pricing announcement and ran it in their first edition? How late could the company wait to go out?

If not today, then surely tomorrow was the last chance. And a Friday Initial Public Offering was almost impossible. Next week was Christmas. You couldn't go public during Christmas week or the week after—the market would be dead. And who knew what the state of the market would be in the new year of 1990?

Could they even go public in January? After all, that would be after the end of the fiscal year. The year would have to be reported. That would take several weeks. And the new numbers would demand another killing road trip around the world to bring investors up to date. Just the thought made Miller's stomach tighten. He wasn't up to another such marathon. The last one had literally almost killed him.

If they didn't make it out today, then it might not be until February. February! The economy could be a disaster by then. The market could go through one of its regular slumps. There was a lot of talk of recession. Hell, the market was already falling. The Marines had invaded Panama the night before and were still fighting.

Or, the company could have a bad quarter. Anything could happen by February. Miller tried not to think about the last set of Silicon Valley firms that had tried to make their first public sale of stock. October 1987. One firm had been giving its road show presentation to New York analysts when the word came that the market had fallen five hundred points. That firm had not attempted an IPO since. And the market had never again been strong for high-tech stocks.

Bob Miller sipped his coffee. There were so many things that could go wrong. As chief executive officer he faced enough challenges just trying to run a high-tech start-up company—especially one such as MIPS Computer Systems, Inc. that had tripled in size each of the last three years. Adding the hysteria of an Initial Public Offering made the job too much for anyone to handle well.

Miller had thought he'd known what was coming, but there was no way to really know until you'd been through it. Looking back, he was proud of the way he'd anticipated the chaos and had divided the top management of the firm; he, chief financial officer Dave Ludvigson, and vice-president and general counsel Joe Sweeney managed the IPO and depended on the rest of the executive staff—Bosenberg, Jobe, Vigil, DiNucci, Hime, and the others—to run the firm.

But MIPS was a new kind of company. Not only did it operate in a realm of innovative technology (its name means millions of instructions per second), but its organization was unlike anything seen before in American business. And experience had taught that if the MIPS business model had one weakness, it was an overdependence in the early stages on the CEO. And for the last two months, this CEO had been pulled almost in two. Thank God, Miller had said many times to himself, that this company has a veteran management. What was the line one industry watcher had used? "The $100 million company with the $1 billion management." The analysts had loved that one. And a good thing it was true, or MIPS might not have survived the last few weeks, what with all the publicity and an angry Securities and Exchange Commission. How did young firms with inexperienced management teams ever make it alive through a Going Public Day?

He finished his coffee in the glare of the kitchen lights. Outside, it was still night, the trees black silhouettes. During the process of taking the company public, Miller had often said the experience was like being the pilot of a jet airliner and trying to land it on Wall Street. You try to finesse it down through the canyons of office buildings on either side of the street . . . and at any second, it all can go terribly wrong. You catch a wing tip on a cornice or a light pole or snag the landing gear on a pothole or high manhole cover—and suddenly you are out of control, breaking apart, the wings shearing off and exploding.

As the debris-spitting ball of flame goes tumbling past, one stockbroker on the street turns to another and asks, "Say, wasn't that MIPS Computer?"

"Yeah, poor bastards."

Bob Miller finished his coffee and dressed in the suit he would wear for the next 12 eventful hours. At five o'clock he kissed his wife, Barbara, goodbye. She remembers saying jokingly, "Don't come back until this is good." Then she added, "I know you're going to nail it; I'll keep my fingers crossed."

"I may need more than that," Miller told her.

The predawn air was cold and misty as Miller drove his Mercedes to the freeway. The lights at the on-ramp were harsh. Just ahead, on the far side of the overpass, lay the darkened campus of 3000 San Hill Road, home of Silicon Valley's venture capital community. Board member Bill Davidow's office was there. And just over the hill, at Mayfield Fund, were the offices of Gil Myers and Grant Heidrich, also board members and the two men who had helped recruit him out of Data General. If all worked out, this would be a big day for them, too.

Miller pulled onto the 280 freeway and headed north in the darkness. On his car phone he called Carol Muratore, a Morgan Stanley principal for Equity Research, at her home in New York City. Do you, he asked, get the *Times* and the *Journal?* No, she said, but I can run across the street and get them. Call me back in 10 minutes. When Miller got her on the line again she reported happily that there was nothing in either paper. That was a relief. One possible disaster had been averted.

But as Bob Miller drove up the Peninsula through the fault-riddled hills toward the Morgan Stanley office in San Francisco, on what could be the pivotal day of his business career, he was haunted by the memory of an event that had occurred a week before. The company's manufacturing employees, a group employed at a building two miles from headquarters, had gathered at a Christmas luncheon.

Most of these employees were assembly line workers, and a large number of them were Southeast Asian, mostly Vietnamese. Miller knew that many of them had experienced terrible ordeals getting to this point in their lives, but beyond that he knew few details. The Vietnamese were hard working, dignified, and taciturn, and it had always seemed rude to pry.

But at this luncheon, Miller sat next to a small, soft-spoken woman who was called by the American name Connie. Miller did know something about her life. He had just learned that she had a husband, a former South Vietnamese army officer, still in Vietnam after 15 years in a Vietnamese political prison. He knew she was planning to use the money she made from selling her stock to buy her husband out of Vietnam.

Not surprisingly, the talk at the luncheon quickly got around to the public offering. After all, many of the manufacturing people, especially the Vietnamese, were among the company's most tenured employees (many had been at the firm twice as long as Miller and the executive team) and thus were fully vested in their stock options. For them Going Public Day would mean an instant leap in personal wealth of $50,000, $100,000, or more.

With the promise of that sort of payday, the manufacturing employees had become very sophisticated in the workings of the stock market. They asked about the underwriters, the opening price, the stock price in the days and weeks after the IPO, even the likelihood of a split. They knew the exact value of their shares at different opening prices and the date, whether it was a week or three years from now, when their options would be fully vested.

Though he tried to be honest, it gnawed at Miller that he was putting too much of a positive spin on the events leading to the IPO. Sure he could provide evidence for everything he said. But was it the truth? Could he be fooling himself? After all, the most recent set of questions back from the SEC had addressed entirely new topics from the previous set. That wasn't supposed to happen; the new questions were supposed to refine the company's answers to the previous set of questions, not start over on new ground. This endless shifting suggested the terrible possibility that the SEC's questions might leap from topic to topic in a process that might take not days but months.

Should he tell the employees his fears? Were the fears realistic or just a product of his own paranoia and exhaustion? He decided to keep up the brave front. Why frighten them with speculation?

But each time he looked into Connie's eyes, Bob Miller was reminded that for some MIPS employees Going Public Day would mean far more than reputation or money. At least one life might depend on it.

The sky to the east was turning pink as he drove into San Francisco.

At about the moment Bob Miller awakened, Bob Latta's plane was just touching down at Dulles Airport in Washington, D.C.

Latta, who prided himself on his ability to sleep aboard an airplane, to nod off as the wheels left the runway and to awaken as they touched down again, had been awake all night. He was running on adrenaline. Of the 50 stock offerings with which he had been involved in his 10 years at the Wilson, Sonsini, Goodrich & Rosati law firm, 25 of them initial public offerings, this MIPS deal was not only one of the biggest, but easily the worst. Every time the turbulence calmed, some new catastrophe would send the team reeling.

Young associates usually carried the papers and amendments to offering documents back to the SEC. But now here he was, the 35-year-old general partner in the most famous Silicon Valley law firm, on a red-eye flight, two boxes of paperwork on the seat beside him and *Dead Poet's Society* showing on the movie screen. What a deal.

Given the history of the case, he had come to expect confusion. On the day before the papers had to be delivered, when John Sandler left Bowne printers to drive back to Palo Alto to be Santa Claus at the firm's Christmas party and then called to see if he should pick up anything on his return, Latta had replied, "Yeah, John, stop at my house and get my wife to give you some clothes for me. Get my London Fog and put the liner in it. And put the gloves in the pocket because I may have to take this if things aren't settled."

And things sure as hell weren't settled. Not after a series of calls back to D.C. during the evening.

Latta had sworn never to make a courier run again, especially in the dead of winter. He could have given the job to Sandler; Sandler always wanted to make the deliveries because he had a girl-friend in D.C. and could get a nice weekend out of the deal. Now Sandler was annoyed, but Latta knew he was right to go.

He had made the decision at 10 o'clock, a half-hour before the last flight out of San Francisco that would reach D.C. before the business day.

Latta turned to Sweeney and Ludvigson and said, "You know, I hate to volunteer for this because I haven't slept in several days and it's really not my idea of a fun time, but maybe I should go instead of John in case something happens tomorrow."

Ludvigson said, "Yeah, I'd really appreciate it if you'd go." But the documents—the amendment with all the pricing data that had to be cleared by the SEC examiner and the box of exhibits in sup-port—weren't ready. The deadline to leave for the airport came and went and still the packages weren't ready. Finally, Latta gave instructions to have the papers meet him at the airport, ran out the door, jumped into his car, and raced to the airport.

As he blasted down Bayshore freeway, Latta reviewed his options if the plane started to leave and the papers weren't in his hands. The most extreme scenario was to find another plane. He remembered the high-rolling days of the early 1980s when legendary venture capitalist Art Rock spent $30,000 to rent a Learjet for Latta's paralegal to get packages on the Diasonics IPO back to the SEC after the regular flights had been missed.

That was an option Latta didn't want to use. How about holding the plane? Trotting through the quiet United Airlines terminal, Latta remembered the time eight years before when, as a young attorney, he'd been assigned to deliver some SEC documents: "We were running to catch the plane and I get there with the package and one of the other guys is buying my ticket. I pop the package up on the counter and announce, 'This is a $60 million package—it was—and you've got to hold the plane for 10 more seconds.'"

"But they wouldn't do it."

They'd made that flight anyway. But the way things were shaping up this time might be even closer. And this was a $70 million package.

Reaching the gate, Latta discovered to his dismay that the plane was on time. "I couldn't believe it. It really pissed me off. The first United flight I'd taken in three years that's on time and it has to be this one." He called Bowne: "Have they left yet? Have they left yet? The goddamn plane's on time!"

Now Latta decided his only chance of holding the plane was a guerrilla approach. Searching the crowd, he spotted a kid wearing a sweatshirt of U.C. Berkeley's law school, Boalt Hall. Perfect. No law student would mind a little embarrassment to make some folding money. Latta walked up and asked the kid if he would be willing to make 20 bucks by faking an epileptic seizure and blocking the ramp doorway.

"The kid wanted more money! So I'm negotiating a price with him when I hear this commotion in the distance. I look over and see Dave Segre running his ass off down the concourse carrying this big fucking box.

"Now I know I'm safe. I've got the exhibits. If worse comes to worse I can have the rest telecommunicated to me.

"So here comes Segre just hauling balls down the people mover. And this is like Gate 90 or something, so he's run like three quarters of a mile or something. Fortunately, he's a biker, rides in the mountains and so forth on weekends.

"So he gets to me and he's panting so hard he can't even talk. He's hanging on the railing. They're loading the plane now and I'm asking him, 'What do I have to know about what's in the package? What has to change when I get to Bowne in D.C.?' And he can't talk. So I start shaking him, yelling 'Talk to me!' and meanwhile the last eight people are getting on the plane.

"Finally, I just say, 'Look leave me a voice mail and walk me through it. I'll pick it up when I get in.' 'Fine,' Segre manages to say.

"About now Patterson, the rep for Bowne—one of the best in the business—finally shows up. And since he's not a jock, he's panting even harder than Segre. But at least he manages to tell me Bowne's street address in D.C. and some other stuff, and next thing I know I'm on the plane."

But the confrontation with United wasn't over yet. "I've got a bulkhead seat in the coach class right by the galley and I'm just standing there, with the box on the seat behind me, sort of hiding it. And I was going to stand there right until take-off. Well, this stewardess comes up and asks me to sit down. So I start schmoozing her, telling her that the reason I don't want to sit is because I've been sitting for about eight days and I've got a veg butt. Well, she buys it and walks away.

"Soon as she's gone I start stuffing this big box into the overhead compartment. Next thing I know another stewardess shows up and starts giving me shit about the box being too big and heavy, and how it should be checked in. And I said, 'No, you don't understand. This is a $70 million package and I'll hold it on my lap if I have to.'

"Right about then the first stewardess appears and says, 'Aw, lay off him. The guy hasn't slept in three days. Be nice to him.' So I got to keep the papers with me."

After all that, the rest of the flight was comparatively uneventful. Sleepless, Latta first used the on-board telephone ("the first time I'd ever had one work") and called Segre and Sandler to find out what was missing from the documents. "I got a pretty good bill for that call later."

Next, back in his seat, Latta set about doing a "washtub" edit of the materials—lawyer's jargon for clearing your mind to proofread, as if for the first time, documents you've already read and edited a dozen times before. After that, amazed to find himself still wide-eyed, Latta watched the movie, even though he had seen it before.

Landing in Dulles, Latta took a cab into the city to the D.C. offices of Bowne, located in the National Press Building, half a dozen blocks from the SEC. He arrived at about seven in the morning, eastern time, read all the faxes from San Francisco, and, following their instructions, set about packaging and organizing all the documents and exhibits according to the right number of copies of each.

At 7:30 Latta finished the tasks and used the Bowne bathroom to shower and change out of the suit he'd been wearing for the previous 30 hours. Outside, a Bowne car with a phone was waiting to take him to the SEC.

As he rode in the car, going over what he had to do, Latta thought that finally everything was beginning to go right.

He was wrong.

"My big mistake was that when I got to the SEC I let the driver go. I never should have done that because it had been eight years since I'd been there and I'd forgotten that there are no pay phones in the lobby of the building. I think it's intentional by the SEC.

"So, I go in. I get to the file desk at five minutes to eight. I wait the five minutes until it opens and I formally file the first set of documents. Now, of course, that doesn't do me any good because no one will see that shit for days. That's why you also carry courtesy copies for the examiners. I've got four of them, but the courtesy desk, which is down in the basement, doesn't open until 9:00.

"There's a reception area on the first floor, with a phone, that I thought opened at 8:30, so I go wait there. I'm watching all sorts of other guys coming in and making their filings at the main desk and then going down to the basement with their courtesy copies. But I know that's a chump move because you'll end up opening too late on the market if there's any problem with the examiner. So I think I'm pretty smart.

"Then 8:30 comes and goes and still nothing's happening in the reception area. So I go and ask a file clerk, 'Hey, what time does the place open?' '9:00.' And I say, 'Oh shit.' I put my jacket back on and I put the coat back on and go out into the cold looking for a pay phone. So here I am. It's now 8:35 A.M. It's also like 10 degrees outside, and I'm huddled in my overcoat walking ever-larger concentric circles around the SEC looking for a pay phone and freezing my ass off.

"Finally, I find one a couple of blocks away in one of those little bombed-out 10-car parking lots between buildings."

Latta dialed the number of the assistant director of the SEC, Howard Morin, the man whose questions were delaying making the public offering "effective" [formally cleared to go public]. Instead of Morin, Latta got a recording: "It was like 'Sally and Suzie aren't home right now. Please leave a message.'

"So I'm thinking, what the hell? So then I call [SEC branch chief] Barthelmes . . . and I get a disconnected number. Then I call the examiner and I get a ring with no answer. What the fuck is happening here?

"So I call Segre in San Francisco and wake him up and get him to check the numbers. He gets up out of bed, looks in the directory and, yep, they're all right.

"So I hang up and try Morin again—'Sally and Suzie aren't home right now.' Then Barthelmes—the line is disconnected. Then, David Thelander, the examiner—no answer.

"It's now twenty to nine and I'm starting to panic. At 9:30 the market opens. I know if I have to wait until the courtesy desk opens at 9:00, the copies won't get to the examiner until 9:30. Then he's got to read it, bless it, pow-wow with Morin—and it'll be 10:30 before we're effective. And that's not what Morgan Stanley wants. They want to go at 9:30.

"I don't know what to do. I can't keep leaving strange messages for Howard Morin with Sally and Suzie. Maybe it's the phone, I decide. So I trot back to the SEC to see if maybe there's a phone there I missed. But there isn't. Just a dozen lawyers standing around waiting for the desk to open.

"So, with no other choice, I run once more out into the cold and start making concentric circles again around the SEC looking for another phone."

The New American Dream

The electronics industry is now America's largest manufacturing employer, exceeding steel, automobiles, farm machinery, and every other type of manufacturing once considered synonymous with the Industrial Age.

At the same time it can be said that the single most distinguishing characteristic of commerce in the United States after the Second World War has been entrepreneurship. Certainly it has been entrepreneurship that has taken the fruits of American technology in the electronics age, many of which have permanently changed human society, and converted them into thousands of companies. It is because of entrepreneurship that most of the 500 largest American manufacturers are companies that did not even exist 20 years ago. And it has been entrepreneurship that has served as the last bulwark against the depredations of foreign competition.

It follows that the Going Public Day of a young electronics company, the day when entrepreneurship is rewarded for its sacrifices and risk taking, is now the emblematic moment of the new American Dream—the day of payoff for gratification deferred, years of eight-hour work weeks, broken marriages, lost career opportunities, grandiose dreams, struggle for personal freedom, huge financial investments, and unshakable loyalty. It is the day when the loyal secretary may become wealthy, the rebel post-adolescent may join the ranks of the world's richest men, the young immigrant may fulfill every fantasy about America heard in the Old Country.

In an egalitarian society that too often exhibits cruel inequalities, Going Public Day often represents a return to first principles. Certainly those at the top of the firm receive greater rewards than those at the bottom, but all receive rewards far beyond those conferred by the society outside the firm. Loyalty, pluck, endurance, faith—all of the qualities Americans profess to hold precious—are recognized on Going Public Day to a degree rarely found elsewhere in the society.

It is estimated that in the instant MIPS went public, 20 employees and directors made more than $1 million. Perhaps 200 more saw their net worth increase by $100,000 to $200,000.

On Going Public Day, the individual employees are rewarded for sacrificing years of their lives, for spurning higher paying jobs elsewhere, and for taking a risk on an enterprise with little chance of survival, much less a payoff. Executives are rewarded as well for taking a flyer on a deal that might sink their reputations. Venture capitalists are rewarded for betting millions on a few pieces of paper and a handful of inexperienced founders.

Most of all, Going Public Day rewards, often with extraordinary riches, the entrepreneur. And that is only fair. It is the entrepreneur who has performed the most magical feat of all: He or she has converted a dream into a real company, producing real products that may change the lives of strangers around the world and providing employment to hundreds of people.

Each Going Public Day is the celebration of a small circle. The odds against a start-up's surviving more than a couple of years are huge. The odds against that firm's being successful enough to reach the $50 million or $100 million it takes to become a publicly owned firm are astronomical.

In Silicon Valley, the heartland of American high-tech entrepreneurship, of the ten thousand or more companies that have been founded in the last three decades, no more than a hundred have gone public. This singular list contains many celebrated names: Hewlett-Packard, Varian, Intel, Fairchild, National Semiconductor, Apple, Tandem, Amdahl, Commodore, Atari, Sun. Now MIPS would join that select list.

Going Public Day also has a ritual value that reaches beyond the individual company into the community itself. A place like Silicon Valley exists on hope, on the belief that anyone with enough ambition, guts, and brains can make it. It is this belief that draws immigrants and ambitious young graduates to the Valley and keeps them there even as they watch companies fail. It keep them there in the face of traffic congestion, pollution, expensive real estate, an exorbitant cost of living that seems forever to grow faster than their salaries. It is this hope that enables them to commute 70 miles and

90 minutes each day to work from their distant homes in California's Central Valley. And most of all, it is this dream that keeps them going in a gypsy-like, rapidly changing, youth-oriented career that may move them to a dozen employers in two decades and make them obsolete before they are 50 years old.

This dream must be regularly renewed, lest it fade and leave visible only the dark side of high-tech life. Every few years, there must be that spectacular reminder that the merry-go-round still offers its riders the brass ring. The stories of Hewlett and Packard, Noyce, Jobs, and Wozniak have enduring power, but must constantly be made current with new, even if lesser, stories of latter-day entrepreneurial successes. When MIPS went public, Silicon Valley was living on the aging stories of T. J. Rodgers at Cypress Semiconductor, Finis Connor at Connor Peripherals, and the crews at Octel, Quantum, and Oracle.

Now, to the considerable relief of many aging and new Valleyites, came the over-the-hill gang from MIPS with their story of the company brought back like Lazarus from the dead and of the billion dollar management. Throughout Silicon Valley, people would open the *San Jose Mercury-News* or the *San Francisco Chronicle,* read of MIPS's spectacular opening market price, and say to themselves that someday they'd find a firm like that and strike it rich. It could be done.

For some those thoughts would be darkened by desperation. One cannot grow old in Silicon Valley. Until the government mandated the 401k program, Valley companies like Apple Computer had no pension plans. Gyms certainly, day care centers perhaps, but no one gives out gold watches in Silicon Valley. A middle-aged public relations woman, a 25-year Silicon Valley veteran, would say about the stock she owned in one of her clients that was planning to go public, "You don't understand. This isn't a bonus. This is my only chance for retirement."

If holding founder's stock on the day a young company goes public is the modern American Dream, then Going Public Day is the nexus of hundreds of individual dreams, all converging on that instant when the company's name appears on the stock ticker.

Then the dreams again diverge, imperceptibly at first, but with an ever-broadening sweep. Some employees, in pursuit of new dreams, leave the firm within weeks or months. Others stay several years before being carried off in the cyclone of electronics industry life. A few, sometimes the least likely candidates, stay for decades, long after the principals of the firm are dead or retired, until, like ancient drummer boys, they are the last surviving veterans of the company's entrepreneurial battles.

Going Public Day is probably the most profound turning point in a firm's history. Before that point of inflection, the people it hired were, by necessity, entrepreneurial to some degree. They were willing to take the high risk and the reduced salary in exchange for equity in the big score. After Going Public Day, the newly hired people are drawn to the firm for entirely different reasons. They are not as willing to take risks; they are more conservative, more political. With no founder's stock available, these new corporate types have different goals than their entrepreneurial predecessors: They want money and power.

In the final weeks before its IPO, a company begins to look like an exhausted marathoner. Growing at a breakneck pace while simultaneously going public takes its toll. Top to bottom, the company is worn out, ready for a vacation, and Going Public Day serves as a perfect mental finish line.

Not surprisingly, many newly public companies go through a difficult period as they adapt to being big corporations. Suddenly, what used to be scarce, money, is abundant, and the challenge becomes not to overindulge every pent-up whim. Too many new corporations immediately launch into new markets, design new products, or build extravagant new headquarters buildings . . . only to find themselves overextended and in trouble.

Sudden wealth can be a problem for the individuals, too. The parking lot transformations after an IPO are famous. Within six months and full stock vestment, the Fords, Hondas, and Toyotas are replaced by Mercedes, Porsches, and BMWs as well as the occasional Rolls-Royce and Ferrari. It can be hard to stay motivated to work till midnight when several hundred thousand dollars is sitting in your bank account.

Finally, there is the entrepreneurial spirit itself. The wildcatting era of the company is over. Those who thrived in those rough and tumble days often find themselves confused and frustrated when the company announces a dress code or publishes an employee manual or begins filling up the executive offices with young Harvard MBAs who've never had to make a payroll. Then, the early days of the firm, no matter how hard and unpredictable, take on a rosy cast, like memories of a pre-empire republic.

This frustration with corporate life can be experienced by veterans from the rank and file right up to the president's office. Soon there will be annual reports and quarterly earnings announcements and shareholder meetings and proxy fights and all the rest of the exposure that comes with being a publicly traded corporation. Some company presidents begin to feel restless, bored, dissatisfied with their work. And some companies begin to feel dissatisfied with their presidents. One of the saddest sights in Silicon Valley life is the entrepreneurial founder who has become a liability to the mature firm he created and has been unceremoniously dumped on the street.

Of course, all of these potential problems, if they ever did arrive, lay in the distant future for MIPS. For now the company was blissfully happy. Everyone tried to work, but beneath attempts to take care of business lay a giddiness that threatened to burst out at any moment. This euphoria wasn't due to the money alone, though obviously that played a major role. For most of the employees, the big payoff they'd just earned would still seem unreal for days. Rather, much of the excitement came from being a participant in a success story, from having achieved a long-sought goal.

Exhausted though it may be, a company will probably never run better than in the weeks before Going Public Day. Morale is high; turnover is low. Productivity, despite the distractions, is excellent. Most of all, for perhaps the only time in the firm's history, every employee shares a mutual and immediate goal. On this common ground, assembly people and vice presidents speak to one another as equals, as travelers on a shared adventure. And on Going Public Day, the company becomes, for that one day alone, a place in which every inhabitant is awarded the winning prize.

As the 600 members of MIPS assembled at the company's of-fices, their dreams converged. By the time they left, their dreams had already begun to fly off on myriad trajectories.

From *Going Public,* New York: HarperCollins, Edward Burlingame Books, 1991.

6

BOB NOYCE

Inventor, Entrepreneur, Statesman

It was not surprising that one wire service, carrying the story of the unexpected death of Robert Noyce, accompanied it with a photo of the wrong man. Generations from now, that mistake will be the punch line to the shocking story of how we, Noyce's contemporaries, didn't appreciate one of the great Americans of the twentieth century, didn't fully understand this protean figure of the modern technological world. Like most myths, it will not be entirely correct. Dr. Noyce was, after all, compared to Edison by several newspapers. And the president of the United States did telephone his widow.

Yet the myth of the unappreciated hero will also have a basis in fact. That Bob Noyce was the co-inventor of the integrated circuit, the most important invention of the second half of this century, would be enough to confer on him a place in human history. After all, in doing so he irrevocably changed the world. How many millions of lives have been saved by this one invention after it was placed in medical equipment and electronic instruments? In computers and sensors? The integrated circuit and its panoply of descendants created revolutions in every sphere they entered, from agriculture to medicine to communication to transportation to the home. It changed the way we see the world, how we think, how we work, and how we play.

How great were these changes? We may not fully know for centuries. Already, electronics is America's largest manufacturing employer. It is the vehicle Japan used to become a world power. Arguably, it was an inability to compete technologically that doomed the Communist regimes in Eastern Europe, a change even tanks couldn't stop. It is having the same effect on the Soviet Union, on China, and on every other country that still believes it can control the lives of its citizens. The little silicon chip, as much as any other force, helped to tear down the Berlin Wall. And its ultimate impact on such traditional constructions as national borders, ideologies, the office, and the city may be so profound as to redefine, in our lifetimes, the very notion of human society.

With a few words in his journal, and with the bull's-eye shaped circuit that came from it, Bob Noyce put quantum physics in the hands of every living person and in the process liberated us. The libraries of kings and resources of giant institutions now sit on the desk of a poor student in Nairobi; and giant super-computers plumb the mysteries at the edge of the universe and in the center of the atom. About no other man of our time can it so unquestionably be said, as it can of Bob Noyce, that he utterly changed the lives of every single human being on earth.

Yes, the co-discovery of the integrated circuit is sufficient to make Bob Noyce one of the great inventors. But it is not enough to make him a great man. And Bob Noyce was most assuredly a great man, a true hero of our time. It is in this difference that we misread the legacy of the man.

In many ways, the invention of the integrated circuit was Noyce's equivalent to a wartime medal for heroism—a glorious moment in youth that amplified, but did not define, all that came after. Furthermore, he wasn't alone. At the same time, at Texas Instruments, Jack Kilby made almost the same discovery; thus history has them sharing the credit. Just as important, the integrated circuit was but a step, if a singular one, in the long march of electronics. A dozen years before it lay the equally signal invention of the transistor by Shockley, Brattain, and Bardeen. A dozen years later saw the invention of the microprocessor—the key to the digital revolution—by Hoff, Faggin, and Mazor at Noyce's own firm, Intel.

To study the story of these inventions is to realize their inevitability. If Noyce and Kilby had not discovered the integrated circuit, someone else eventually would have. This, of course, does not diminish their achievement: How much would have been lost in the intervening months or years? That's why these two great inventors, in what will be another damning piece of evidence for future generations, should have received the Nobel Prize for physics (and peace, for that matter). But Nobel Prizes tend to be given only to those who didn't dirty their hands with commerce, who don't spend each day preserving a livelihood for tens of thousands of workers and their families.

When Bob Noyce invented the integrated circuit, he didn't set out to change the world but only to improve the competitiveness of his fledgling company. It was essentially a challenging engineering problem to be solved. And Noyce, though he appreciated the impact of the integrated circuit as much as any man alive, always seemed to treat this role in this historical turning point as just that.

By comparison, for the rest of his life, Noyce did set out to change the world. To accomplish that he had to ignite one social revolution after another. He had to revise himself over and over to match his growing responsibility and influence. And, just to start, he had to invent Silicon Valley.

That he accomplished all of these things, and did so gracefully, earning a seemingly boundless reverence from his employees and even from his competitors; that rival and one-time subordinate Charlie Sporck would order the flags at National Semiconductor lowered to half-staff; that engineers at arch-opponent Japanese firms would reportedly not wash their right hands for days after shaking Noyce's hand—*that* is Robert Noyce's true claim to personal greatness, the moral we should read in his life. His is the ultimate epitaph: He changed mankind, yet left no enemies.

The early years of Noyce's life have all the elements of a myth in the making—and one can already picture how the story, embellished with numerous anecdotes from our own time, will be broadened and inflated with time, until the real Bob Noyce will be nearly lost.

As with many such figures, his success has no real antecedents. His father, as were both his grandfathers, was a preacher, moving among the towns of Iowa. The family was poor, a situation exacerbated by the Depression, and Noyce, the third of four brothers, shared the humiliation of living off hand-me-downs and produce from church members.

At 11, Bob Noyce's father was awarded the distinguished (but low-paying) job of associate superintendent of the Iowa Conference of Congregational Churches, and the family finally settled in Grinnell, a college town and Congregationalist center. For the first time, young Bob could settle in everyday community life, join the Boy Scouts, meet girls, and compete on the swim team.

After school, he worked detasseling corn and hoeing beans, and delivered papers and special delivery letters. The only clues to any technological acumen were a hang-glider—more properly an oversized box kite—that nearly killed him and his brother; and a homemade "car" powered by an old gasoline motor from a washing machine. There was no question of Bob's intelligence, except perhaps in his own mind. Though he graduated at the top of his high school class, it was only in his final years of high school "that I began to feel that maybe I had a little bit more than average ability." Bored with high school classes, he took college physics classes at nearby Grinnell College.

After graduation, the Noyces decided to move to Illinois. But Bob chose to stay behind and finish his studies in physics and mathematics at Grinnell.

As chance would have it, this little prairie university happened to have one of the best physics programs in the United States. Bob rolled through the program at the top of his class, still having enough time to earn a varsity letter in swimming (which he seemed to consider one of his proudest achievements) and win the state diving championship.

But, in his senior year, in an event that is already part of the Noyce legend, Bob suddenly found himself facing expulsion and possible criminal charges. Apparently, to reproduce a then-popular South Sea roast pig luau, Noyce and another student had stolen a 25-pound porker from a neighboring farm and cooked it for the dorm.

Iowans did not find pig stealing amusing in 1948, and Grinnell suspended its top student.

Chastened, Noyce spent the next six months in New York, working in the actuarial department at Equitable Life and hanging out with his eldest brother, a student at Columbia. Because he was already so far ahead of his classmates, Noyce was able to return to Grinnell in early 1949 and still finish on time. It was during this last semester, under the tutelage of Professor Grant Gale, that Noyce devoted himself to understanding the wonders of the newly invented transistor: "I began to look at the transistor as being one of the great phenomena of the time. And that it would be something good to exploit—well, maybe 'exploit' is the wrong way to put it—but I saw it as something that would be fun to work with."

That pursuit led him to the doctoral program in solid state physics at MIT, where he was stunned to find the school woefully lacking in expertise in transistors. Forced to pursue other studies, Noyce fortuitously chose physical electronics, eventually writing his dissertation on "A Photoelectric Study of Surface States of Insulators." Up to this point in Bob Noyce's life, we have the not-atypical story of a brilliant, and slightly wild, young man. But now, he made a series of crucial decisions that set him on a singular trajectory.

The first of these was his choice of a job. With his curriculum vitae, he could have gone to any of the great research laboratories—GE, Bell, RCA—but instead chose lowly Philco for less pay. His reasoning give us a hint of the utter self-assurance, the sense of his own importance, that always hid behind the adult Noyce's self-effacing style: ". . . the way I put it to myself at the time was that they really needed me. At the other places they knew what was going on, they knew what they needed."

Soon, like every company with which Noyce would be associated, Philco became known as a technological innovator. He stayed three years. Then in 1956, having heard a Noyce presentation at a technical conference, William Shockley called. Schockley was leaving Bell Labs to return to Northern California and start a company. He was gathering together the best and brightest young minds in solid state physics. Would Bob like to join them?

A second hint at the inner workings of Noyce's mind is that he flew out to the Bay Area and bought a house in Los Altos that morning even before the interview with Shockley in the afternoon.

At Shockley Semiconductor, Noyce joined a charmed circle at the cutting edge of microelectronics. Among these powerful minds, Noyce was soon first among equals, Shockley's favorite. At first the experience was exhilarating. Shockley was an extraordinary thinker, sometimes compared with Newton and Einstein. But he was also a brutal boss, paranoid, vindictive, and unpredictable. The seven other young geniuses of the company decided to quit en masse. They had even found an investment banker, who, after being turned down by 22 firms, at last found an interested party in New Jersey's Fairchild Camera & Instrument. But the seven realized they would have no hope of a deal without the eighth man, Noyce, the only natural leader in the group.

Noyce, Shockley's golden boy, joined them in the mass resignation. Shockley, furious, forever labeled them the Traitorous Eight. But tellingly, though it took 20 years, even he forgave Noyce.

Most histories of Silicon Valley will point to the Traitorous Eight and their formation of Fairchild as the moment modern Silicon Valley was born. But in truth that moment really came with the most heroic, and least appreciated, decision Bob Noyce would ever make. Just 28 years old, he was now the general manager of what would soon be the most influential company in the world. How would he run it? How should a semiconductor firm be managed?

The only model close was Shockley Semiconductor. It would have been easy for Noyce to simply temper that style slightly to reduce turnover and be on his way. That would have been congruent with the business models of the day.

But Noyce chose to turn his back on all the models. Like Hewlett and Packard before him, he decided to trust his people. But going even further, he let them take their own lead, allowed their eccentricities (and with it their strengths) to emerge and eschewed the rigid East Coast organizational style. Fairchild, thanks to Noyce, would become the most democratic company of its generation, a fact properly celebrated by Tom Wolfe in his *Esquire* profile of Noyce a decade ago.

It is difficult now, when the Silicon Valley "management style" is so firmly incorporated into our culture, to fully appreciate the courage of Noyce's decision. He had everything to lose and no evidence of potential gain. He seems to have made the choice simply because it was the decent and proper way to treat people.

Fairchild these days is best known for the circumstances of its demise, blowing up and scattering entrepreneurs over the Valley floor to sprout scores of new companies. What is forgotten is that somehow, for a decade, Noyce managed to hold together this seemingly impossible collection of talent, idiosyncrasies, and egos, of future Fortune 500 CEOs and engineering legends. And he might have held them together forever if Fairchild corporate had acceded to his requests for employee stock options.

After leaving Fairchild, Noyce, with Gordon Moore and Andy Grove, founded Intel, and in the process gave the local high-tech venture capital industry its first great victory. With Intel would come the invention of the microprocessor and, in time, Intel's preeminence in the world of digital microelectronics.

But by then, Noyce had moved on to the national arena, as spokesman for the U.S. electronics industry. In the history of American business, there have been only a handful of men and women who have been able to cross over from being inventors to successful entrepreneurs. Of these, only a small fraction have been able to grow with their enterprises, remaining in command as the company reached $1 billion in sales. And of these, only David Packard and Bob Noyce have managed the last step of becoming statesmen.

The difficulty of their achievement is nearly impossible for the rest of us to imagine. Each step along the way required a nearly complete change in management, personality, and priority. And it did not come without cost: Noyce was married twice. He chain-smoked, which probably led to his early death. And, in the last few years, as he fought for more of a national industrial policy in electronics, Noyce found himself facing unrelenting opposition from his own industry, even from executives who had modeled their lives after him.

He led the fight for Sematch, the industry research consortium, and when no suitable president for it could be found, he took the thankless job himself, packing up his National Medal of Science and his Grinnell mementos and leaving his creation, Silicon Valley, forever. At a time in his life when he might have harvested his laurels, he bet his reputation one more time. He assumed the onerous schedule of a young man. A business meeting had even been scheduled on the Sunday he died.

In person, Noyce was not a commanding figure. He was a relatively small man, with a rumbling voice and the compact build of an aging athlete. He was genial and unaffected, swore with care, and had a keen sense of irony that would result in a chuckle and crooked grin like that of a mischievous schoolboy.

What is not easy to explain is the man's presence. He filled any room he entered with a bewildering impression of power and command. He appeared neither humble—he well knew his place in history—nor arrogant. He was just his own man; slightly reserved, ultimately unknowable to everyone but those very close to him. The only real clue to what lay inside was when he was angry or intellectually engaged. Then his eyes would seem to go black, burning a hole through your forehead to pin you to the chair behind.

But perhaps the best way to describe Bob Noyce to those who will never meet him, is that before and after everything else, he was a swimmer. And that fact, more than any of his famous achievements, may be the most telling characteristic of the man. In swimming there is the seamlessness of action, the balanced use of every part of oneself, the pursuit of perfect motion, the essential solitude.

Dr. Noyce dived competitively at Grinnell, scuba dived throughout his life, and turned the backyard of his Los Altos home into a swimmer's paradise. Even his voracious winter pursuit of skiing throughout the world seems consonant with his love of water and fluidity of motion.

Bob Noyce spent most of the few spare moments of his life swimming, and with a kind of noble symmetry, his fatal heart attack came after a morning swim. One imagines him on those last laps in the pool, even after a lifetime still patiently working to refine his stroke, to perfect his movement through the water until he just left the slightest of wakes. And, one imagines on the fateful morning, as always, Bob Noyce made it look effortless.

From *Upside Magazine,* July 1990.

7

SILICON SUBURBIA

Silicon Valley in 1965, at the time when Steve Jobs was attending Monte Loma elementary school in Mountain View, was a tense combination of opposing demographic forces.

Strictly speaking, Silicon Valley didn't yet exist. Sure, Fairchild was there, but it became mythic only in retrospect. If you were to drive down Ellis Street in Mountain View past its headquarters, you never would have known that this little company was already changing the world.

Hewlett-Packard, of course, was there. By 1965 it was already more than 25 years old. At night, driving up El Camino Real in Palo Alto heading to the young Stanford Shopping Center, you could see its sawtooth roof glowing atop the hill up Page Mill Road. But HP was, and is, as hermetic as a church. If your father worked there, you were embraced within the HP family, you met Bill and Dave and attended the company picnic, and lived in an Eichler home in Palo Alto. Your neighbors were college professors from Stanford, other HPers or engineers and scientists who worked near HP in the Stanford Industrial Park at companies like Varian Corp., Watkins Johnson, or Syntex.

But more important than HP was Lockheed Missiles & Space (LMSC), a city in itself rising alongside the Bay next to the Moffett Naval Air Station and NASA's Ames Research Center. Each day at 7 A.M., Lockheed's 25,000 employees would leave their homes in Mountain View, Sunnyvale, Cupertino, and Santa Clara—from housing developments that had been built specifically for them by smart developers—and crowded the streets heading east into the morning sun toward the two LMSC gates. And each day at 3:30 P.M., the process would reverse, giving the Valley a distinct work cycle that would dominate the area for 20 years.

More than any other force, Lockheed was the dynamo that made Santa Clara County (the western cities of the South San Francisco Bay from Palo Alto to San Jose) the fastest growing place in America. Young men, new families in tow, arrived by the scores each day, armed with a GI Bill degree in aeronautical, electrical, or mechanical engineering, and looking for a piece of the aerospace future. They bought their ranch-style house—or, if they were adventurous, a Bauhaus-for-everyman Eichler with an atrium—and drove off every morning to build ICBMs for Lockheed.

Those who now call that world stultifying, conformist, or retrograde weren't there. It was, in fact, as progressive in its way as any place on earth. The men and women who populated Silicon Valley in the 1960s were optimists. They believed that they were not only constructing the future, but creating a perfect world for themselves and their families in the process. They would be famous and rich, have beautiful children and live in a Winterless Paradise and own a modernistic house and collect fine wines—all at the same time.

The betrayal, the depression, and the self-doubt only came later, after Lockheed laid off at least one breadwinner on every residential block, after their kids grew their hair long and despised them and, worst of all, after these young men and women of infinite promise became divorced, career-stalled middle-aged men and women with a ceiling on their hopes.

It came after the counterculture revolution, Vietnam and recession, and after Silicon Valley had become a single monolithic urban stretch of high-tech communities 30 miles long and 10 miles wide. In 1965, though, these professional communities were still tiny enclaves of (mostly) White, (mostly) Protestant, (mostly) engineers embedded in vast stretches of old Santa Clara Valley: blue-collar, rural, orchard-based, seasonal, immigrant, Catholic.

Mountain View was one of the oldest of Valley communities. Originally the Castro family land grant from Mexico, it was a well-developed farming community by the beginning of the twentieth century. The children and grandchildren of these farmworkers were enjoying the postwar prosperity by moving up to the new suburban housing developments, like the square mile of ersatz Eichlers built by Mackay Homes on the edge of Mountain View along Alma and San Antonio roads hard by the southern tip of Palo Alto.

For the local families that moved into this development in the early 1960s, these homes were the culmination of an assimilationist dream that in some cases reached back a century. It was the family's first toehold in the middle class, thanks to new jobs in auto repair shops, assembly lines, and retail stores. Yet they soon found their shiny dreams tarnished by the arrival of new neighbors from the East Coast or the Midwest; arrivistes who drove their foreign cars every Friday night to San Francisco in search of real culture, and who owned not just college diplomas but graduate degrees in unimaginable disciplines like solid-state physics and semiconductor electronics.

For these newcomers, the neighborhood was not a culmination but a flagstone on the path to bigger houses in nicer neighborhoods in Sunnyvale or Cupertino, and then, with luck and some stock options, Los Altos Hills or Saratoga. For now, they merely demanded that the schools improve their facilities, that local stores offer more diverse merchandise and that the constabulary protect their children from the predations of the tougher working-class kids down the street.

It was a situation guaranteed to provoke friction and hostility. The upwardly mobile new Silicon Valleyites saw the natives as uneducated, unsophisticated, and slightly dangerous, and the old Santa Clara Valleyites saw the newcomers as arrogant, pushy, and, worst of all, a threat to their hard-fought prosperity.

It was in this tense milieu that nine-year-old Steven P. Jobs found himself in 1965. And within this sensitive and often irritating boy the schisms went even deeper.

His father, Paul Jobs, grew up on a farm in Germantown, Wisconsin, dropped out of high school, then knocked around the Midwest in search of work. After Pearl Harbor, he made the odd decision, for someone at the land-locked center of the country, to join the Coast Guard. As the war ended, he found himself in San Francisco on a decommissioning ship, and in yet another one of the compulsive moves that would characterize his life, Jobs bet a shipmate that on one of their upcoming leaves he would find himself a wife.

He did just that, on a blind date. Feckless he might be, but Paul Jobs was also a persuasive man; a natural salesman. Unfortunately, he had one disastrous flaw for a salesman. He hated kowtowing to customers. He talked his new wife, Clara, into moving back with him to the Midwest, a decision that ran precisely counter to the great migration of ex-GIs. Needless to say, it was a bad strategy, and after struggling as a machinist and then a used-car salesman, Paul finally, in 1952, caught on to the spirit of the era and he and Clara headed back to San Francisco.

Despite the fact that California wasn't as golden as he expected, and Paul jumped from one lousy job to another—bad-debt collector, car repossessor, loan checker—he and Clara were now feeling suitably stable and settled to start a family. In 1956, they adopted a baby boy, Steven. Five months later, before the adoption legalities were even complete, the family moved to South San Francisco.

There was in Paul Jobs an unusual, though not rare, combination of romanticism, unreality, hard work, ego, and self-doubt. He was, in a sense, an entrepreneur who missed his calling, a lone wolf who chafed in every organization in which he worked, who resented being subordinate to anyone, who felt he was destined for important things but always arrived at the station just as the train pulled away, and who was perpetually ashamed about his lack of success. No sooner did he construct a new hopeful reality than it would crash around him and he would set off again.

In 1960, the finance company Paul was working for transferred him to Palo Alto. It was a good place for a man approaching middle age. The economy was booming and jobs were waiting unfilled. As they moved into their new home in Mountain View, it seemed that Paul Jobs had finally made it. Marking this new phase in their lives, Paul and Clara adopted a daughter, Patricia.

Now the Jobs family was in the very embodiment of a Postwar Upward Mobile community. It was as diverse a neighborhood as any the Valley would ever know. On a single block one might find a psychiatrist working at Agnews State Mental Hospital, a high school janitor, a naval officer flying P-3 sub chasers out of Moffett Field, a gardener from the Philippines who worked for the city, a Pakistani PhD in geology analyzing moon rills at NASA-Ames Research Center, and a computer scientist who would one day be a vice president of Hewlett-Packard.

In the midst of all this was a brilliant little boy, often distracted, something of a discipline problem, and accustomed to being the center of attention. He was the inevitable star of neighborhood home movies, birthday parties, and picnics. Not only was young Steven doted on by his parents, but as the years went on he increasingly became the surrogate for his father's frustrated career desires.

The result would likely have been an arrogant chronic overachiever, the kind of obnoxious personality type that fills the senior, but not top, management ranks of Silicon Valley. But there were two other factors at work as well. One was that young Steven, the adopted child, was simply *different* from his family. Where his old man was tough and gregarious, the kind of guy who could repossess cars all week, then spend the weekend rooting around junkyards for parts for the classic cars he rebuilt in his garage, his son was sensitive and withdrawn. The boy was a discipline problem at school, while still managing to have few friends. He would go with his dad to the junkyards, obviously enjoying the dickering, but once they returned home, he showed no interest in getting his hands dirty bolting on carburetors and fenders.

Worse, Steven was also a whiner. When he took swim lessons at the Mountain View Dolphins Swim club, one of his classmates, Mark Wozniak (yet more evidence that Silicon Valley has always been a very large small town) would recall: "He was pretty much of a crybaby. He'd lose a race and go off and cry. He didn't quite fit in with everybody else. He wasn't one of the guys." In fact, he was one of the boys, found in every class, who get the stuffing knocked out of them on a regular basis.

Out of place at home and at school, Steven turned to others in the neighborhood for friendship. It was possible in those days to walk down the street on a Saturday morning, past all the open, well-stuffed one-car garages and see the neighborhood men at work on their hobbies. And these extracurricular activities were as diverse as their careers. For every two Paul Jobses installing new lifters on engines, there was at least one man surrounded by used oscilloscopes, multimeters, waveform generators, oscillators, and all the other detritus of the vacuum-tube age of electronic instruments. Many of these obsolete devices had been lifted out of dumpsters at the office and were now being put to use on televisions, stereos, and, identified by the telltale antenna masts swaying over the house, ham radios.

Steven had just such a neighbor, a Hewlett-Packard engineer. One Saturday, while the boy was desultorily working with his father on a car, this engineer hauled a carbon microphone, a battery, and an old stereo speaker out on the driveway, hooked them up and shook the street. Steven's eyes lit up. How does that work he asked his father? Paul Jobs shrugged. He didn't know. So Steven ran to the engineer's house to ask. From then on, almost every Saturday, Steven stood in a new garage, peppering his new role model with questions.

His son's attention wasn't the only thing Paul Jobs lost. His job, he was convinced, was going nowhere. It didn't help that one by one the professionals among his neighbors began to move away to smarter, more expensive neighborhoods in Palo Alto and Los Altos. Unhappy and desperate, Paul Jobs decided once again to make a career shift. He took courses in his off-time and earned his realtor's license.

It was, in fact, a brilliant move. With the economy surging, the cost of living starting to climb, and one more old cherry orchard being covered by a new housing tract almost by the week, real estate was one of the most lucrative professions in the Valley. Had he stuck with it, Paul Jobs, like many others, might have made himself wealthy over the next 20 years.

Instead, he detested the work, a fact he might have realized long before he got into it. He didn't like making nice to every idiot with a buck in his pocket, he despised the whole phony nature of the profession and, most of all, he really hated not knowing when the next check was coming in. And they came in less and less frequently as his attitude spilled into his work and scared away clients.

The family was now caught in a downward spiral, made worse by the success of everyone around them. To stay afloat, the Jobses had to mortgage their house. Clara even took a part-time job. And when Steven took up swimming, she added babysitting to pay for his fees. Vacations were canceled. The car grew old. And in perhaps the ultimate statement of defeat in 1960s California, when the Jobses' color TV broke it was replaced with a black-and-white version. Eventually, to everyone's relief, Paul Jobs bailed out of real estate. But his only career choice now was to go back to work as a machinist with no seniority. He managed to find a job 20 miles away in San Carlos and the family struggled on.

Steven, now nine years old, watched in despair as the world around him, *his* world, began to crumble. Already alienated from his parents and his schoolmates, he was now, in a way he couldn't fully appreciate, also losing touch with his social class. It came to a head one day in school when his teacher asked a simple astronomy question: "What is it in this universe you don't understand?"

Little Steven Jobs, hovering over a cosmic abyss the teacher couldn't understand, answered abjectly: "Why is my family so broke?"

▼▲▼

Although the smartest kid in his class, Jobs became so difficult and obnoxious that he was thrown out of his fourth-grade class. Luckily, another, better, teacher took him in. Years later, Jobs would recall that the teacher found a quick motivational tool for the young man: bribes. Especially money. With the prospect of a payoff down the line, Steven Jobs could do amazing things. So amazing that he skipped fifth grade altogether.

But skipping a grade was both an honor and a curse, because the troubled, socially awkward boy was now a year younger than his classmates. Worse, jumping to sixth grade brought Steven one year closer to Crittenden Junior High School.

Monte Loma was paradise compared to Crittenden. Located in a poor neighborhood a half mile closer to the Bay, drawing from the middle class all the way down to the bottommost economic strata, Crittenden was a school where the daughter of an astrophysicist might sit at a desk next to the deeply disturbed son of a parolee. Fights were a daily occurrence; as were shakedowns in the bathrooms. Knives were regularly brought to school as a show of macho. The year before Steven arrived, a group of eighth-grade boys had gone to jail for gang rape. During Steven's seventh-grade year, the school lost a wrestling match to Sunnyvale's Mango Junior High and proceeded to demolish that school's team bus.

Among the students, there were two ruling elites: the hoods, mostly Hispanic, in pointed high-heel shoes, pegged black pants, white shirts, DAs; and a small number of surfers, with long blond hair, knit shirts, baggy pants, and deck shoes. Everyone else cowered in fear. And Steven Jobs, a year younger than his classmates and thus the youngest kid in school, a pariah even among the pariahs, was in the sorriest spot of all.

That summer, Steven dreaded September more than anything he'd ever known. Finally, he couldn't stand it any longer. He told his parents that if he had to go back to Crittenden, he would quit school.

What happened then was a turning point in Steven Jobs's life. He wasn't alone in fearing his school. In his neighborhood scores of families, worried about the quality of education and the threat to their children represented by Crittenden, had picked up stakes and moved elsewhere. But these were upwardly mobile families; most had planned to leave for months, even years, and the quality of schooling proved to be the trip wire.

An even greater number of kids in the neighborhood, when they expressed the same fear, or came home with a split lip and missing lunch money, were told by their less affluent parents to buck up and not be pushed around.

But when Steven Jobs made his ultimatum, the most amazing thing happened: his parents agreed. His family *moved* to a safer, and more expensive neighborhood in Sunnyvale—despite the fact that they were working extra jobs trying just to stay solvent, despite the fact that it meant an even longer commute for his father and that it meant pulling his sister out of elementary school.

This was power. And Steven Jobs learned its lesson.

From *Infinite Loop*, by Michael S. Malone, copyright © 1999 by Michael S. Malone. Used by permission of Doubleday, a division of Random House, Inc.

8

THE MACINTOSH INTRODUCTION

The "1984" commercial ran as scheduled for the one and only time to a wide audience (it was actually shown to a small midwestern audience in December to make it eligible for awards) during the third quarter of the Super Bowl.

Wozniak, with characteristic naiveté, nearly wrecked the plan. Invited to appear on *Good Morning America* a few days before the Super Bowl, he decided to take a copy of the commercial with him to show on the air. Luckily, he was caught in time.

Apple had wanted to make a splash with "1984." What it got was Eniwetok. The biggest single splash in the history of television advertising. Only one other commercial had ever had such an impact from a single showing, and that was the infamous Johnson political attack ad against Barry Goldwater showing a little girl pulling petals off a daisy as the voice-over began the countdown to a nuclear explosion.

On this Sunday afternoon in the winter of 1984, 43 million Americans saw the corporate analog of that infamous commercial. The bleak, gulag-like world. Big Brother on the screen intoning:

My friends, each of you is a single cell in the great body of the State. And today, that great body has purged itself of parasites. We have triumphed over the unprincipled dissemination of fact. The thugs and wreckers have been cast out. And the poisonous weeds of disinformation have been consigned to the dustbin of history. Let each and every cell rejoice! For today we celebrate the first, glorious anniversary of the Information Purification Directive. We have created, for the first time in all history, a garden of pure ideology, where each worker may bloom secure from the pests of contradictory and confusing truths. Our Unification of Thought is a more powerful weapon than any fleet or army on earth. We are one people. With one will. One resolve. One cause. Our enemies shall talk themselves to death. And we will bury them with their own confusion . . .

If it was gibberish, it was also just coherent enough for the audience to understand. Never before had a major U.S. corporation been described in such a way: evil, brainwashing, antidemocratic, totalitarian. Hundreds of thousands of jaws across America dropped in unison.

And then the Avenging Angel ran on-screen in her tank top and gym shorts. She flung her hammer, shattering the projected visage of Big Brother, unleashing a windstorm of shattered glass—stunning and awakening the sleepwalking prisoners like a shaft of sunlight bursting into Plato's Cave.

Then the final voice-over: "On January 24, Apple Computer will introduce Macintosh. 1984 won't be like *1984*."

In 10 million households from coast to coast there was a collective gasp, then, echoing the on-air words of one of the sports announcers, "Wow, what was *that?*"

The next day, the world was still talking about it. It was on the evening news. Millions of unfortunate people who had been in the kitchen or bathroom at the moment still claimed they saw it, so as not to be left out. In one minute's time, Apple, still a cult company to much of the consuming world, had become the coolest place on earth.

It was, indeed, insanely great. The commercial, which would never be broadcast again, thus adding to its legend, would go on to be the first American commercial to win a Grand Prix award at Cannes.

Now Apple needed a closer: the formal introduction on Tuesday. The commercial had primed the marketplace. It had done everything Jobs had wanted for it. Now he had the chance to capture the culture itself

With the help of Regis McKenna, a willing press, and a perfect historical window, he did it. The Macintosh introduction was the great set piece of the digital age. All others that aspire to the title are in some way deeply flawed. The Windows 95 introduction 11 years later drew thousands to all-night vigils in computer store parking lots around the world. But it was an act of submission: desperate users awaiting the largesse of a monopoly. The Intel Pentium Bug debacle certainly shook the electronics world and beyond, reminding the semiconductor industry that it was now a global consumer force, with all the responsibilities that flowed from that role—but it was also essentially a boneheaded screwup.

The Macintosh introduction, by comparison, was uplifting, transcendent. Sitting there in the Flint Center auditorium on the De Anza College campus, just a block from Apple's first office, there was the sense of being part of history, of being present at a thrilling discontinuity in the story of computing. *This* was what a computer was supposed to be. Plucky little Apple, already being written off by industry cynics, had somehow managed to jump to its feet and throw a fast one right into the chin of the biggest, baddest corporate Goliath of all. You couldn't help but laugh, it was so outrageous. And then the computer itself turned out to be so god-damned *cute*.

It really was a turning point. Before the Macintosh, electronics companies were institutions that aspired to the stature and gravity of their manufacturing counterparts. When they introduced products, it was almost always at a staid press conference before an audience of tech insiders who looked at the spec sheet before they looked at the product itself. After Macintosh, every tech company, to prove that its product was important, was forced to create some sort of extravaganza, develop a unique logo and motif, and try to link its product to the train of history.

But they would never pull it off. They couldn't, because no matter how great the product or how elaborate the promotion, those later companies could never recapture the delirious shock of experiencing such a moment for the first time. Even Apple would fail in the years to come to conjure up the old magic, until near the end its big events became only sad, forced parodies of the past.

Flint Center could hold two thousand people, but the event drew only about half that—less than attended a travelogue a few days before. But the empty balcony was nearly invisible, so the room seemed full. Of the crowd, fully half were Apple employees serving as shills. But that was still more people than any comparable event before, and those non-Appleites who were there were the cream of high-tech investment, analysis, and reporting. Regis had seen to that, and he had made sure that each had received a packet containing not only a press kit but other freebies, notably a T-shirt with a cleverly simplified (and groundbreaking) graphic of the Mac.

The day before, during rehearsals, the dark side of Steve Jobs had emerged. He belittled the hardworking stagehands, yelling at their every mistake while flubbing his own lines over and over. He changed his speech, tossed out and reinserted slides, and generally cast a pall over the proceedings. More than one Apple employee left Flint that night praying the next day wouldn't be a complete disaster.

But it was the other Steve who stood behind the curtains the next day. He privately confessed, "This is the most important moment of my entire life. I can't tell you how I feel. It's the most incredible thing I've ever had to go through and I'm really nervous."

Then he walked out from behind the curtains, apparently calm, with the smirk so tiny that it seemed less contemptuous than ironic at the sheer unlikeliness of it all. This was the new Steve Jobs, only a decade older but a million years from the smelly ascetic, now sleek and chic, wearing a double-breasted, European-cut charcoal-gray suit and a bright red bow tie that managed to look at once intellectual, revolutionary, and arch. He cut a striking figure, one that was nearly as significant to the audience as the product he was about to introduce: *Jobs is going for it!*

There was a murmur of expectation. Then Jobs, the last child of the 1960s, began to recite Bob Dylan's famous lines about "the times they are a-changing" for the last famous time.

It was a tocsin to the Woodstock generation: *Don't sell out! Don't forget the dream! Stay free!* And in that hall filled with boomers, both from Apple and from the press, most of them now with babies and first mortgage payments, receding hairlines and business suits, a thrill shot through a thousand hearts. *Yes! We've been sleepwalking. Wake us up!* There was a hush of expectation. Where will the Pied Piper lead us?

But Jobs had already slipped backstage. The audience, ready to rise up and rush the stage, instead had to sit impatiently through the company's annual meeting. Quarterly earnings and announcements of new facilities and joint ventures. Yeah yeah yeah blah blah blah. Even the reporters put down their notebooks. They could get all this financial garbage off the press release. *Where's Steve?*

Then, as suddenly as he had disappeared, he was back, gleaming in the white spotlight. He spoke with the disarming, confiding earnestness he used for his biggest seductions. His head was cocked just slightly, his body rigid, but his arms and hands punctuated every sentence. He began almost lightly, but, feeding off the embrace of the audience, seemed to grow more confident and powerful with each paragraph. He was 29 years old and this was the greatest moment of his life:

It is 1958. IBM passes up the chance to buy a young, fledgling company that has just invented a new technology called xerography. Two years later, Xerox is born, and IBM has been kicking itself ever since.

It is 10 years later, the late 1960s. Digital Equipment Corporation and others invent the minicomputer. IBM dismisses the minicomputer as too small to do serious computing and, therefore, unimportant to its business. DEC grows to become multi-hundred-million dollar corporation before IBM finally enters the minicomputer market.

It is now 10 years later, the late 1970s. In 1977, Apple, a young fledgling company on the West Coast, invents the Apple 11, the first personal computer as we know it today. IBM dismisses the personal computer as too small to do serious computing and therefore unimportant to its business.

The early 1980s—1981. Apple 11 has become the world's most popular computer, and Apple has grown to a $300 million corporation, becoming the fastest growing company in American business history. With over 50 companies vying for a share, IBM enters the personal computer market in November of 1981 with the IBM PC.

1983. Apple and IBM emerge as the industry's strongest competitors, each selling approximately $1 billion worth of personal computers in 1983.

. . . The shakeout is in full swing. The first major firm goes bankrupt, with others teetering on the brink. Total industry losses for 1983 overshadow even the combined profits of Apple and IBM for personal computers.

It is now 1984. It appears IBM wants it all. Apple is perceived to be the only hope to offer IBM a run for its money. Dealers, initially welcoming IBM with open arms, now fear an IBM dominated and controlled future. They are increasingly turning back to Apple as the only force that can ensure their future freedom . . .

Jobs paused, as if steeling himself for the enormity of the task ahead. He looked out at the audience, as if asking them to join him at the battlements of computing freedom. Then his voice dropped a half octave, as if at the sheer magnitude of corporate evil, oh the humanity . . .

IBM wants it all and is aiming its guns on its last obstacle to industry control, Apple. Will Big Blue dominate the entire computer industry, the entire information age? Was George Orwell right?

"NO!" shouted the audience. "No!" shouted the first five rows, filled with the Apple team. "No!" shouted the other Apple employees and the analysts and the distributors and dealers and retailers and shareholders . . . NO! said the assembled journalists secretly to themselves.

Steve Jobs smiled. Enough with that Zen bullshit about the "journey being the reward." *This* was the reward.

He walked over to a table bearing an ominous-looking bag. With a flourish, Jobs unzipped it . . . and there, the color of brown stone, like a little primitive totem, a friendly phallus, was the Macintosh. An appreciative murmur went up from the crowd. It was instantly drowned out by the amplified theme from the movie *Chariots of Fire*. It was corny, but nevertheless spine tingling.

"Today," intoned Steve Jobs, "for the first time ever, I'd like to let Macintosh speak for itself." That couldn't be true: Apple had never actually tested speech synthesis on the Mac until this moment. But what the hell, go with the flow. It was all too exciting to quibble.

Jobs touched a key, and in a quivering little voice—its very crudeness perfect in its antithesis to Big Brother—the Mac announced:

> Hello, I am Macintosh. It sure is great to get out of that bag. Unaccustomed as I am to public speaking, I'd like to share with you a thought that occurred to me the first time I met an IBM mainframe: Never trust a computer you can't lift. But right now I'd like to sit back and listen. So it is with considerable pride that I introduce a man who has been like a father to me, Steve Jobs.

"Like a father" was the appropriate phrase, as Mac's real father was at that moment living in the Santa Cruz mountains. And it was a bit cheesy to even steal Jef Raskin's line about not trusting computers you can't lift. But it didn't matter. The crowd laughed and cheered—even those in the front row who knew better.

It went on like this for another 20 minutes, losing momentum by the minute. After all, how could you top the introduction of one of the greatest products of the century? Still, those final depleted minutes did manage to establish a second turning point in the history of personal computing: This was the day the press, especially the computer trade press, formally and publicly, sold out.

It was hard to resist. After all, Apple was now the underdog, and the press loves underdogs. And the Macintosh represented such an unbelievable comeback. And IBM was a tight-assed pain to deal with, with its PR department keeping a database on every reporter and firing off angry notes every time you suggested the company was bigger than the corner drugstore—while Apple was young and brash and answered the phone and was always good for a quote. And almost everybody in the press owned an Apple at home even though they had to use IBMs in the newsroom. And, not least, Apple bought a lot of advertising pages, especially in the last month.

It was just so easy to succumb. And never more so than at this moment of triumph for Apple. Onstage, the company introduced the publisher of a new, purportedly independent magazine called *Mac-World,* dedicated entirely to the Macintosh. It was an amazing moment in modern journalism, and nobody seemed to notice. On the contrary, the reporters reminded themselves to get subscriptions.

If the electronics trade magazines, dependent on Apple advertising revenues, finally revealed themselves as lickspittles at the Mac introduction, the general press was only slightly more reserved. Esther Dyson, who had taken over Ben Rosen's newsletter and was on her way to becoming the preeminent opinion maker in personal computing, actually sat through the event wearing her free Mac T-shirt. The story passed around that she had changed into it while driving down from the San Francisco Airport—to the entertainment of the men in nearby cars. Other writers were discreet enough to wait until they got home before putting on, literally and journalistically, Mac shirts of their own.

Then it was over. Jobs, drained and tearfully happy, made his way back behind the curtain. "It's really happened," he said. "Mac is a real product now."

The press rushed the stage, where Apple representatives, from publicists to Art Rock, held forth in little clusters of reporters. When will the Mac be available? What different configurations are available? How much market share do you think you can take back from IBM?

In one of the largest of these clusters, Regis McKenna held forth. "Where are the cursor keys?" asked a reporter. "It doesn't have any cursor keys." "I know," said Regis, reliving an argument he'd had a few months before. "I tried to talk them into it. But they wanted a mouse and a mouse alone." He shrugged and smiled, as if to say: I know it's nuts, but what are you going to do? It's Apple.

By now, the January afternoon had turned gray. The reporters rushed off to file their stories. The Apple staffers wandered back, down the street to their offices. And no one had the slightest doubt that a new era had begun.

From *Infinite Loop,* by Michael S. Malone, copyright © 1999 by Michael S. Malone. Used by permission of Doubleday, a division of Random House, Inc.

SILICON TOWN

9

THE REAL SECRETS OF SILICON VALLEY

I think that maybe in every company today there is always at least one person who is going crazy slowly.

—Joseph Heller

One of the cruelest myths we serve up to our children is that we, somehow, choose our own careers. We ask them, "What do you want to be when you grow up?" and then, with a straight face, nod at their hopelessly wrongheaded answers.

Perhaps that is because none of us has that requisite Olympian *sangfroid* to calmly listen to their answers, then reply, "Well, I'm sorry, son, but the Yankees usually have only one centerfielder per decade and you're not even the best hitter in your third-grade class;" or, "Yes, but sweetheart, being a nurse means that you will be underpaid, underappreciated, spend half your life zombified by working the graveyard shift and then, if that isn't enough, you'll be regularly psychically bruised by emotionally juvenile doctors and chronically selfish patients."

And, if we are unwilling to honestly disabuse our children of their dream careers, how could we ever tell them honestly about the reality of adult work? How shocked we would be if our child, suddenly wiser than we, were to reply to that inevitable question, "Well, Daddy, I'd like to be a cowboy, but I suspect I'll become a frustrated middle manager in charge of wafer fab at a second-tier semiconductor company."

We would be surprised because we are unwilling to admit that reality to ourselves. Nobody dreams of growing up to be an advertising executive, or a supervisor of accounts receivable—or, for that matter, a freelance writer. We end up there because, as in a coin sorter, the tens of millions of us in the workforce separate out into the available slots. There are thousands of these slots, but only a handful of really good ones: business tycoon, U.S. senator, bestselling author, famous surgeon, prize-winning scientist, rock star, movie queen—and, because these slots are so shallow, they fill up much faster than the rest. Frankly, that is probably for the best, because most of us never have to face the fact that our coin wouldn't have fit.

So, we march on. The rent or mortgage still has to be paid, the car payments made, food put on the table, and stainless steel wired to little Susie's molars. We take a job . . . and we dream of what might have been. And then we scheme ways to make the career we've found more fulfilling, more rewarding. Ambition colors our lives—an all-consuming, fundamental ambition to somehow reach a better slot. This ambition is a universal disease. Politicians dream of becoming president, priests of being named pope, apparatchiks of becoming commissar, commoners of being crowned king.

But I digress . . . in fact, this entire article thus far has been one long digression. It's just that when one speaks of work, it always comes back to dream versus reality, to envy and ambition. But most of all, it comes back to *self*.

This is understandable, but also deadly. Too often we are so busy contemplating our splendid selves, congratulating ourselves over some minor, meaningless victory ("The Boss remembered my name! My future is made.") or chastising ourselves over some inexplicable defeat ("The Boss forgot my name! I'm human trash. I think I'll kill myself.") that we fail to look around. More often than not, that is where our real problem lies.

The Job. The *Company* you work for. We shed a tear over Dickens' horrific workhouses, then fail to notice that our own company makes Scrooge & Marley seem like Club Med; or that, next to our boss, Fagin is Mother Teresa.

The fact is that there are career slots and then there are bottomless pits, stamping presses, and acid baths. The same job that at one firm is like a gentle barge cruise down the Nile at another can be a screaming barrel ride over Niagara Falls. Your boss at one place may have the concern, dignity, and tactical wisdom of Robert E. Lee, while at another be as monstrous, perverse, and drug-addled as Hermann W. Goering. Yet both hold the same title —and the same rule over your fate.

We're not just talking high-tech companies, either. The Silicon Valley Psychopathia is widely infectious: from restaurants to car dealerships to hotels to this newspaper, all of us are cursed with hyper-extended workweeks and the mindless taskmaster of technologic change. You no longer have to be an M.S.-E.E. to suffer.

This article is designed to be a ladder-a rickety, crooked one at that—to help all of us climb above the roar and dust of our everyday lives and get some perspective over what it means to work in Silicon Valley; of the various forms the companies out there take. This article (primarily because the author has no job to be fired from, only years of vilification and personality assassination to look forward to) will not only describe each of the corporate types that make up Silicon Valley, but, thanks to the recommendations from various Valley headhunters (who should know better than anyone else), will actually list those companies that best fit each category.

You will note that some firms appear in several categories. Others have changed categories over the years. Still others, defeated by the Valley, have all but moved away. But if there is one truth to Silicon Valley, it is that, like bad pennies, old companies and old names forever resurface. Forewarned is foreresumed.

The Grand Army of the Republic

I shall push the enemy to the wall.
—General George McClellan

This is the company, large or small, that spends all of its time getting organized, practicing drills, developing organization charts, marching around the parade grounds, holding fancy public events, tastefully decorating executive offices, hiring graphics firms to design beautiful logos and letterheads, making ringing speeches to the troops about the Great Campaign Ahead . . . and then marching out to be utterly and completely annihilated by the competition.

The model for this kind of company is the Union Army of the Potomac at the beginning of the Civil War, which, with limitless supplies, fancy new uniforms, and a plentitude of officers and soldiers, was regularly whacked by a rag-tag Confederate Army half its size, but boy, could it ever march.

Silicon Valley regularly sees spanking new companies pop up with plans to take on the world. Typically, they are backed by some giant East Coast corporation. And equally typically, they are run by some former v.p. of finance or sales. Up goes the fancy building, out come the canapés for the distinguished visitors to the open house, in goes the Hermann Miller furniture, up go the pompous predictions of success, out (six months late) goes the first product, down goes the corporate stock, out go half of the employees (whose only crimes were loyalty and having worked hard for an incompetent management), back goes the new Silicon Valley division to the East Coast, and up goes the For Lease sign on the fancy building.

Oh, and lest we forget: down goes the county employment rate and out extends the line at the Employment Development Department. For an epitaph, all those jobs and all those dreams wind up as a "Write-Off for Discontinued Operations" in the back pages of the next corporate annual report—right next to a salary increase for company directors for a job well done.

But hey, thank you for your support.

How to Spot

Corporate limousines for the honchos. Too many Ferrari models in executive offices. Executive dining room. Glossy divisional newsletter. General manager is a CPA or former national sales manager. Visiting corporate CEO says "Silicone." Equipment in R&D lab still has shipping labels after six months. 80-pound matte finish 100 percent rag off-white stationary. General manager and most of the top staff live in San Francisco. Introduction date of first product is bumped three times and no one has been canned.

Bedford Falls

> Such is our comfortable tradition and sure faith, Would he not betray himself as an alien cynic who should otherwise portray Main Street, or distress the citizens by speculating whether there may not be other faiths?
>
> —Sinclair Lewis

The title comes from the most evil and dangerous movie ever made: Frank Capra's *It's a Wonderful Life*. You remember: Jimmy

Stewart discovers that his life wasn't rendered meaningless because he stayed in his hometown. On the contrary, in a dream he learns that had he never been born, sweet Bedford Falls would have become evil Potterville.

Sure. This disgusting corporate propaganda is jammed down our throats along with the other turkey every Christmas. In reality, what pretends to be a good-hearted little morality tale about personal responsibility and community is actually a pernicious attempt to enforce career conformity. It really says: Stick with your job, no matter how much you hear the siren call of adventure, no matter how disappointed you are with yourself, because—trust us—in the end you'll be proven right.

In fact, the more you watch *It's a Wonderful Life* the more you realize the real hero is party-girl Gloria Grahame, who makes her own rules, kicks up her round heels . . . and when things grow too hot, gets the hell out of Dodge. And on the bank's money to boot.

There are a number of companies in Silicon Valley that resemble the idyllic small-town life of Bedford Falls. The most famous, of course, is the Country Club itself, Hewlett Packard Co. HP is a corporation of scoutmasters and Little League coaches, Mormon elders, and just generally nice, hard-working, impossibly decent human beings. Not only will they never lose their jobs, but frankly, they never should. All will proudly wear their 30-year pins at their retirement dinners. This is marzipan land.

For those who fit, of course. The ugly little secret of companies like HP is that it is a wonderful life only for those who conform. If you have even the slightest desire to occasionally walk the noisy sidewalks of Potterville, such a place as Bedford Falls can be an endless torture. That's why the most creative, independent employees of HP, like Steve Wozniak, have always left. Not driven out, mind you, these companies are too damned decent for that; it's just the growing gut sense that you simply don't belong, that your psychic fly is down. That's why the quote above comes not from the movie, but from Sinclair Lewis. You see, hidden behind every Bedford Falls is not something as obvious as Potterville, but rather the smug, intolerant rectitude of *Main Street's* Gopher Prairie.

Hey, Gloria! Wait for me!

How to Spot

Top execs eating in the employee cafeteria. Absurdly high employee satisfaction ratings. Low turnover and long employment waiting lists. Friday beer busts that don't turn bitter. Casual dress on Fridays. Morning doughnut and fruit breaks. Prayer groups. Holiday Open House nights. Bike paths and par courses. A too-normal chief executive.

The S.S. Pequod

> Aye, aye! and I'll chase him round the Good Hope, and round the Horn, and round the Horn and round the Norway Maelstrom, and round perdition's flames before I give him up. And this is what ye have shipped, for men! to chase that white whale on both sides of the Earth, till he spouts black blood and rolls fin out. What say ye, men, will ye splice hands on it, now? I think ye do look brave.
> —Captain Ahab (Herman Melville's *Moby Dick*)

This is the company that initially seems like a wonderful cruise line—until little clues begin to give you the gnawing fear that there is a demented, obsessed captain in control of the tiller—and that you have booked passage on a Death Ship from Hell.

What is so frightening about this kind of company is that in the early stages it is almost completely indistinguishable from a hot start-up that soon will be a household word and make everybody involved rich beyond their greatest fantasies. After all, no sane person would stay in this valley without the prospect of becoming a tycoon.

So, we stick with these little corporate nuthouses, these Silicon Valley versions of Mr. Dark's Pandemonium Shadow Show, because we want to believe they will pan out and all the insanity will have been worth it.

And so, as we watch the company CEO begin to wear only white (Ampex) or soak his feet in the men's room toilet (Apple) or code name prototypes after well-built female employees (Atari) or slowly become a mad Ahab pacing the quarterdeck on his ivory leg, we keep whispering to ourselves, "Be cool, be cool, don't worry about it. I mean, entrepreneurs are supposed to be a little flaky. Right? Right?" And secretly, we pray that ours won't be the fate of poor Ishmael, the Pequod's sole surviving orphan, clinging to a flotsam coffin in the middle of a great lonely ocean.

How to Spot

Explanations of the founder's eccentric behavior as, "Well, he is a genius, after all." A meeting in which an exec makes a statement so wacky that you start to laugh—only to discover that everyone else in the room is taking notes. Wholesale revamping of job titles ("area associate" for "secretary") and other forms of social engineering (such as calling everyone by his or her first name) to create a spurious notion of equality. An inverted dress code, in which the subordinate exhibits a better wardrobe than the boss. A personnel philosophy that places the corporate "family" before one's own. The eerie sense that you have not joined a company, but a Glorious Cause.

Modern Times

> Thou shalt break them with a rod of iron; thou shalt dash
> them in pieces like a potter's vessel. Be wise now therefore,
> O ye kings: be instructed, ye judges of the earth.
> —Psalms 2: 9–10

The title suggests the image—Chaplin's Tramp being dragged through the gears and sprockets of an automated factory—and the image suggests in each reader's mind a handful of companies that fit the bill.

One of the interesting features of the human imagination is that our worst nightmares rarely come true, but that our nicest dreams usually do—and turn out to be even worse.

Fifty years ago, sociologists, labor leaders, and futurists all bleakly predicted that the fate of the average American man would be that of *Modern Times,* as an exploited assembly worker, Taylor, planned into a mindless automaton and ground up by the heartless industrial machine. Wouldn't it be so much finer, they said with a sigh, if each of us could work in handsome, clean buildings, in our own private work cubicles, performing felicitous tasks of the mind and not the body, and calling one another by our first names? It was enough to bring tears to the eyes of the most hardened Wobbly.

Well, folks, we got our wish. What the dreamers forgot to consider was that these newfangled factories could be as stressful, totalitarian, exhausting, and physically ruinous as a West Virginia coal mine. At least, down there in the dust of a coal mine, as long as the work got done, you could allow your natural personality to shine through. Try that in the scrubbed air of some Silicon Valley tilt-up corporation.

Of course, we did the decent thing and opened up the opportunity to women. Now, we all can participate in the workforce and enjoy the fruits of the technological revolution: quadruple bypass surgery, Valium, Cokenders, and Porsche leasing programs.

The great bugaboo of past reformists was the quota system. Who can forget the poor Tramp, so dazed from torquing down bolts on the assembly line that he uses the wrench to tighten parts of the foreman's anatomy? Thank God we got rid of quotas! Of course, we've replaced that with Innovation—which means that now you have to beat the competition not only at the end of the month, but well into the next century.

Ah, Progress! It used to be only nations that were wrecked in the name of an idea. One wonders if high schoolers of the future will study the 80-hour work weeks, the divorces and drug abuse, the pathological struggle to stay on "the leading edge" that make up the fabric of Silicon Valley life, and recoil with the same horror we do reading the horrors of the Packingtown plant in Upton Sinclair's *The Jungle?*

"But why," the teenager will ask, "Did people stay?"

"I don't know," his parents will reply, "I guess people just didn't know any better back then."

How to Spot

Glandular, even chromosomal, fear of what "the Japanese are up to." Full parking lots at lunchtime. Sunday morning meetings. Simpering reverence for technical types. Abuse of anyone in a staff position. Corporate newsletters that devote more space to new products than to people. A sizable percentage of the employee population that speaks Japanese or Hindi. The need to wear a bunny suit when entering half of the company's buildings. Occasional evacuations and/or lawsuits over toxic leaks. A chief executive with a PhD in electrical engineering, chemistry, or computer science. A complete product line that would neatly fit into a briefcase with room left for a bag lunch.

The Magic Mountain

> I have dreamed of man's state, of this courteous and enlightened social state; behind which, in the temple, the horrible blood-sacrifice was consummated. Were they, these children of the sun, so sweetly courteous to each other in silent recognition of that horror?
>
> —Thomas Mann

In the novel that bears the title of this section, there is a scene in which Hans Castorp, a tuberculosis patient staying in a Swiss sanitarium goes out hiking in the Alpine snow—only to find himself trapped in a storm and dazed with the cold. In his delirium, he imagines himself in a paradise on earth, where beautiful people cavort in a garden-like setting. As he explores this Elysium, he comes across a temple. Curious, he enters . . . to find two old witches ritually murdering an infant: the hidden cost of the perfection outside.

It is no small irony that some of the best employers in this Valley, the most people-oriented, benevolent companies around, are built on a dark and dreary foundation.

The most obvious examples are the firms that build weapons and their delivery systems. However one feels about the military and defense, to devote one's life specifically to building instruments of destruction is bound to induce occasional twinges of doubt as, conversely, should a career spent hiding from one's responsibility to defend one's family, country, and beliefs.

Of course, it is always easy to pick on military contractors while one blithely spends 10 hours a day designing video games to implode the brains of America's youth, or developing ad campaigns to manipulate people into acquiring products they don't need, or sitting in board meetings discussing how to hide the upcoming company stock crash from all those thousands of fixed-income retiree shareholders out there—or, for that matter, discussing how to dismiss a lifetime of hard work with two paragraphs of newsprint.

So don't think about it. Enjoy the beautiful day, the ripened fruit, the fragrant flowers. And if you hear any noises coming from the temple, just tell yourself it's the wind, the wind.

How to Spot

Defense: Descriptions of company products that never address precisely what they do or what they're good for. Class-action suits by consumers or shareholders. Ongoing unionization efforts. Classified areas. Regular EPA inspections. A general unwillingness on your part to tell strangers what you do for a living. An intermittent desire to give it all up and go work as a volunteer in a homeless shelter.

Consumer: A tendency to justify one's work with: "So what's wrong with people having a little fun?" or "Whatsamatter, didn't you play with toy guns when you were kid?" or "I think it's good that kids have a place to go—it's certainly better than having them running around on the streets" or "It's important for a child to have a healthy imaginary life; it's the job of the parents to make sure it doesn't become unhealthy."

The Berlin Bunker

> The bunker and its atmosphere were stifling and unreal. Heinrici had the disquieting feeling that the men around Hitler had retreated into a dream world in which they had convinced themselves that by some miracle catastrophe would be averted . . .
>
> —Cornelius Ryan, *The Last Battle*

I thought about calling this the Seventh Calvary. You know: "We'll just ride down the hill and kick some Sioux butt." But our century has provided us a more appropriate image. This is the company that is in terrible straits yet won't admit it to itself. While artillery rounds explode overhead, down in the corporate bunker middle-managers still dream of glorious campaigns to come; of hot new products that will regain all of the lost markets. Meanwhile, out on the streets, the line workers and secretaries fight savagely house-to-house for a cause no one has told them is already lost.

Where does such self-delusion come from? The top, of course. The executives have no such fantasies. They read the sales numbers; they see the analysts' reports. They know the company is doomed—that's why they put their résumés out on the street three months ago. As they exhort the troops to fight to the last man for the Fatherland, they are standing with one foot through the hatch of the submarine that will take them (and their gold) to Paraguay.

A friend of mine once applied for a job at a local defense electronics company. The interview went well, the unctuous v.p. of personnel explaining why the firm was such a wonderful place to work, until my friend was asked if he had any questions.

"Yes," he replied, "if this is such a well-run place and if your products are so competitive, why have you been losing money for the last three quarters?"

The v.p. blanched, then grew angry. "Obviously," he replied through clenched teeth, "You are not a *team player.*" The magical two-word kiss of death. Interview over.

Two weeks later that same v.p. took a job at another company. For more pay. Most of the people he hired were laid off.

How to Spot

A president's letter in the company newsletter that includes quotes like, "We've had some setbacks, but we're coming out of it." An early retirement party in the personnel department on the day you interview. Signs and posters in the lobby proclaiming "Welcome to the XYZ Co. Family!" A seething companywide paranoia about the terrible things being said about it in the press. A growing number of stock analysts that no longer cover the firm. An annual report that deemphasizes lousy financial figures to focus on "The Wonderful People Who Make up XYZ Inc.," No overtime, no business trips, no seminars except, of course, for company execs.

Beyond the Inner Station

The Horror! The Horror!
—Joseph Conrad

Both of you English majors out there will recognize the title of this section from Joseph Conrad's *Heart of Darkness*. By the way, what are *you* people doing in Silicon Valley? There's no work for you here. Run away! Run away! Beyond the Inner Station was where Kurtz ran his evil empire, a sort of Fortune 500 business in ivory and slaves, where employees' heads typically wound up on poles around the lobby.

The companies of this category exist in the seventh circle of corporate inferno. Abandon all hope ye who are hired here.

To paraphrase Leo Tolstoy (you still there, English majors?) all happy companies are the same—but all unhappy companies are unhappy in their own way. Thus, each of the companies from Beyond the Inner Station, the companies that fill the Infernal Industrial Park, reached their present decadence along their own unique paths. Some were just born bad-bad: Venture Capital genes perhaps, or maybe the founders were frightened by a ghost while the company was being born. Others were once good companies, but have been hijacked by a cabal of bad men. Others, facing the horrors of competition have just snapped, gone over to the Dark Side, embraced the Great Satan of survival at all costs—even if it means shipping mainframes to Dubrovnik in boxes marked Lee Press-On Nails.

Working for a company from Beyond the Inner Station is something you never quite get over, akin to the rare, but unforgettably chilling experience of meeting a true psychopath. Companies like these are not the raw material for amusing anecdotes years hence. Rather, they are the blank few months in your job history you never, ever want to talk about. These are places so palpably malevolent that within minutes after arriving you sense that something truly awful is going to happen—and maybe to you.

You'll notice I'm not being funny here. That's because I've gotten the phone calls from employees on the verge of nervous breakdowns, talked with executives who have been hidden in hotel rooms waiting to turn state's evidence before a grand jury, and most of all, seen the set mouths and frightened eyes of the survivors. I also got sued once by one of these companies for $1 million (well, actually, it was me and the *Mercury News*, but that's close enough, believe you me), so don't expect to see below the names of companies that still exist—at least not until I can get my few meager assets put in my cat's name.

How to Spot

Extremely limited access to the shipping room and loading dock on certain days. Line workers who disappear every time a government vehicle drives up. Late-night meetings between company executives. Foreign engineers who have been promised extraordinary bonuses. Almost no attention by the press or analysts for a firm its size. Government inspectors taken for long lunches. Visibly frightened female employees. High wages combined with no prepared materials on company benefits. Hints of drugs on executive row.

The Longest Running Show on Broadway

Donny Osmond *is* Joseph and the Amazing Technicolor
Dream Coat!

You know how it goes: Some musical or play gets all the big reviews from the New York papers, sold-out houses for months and months, a Tony or two, and fame and glory for its stars. But by the time you finally get to Broadway to see the thing, or it arrives out here in a road show, the sets are cheap and the principal players long gone. You end up with Red Buttons instead of Kevin Kline, Eve Arden instead of Bernadette Peters.

So it is with many Silicon Valley companies, including some of the most successful. The days when their reputations were made as dynamic, iconoclastic, cheeky corporate mavericks are long gone. The famous founder, the subject of endless memorable anecdotes, got booted out of the firm long ago and is now running a competitor down the street. The hirsute, besandled computer jockeys that changed the world have been supplanted by intense, slick GQ clones with MBAs. The only thing that survives is that cute little logo, and, of course, the cynical ads that continue to play off the company's old image.

But don't be disappointed. Actually, the old firm was a place of runaway egos, fistfights in the hallways and gut-churning chaos. By comparison, the new firm is predictable, safe, and prosperous. And though, for all of its faults, you would have happily given your life for the old company; the new company you will come to hate with every cell in your body.

How to Spot

Company publications, posters, even museums, cherishing the memory of a founder who long ago was driven away. The executive of a competing firm who happens to have the same last name as this company. People in company ads who look nothing like people who work at the company. Testy replies like, "Yeah, that's true, but I'd rather be working for the company *these* days." or "Sure, we've had a great past, but this company's future is *just* as exciting." Company logo window or bumper stickers. Adults who identify with the company in the embarrassing manner of children with rock groups. A sort of Soviet paranoia about Evil Giant Competitors ever ready to destroy this Peaceful Little Kingdom. Headquarters in the Stanford Industrial Park or on Ellis Street in Mountain View. A new company president who knows nothing about electronics but more than any human should about retailing.

Corporate Laputa

Their houses are very ill built, the walls bevil, without one right angle in any apartment; and this defect ariseth from the

contempt they bear for practical geometry; which they de-
spise as vulgar and mechanick, those instructions they give
being too refined for the intellecks of their workmen; which
occasions perpetual mistakes.

—Jonathan Swift

These are companies that have taken the Silicon Valley philosophy to its logical conclusion: They are so far out on the leading
edge they've fallen off. The title and quote come from *Gulliver's
Travels,* of a people so intellectualized and out-of-it that they had
to be escorted by assistants who regularly hit them with bladders
filled with pebbles to remind them to speak or listen. (Swift, you
may notice, also had a way with Spanish puns.)

One only has to peruse the trade press to appreciate that Silicon Valley is filled with companies working in technologies so ar-
cane that one doubts even they can understand them. These
Laputans take several forms:

1. Established companies that announce new products that will
never, ever see the light of day. These firms (and their name is legion) are moderately interesting as examples of business fraud and
can be found in almost every category in this list but typically are in
the software business—which isn't particularly real in the first place.

How to Spot

New product announcements that contain no information on price
or delivery. Stunned reactions by industry leaders over the announcement, followed a few days later (after apparently considerable research) by a certain smugness. Profound quiet thereafter
from the company making the announcement.

2. Companies operating in fringe or niche markets only they
seem to understand or want to participate in. As reporters rarely

understand what they do, they are rarely mentioned in the press—
often making their sheer size a surprise even to Valley veterans.

How to Spot

Any company in microwave products or linear devices. Firms that
are hiring when everybody else is in deep recessionary despair and
layoffs. Regular appearances in trade magazines you've never
heard of. Engineers still at the forefront of their profession after
age 35. Non-appearance in local newspaper business sections except on the stock page.

3. Research laboratories. These are places designed from the
start to be essentially worthless. Their products typically being
very expensive reports that few read and no one ever puts into action. One positive side effect, however, is that these institutions (in
every sense of that word) keep college professors and doctoral candidates away from both undergraduates and real corporations,
where they may do considerable harm.

How to Spot

Research reports that look suspiciously like old dissertations with
new title pages. Research projects that don't quite match what you
paid for. An unsafe level of Stanford Ph.D.s in the hard sciences.
Government contracts that aren't put up for bid. Scores of apparently intelligent people not actually doing anything. General college faculty-like contempt for secretaries, clerical staffers, and any
others who make productive use of their time. KQED window
stickers on Volvos.

4. Companies that never actually do anything. These firms are
intriguing because one senses that their executives actually *believe*
they are working on something important. The founders meet and
scheme, write business plans, and in time actually convince venture

capitalists to put up millions of dollars. Then they rent a building, put a company sign out front, and set about filling the place with people and equipment. In every way, they are a perfect copy of a real, producing company. And yet, nothing happens. They fall into themselves, dry up and blow away like chaff on the fiscal winds: Employees, who until the day before had been told everything was going just great, stand in the parking lot, stare at the For Lease sign, and wonder what just hit them.

The most amazing thing about these introverted, ill-fated companies—the most famous being Trilogy—is that when it's all over, the realization suddenly hits everybody that the project was doomed from the start. Like the Laputan scientist trying to breed hairless sheep, these companies all suffer from some fundamental flaw in their plan, be it technology, product, market, or management. Some are almost touching in the immense amount of time, money, and sweat they expend, none of which forestalls oblivion by as much as millisecond.

Touching, of course, unless you've been suckered into working there.

How to Spot

Unwarranted optimism in the face of new competition. Regular daily visits from sober-looking venture capitalists and bankers. Sudden disconnection of the phone system or cut-off of power. Yellowing drawing of the planned product in the lobby. Execs prone to extended reminiscences or telling you how much they "appreciate your loyalty to the company." No product brochures, no product data sheets, no product. Sudden talk about a new direction for the company.

The Hidden Fortress

Just as George Lucas' *Star Wars* was a flashy knock-off of Akira Kurosawa's *The Hidden Fortress,* so too by comparison do American

high-tech companies seem clever and shallow next to their mysteri-
ous and complex Japanese counterparts. Equally the tiny outposts of
Japanese firms we see in Silicon Valley can disguise megacorpora-
tions at home.

Discovering just what these outposts are all about can be a
challenge even to the Americans who work for them. Some are
here to help set up local distribution programs; others to stake out
U.S. manufacturing in case we finally get tired of their predatory
behavior and set up tariff barriers. Still others exist primarily to
hire us locals to suck our brains out. What may seem like a good-
paying gig and a safe haven from the next Valley downturn may
turn out to be Nightmare on First Street. That's particularly true
for women, whom many Japanese executives consider to be slightly
less evolved than office plants.

So don't say you haven't been warned. After all, our equivalent
characters in *The Hidden Fortress,* the one on which R2D2 and
C3PO are based, happen to be slaves.

On the other hand, if the job does turn out great, each night
before you go to bed, be sure to remind yourself, as a citizen, of
just how much you are doing to help America compete against its
greatest threat since . . . well, Japan.

How to Spot

You've got to be kidding. And don't let the "America" or USA in the
name fool you.

Life on Pluto

> Death is absolute and without memorial, As in a season of
> autumn, When the wind stops . . .
> —Wallace Stevens

Any mathematician will tell you that, just like the eye of a hurricane, any closed system in motion will have a dead spot somewhere.

Such are the companies in this category, so far from the heat and light of the Silicon Valley entrepreneurial sun that they assume it's just another distant star.

Many of these companies once themselves burned brightly, but have cooled into torpor. Others were dead from the beginning, having found a nice safe corner to build a nest and sink right into eternal hibernation.

There is nothing especially wrong with these companies. In places like Detroit and Philadelphia they make up the majority. But here in Silicon Valley, where everything moves at twice the normal pace, these joints are as close as you can get to Night of the Living Dead—the kind of places you only admit to working at if you can endure nervous coughs.

Now don't get me wrong. Corporate retirement villages are a crucial niche in this area's ecology. After all, Silicon Valley eats its old. Betray a little human weakness, show a wrinkle here or there, ask to cut your workweek down to six days, and the next thing you know the tribe has left you on the far side of the river with two pieces of flat bread and a prayer wheel.

That's when you, an aging Silicon Valley courtesan, show up at the front door of one of these companies, pleased to know that there still exist firms that will love you for your experience, not your energy.

How to Spot

"Years with the Company" lists that take up most of the corporate newsletter. A majority of the employees owning their own homes. Electric typewriters. Enclosed offices. White short-sleeve shirts. Weekly retirement parties and regular return visits by those who've left. Greater interest in profit sharing than in new products. Bikinied women and 1950s-style layouts in corporate ads. Regular non-appearance of the company's name in trade journals. Metal furniture. A company name without a prefix like sili-, in-, trans-, super- or semi-, or a suffix like -tron, -tronics, -ics, or -ix. A company history book that's already out of date. Anyone with the title "emeritus."

There you have it. You have now been vouchsafed the *real* company secrets of Silicon Valley.

But a warning, gentle reader: Remember the lesson of Plato's Cave. In the land of shadow and illusion, you have been given the opportunity to climb out into the light and see this place for what it truly is. But when you return to the corporate cave tomorrow morning, do not tell your workmates what you've learned. Don't turn to the person at the next desk and loudly announce, "You know, this place really sucks." Such philosophical honesty may result in your living in a damp cardboard box under the San Fernando Street overpass and wearing somebody else's underwear. Just keep your mouth shut and remember: Given the present state of Social Security, you can never, ever retire.

So good luck! And don't forget to pad that next job application.

From the *San Jose Mercury News West Magazine*, November 6, 1988.

10

GOING UNDERGROUND IN SILICON VALLEY

John Henry Jackson, 44 years old and known as One-Eyed Jack, is waiting for his trial to begin, where he will face charges of grand larceny, conspiracy, and "the buying, receiving, and possession of stolen and altered property." The courtroom setting is familiar to Mr. Jackson, who is currently out on bail. He has been convicted four times on lesser counts, involving passing bad checks, forgery, and burglary.

But this trial is different. In pretrial hearings over the last year, One-Eyed Jack has not been listening to the district attorney's office describe him as a small-time criminal, but rather as a kingpin in the electronics underground. Mr. Jackson has pleaded not guilty to all the charges.

The case against Mr. Jackson alleges that he both led a crime ring that stole 10,000 memory chips from the Intel Corporation, Silicon Valley's giant semiconductor manufacturer, and remarketed as many as 100,000 other similar devices, most of them stolen. The chips he is accused of stealing are Intel's 32K Eprom's, a highly specialized computer chip, worth $100 apiece at the time. But more important to the prosecutor's office and federal investigators is the range of their application in electronic equipment—from harmless video arcade games to guidance systems aboard fighter aircraft.

The Jackson trial marks the most important case to date involving the so-called gray market in electronics. The gray market has in recent years grown into a vast underground of electronic devices and computer chips, some stolen, some merely surplus. Law enforcement officials contend that the market is both undermining national security and leading to growing criminal activity in the previously peaceful electronics industry.

It is called the gray market because much of the business of selling surplus chips back and forth is entirely legal, but an increasing portion is becoming a true black market.

When asked to estimate the size of the gray market in the United States, most police and federal agents guess $20 million, then quickly add that the number may be three or four times greater. What does appear certain is that though loosely knit, it is becoming increasingly organized; that it suffers the same economic cycles as the rest of the electronics industry, and that it is a key source of goods for less scrupulous domestic manufacturers, for foreign competitors such as Japan, and for embargoed countries such as the Soviet Union.

Indeed, concern over the impact on national security of such activities was raised last year in a speech by William H. Webster, director of the Federal Bureau of Investigation. "United States technology," he said, "whether it's military or purely industrial, is spy target No. I for foreign intelligence operations. I don't think there has been another time in our history when America's business has been under such a sophisticated espionage attack."

Many of the details in the Jackson caper come from Mr. Jackson's own statements to the police at the time of his arrest, as well as from statements by his accomplices, including Mr. Jackson's secretary. However, it is expected by the district attorney's office that Mr. Jackson's attorneys will move to have those statements ruled inadmissible in the trial.

The Intel chips were allegedly stolen from a fenced storage room protected by alarms, 24-hour security guards, an employee badge system, after-hours sign-in logs, security audits, spot checks, and closed-circuit television. The police say that Mr. Jackson circumvented all the security by having an Intel security guard as an accomplice—Albert Williams, who is also charged in the case and has also pleaded not guilty. Allegedly, Mr. Williams carried the chips out of the storeroom in the lining of his leather jacket, and, at times more blatantly, in plastic garbage bags.

(The recruiting of security guards into the underground is a growing problem in Silicon Valley, law enforcement officials say, and they add that thus far, little has been done by the companies themselves to blunt this activity.)

According to early statements by Mr. Williams, he and Mr. Jackson got cooperation in the heist from a highly placed unnamed executive at Intel. Mr. Williams said that this executive prepared the necessary paperwork to initiate the production of the 10,000 memory chips to be stolen, and by later destroying the papers, made the theft possible without Intel's records showing the loss. The executive was never prosecuted, much less named, and references to him do not appear in the court records.

The use of inside agents was the most effective technique available to Mr. Jackson. But when that was not possible, he had others. In a secretly taped interview with a private investigator, one Jackson employee described how his boss would sometimes use a pretty girl to distract workers at the loading dock, while someone else carted off goods. According to statements by Mr. Jackson, 90 percent of all theft occurred during the shipping and storing of chips.

The stolen chips, which were fresh off the assembly line and as yet unmarked and unculled for the standard 40 percent rejects, were then taken to a Sunnyvale, California, apartment and stamped with the Intel logos. From there, the chips were taken to Southern California and sold to any buyer with cash, and thus began their long journey through the electronics gray market.

But the alleged Jackson theft was not the first time Intel had been hit by thieves. In April 1980, Michael Moe, a maintenance supervisor at Intel, carried thousands of dollars in memory chips out of a storage area in the false bottom of a box. Mr. Moe was convicted in May 1980 of grand larceny and given three years probation—In the same case, Glen Johnson, owner of Glen Manufacturing Inc., an electronics manufacturing company of Stockton, California, was convicted of buying thousands of stolen chips from Mr. Moe, and was given six months in prison, four years probation, and fined $5,200. In trial testimony, Mr. Johnson contended that the eight-month lead time on receiving Intel chips pushed him into doing business with Mr. Moe.

"We now monitor the gray market locally," Roger S. Borovoy, Intel's vice president, general counsel, and director in charge of security, said. "And it's been very successful. Those little shops that used to sell Intel parts don't have them anymore."

But, Mr. Borovoy admits, a concerted industrywide effort to fight the gray market has yet to occur. "I'm afraid that we're still pretty much alone in fighting this thing," he said.

Since the electronics industry has always been cyclical and subject to sharp peaks and troughs, during boom times, key products, such as memory chips and microprocessors, experience extraordinary demand. Delivery times can stretch from a few days to as much as a year, and panicky customers with bottlenecked assembly lines desperately search for any source of overlooked parts. During downturns, the long lead times dwindle and manufacturers are stuck with swollen inventories that they must sell to maintain their cash flows.

Gray marketeers perform a useful and legitimate service by acting as a kind of broker. And for that reason, they are supported both by manufacturers and their customers. During down periods, the gray marketeers acquire excess inventory at a discount, betting that these particular models will eventually be in demand. When the boom hits, those who have bet right can make a killing on skyrocketing prices. Those who have guessed wrong can still use their network of contacts to locate pockets of unused parts throughout the world that can be resold to hungry customers.

But sometimes demand is so great that it outstrips even the ability of gray marketeers to meet it, a situation that has tempted some in the gray market into thievery. The Japanese video game boom of 1977–1978 was the latest event to set many on their criminal paths.

According to one Silicon Valley gray marketeer, scores of small Japanese manufacturers popped up to meet the demand for video games. And, as it turned out, a critical memory chip, the semiconductor ancestor of the kind Mr. Jackson allegedly stole, was available only in the United States. Orders flooded the American semiconductor companies.

When the enormous demand could not be met by the manufacturers or the licensed distributors, Japanese businessmen began arriving in Silicon Valley offering $20 cash and more for semiconductors worth $3, no questions asked. One gray marketeer, who insisted on anonymity, recalled meeting Japanese executives at the San Francisco airport carrying suitcases filled with as much as $1 million in cash.

The huge profits turned some shrewd gray marketeers into millionaires, others into outright criminals. But for the majority, according to law enforcement officials, it gave them a taste for illegal games that has led them to cross back and forth beyond the law ever since.

Doug Southard, deputy district attorney in Santa Clara County and the one who is prosecuting the Jackson case, estimates that there have been 30 to 40 successful prosecutions of illegal gray market activity.

Of the 100 to 200 gray marketeers, he says, "most independent brokers are legitimate." But adds, "The problem is in that particular business, it's like pawnbrokering, it provides an opportunity to buy stolen goods when they are available. Even the most honest brokers will turn their heads from time to time and purposefully be fooled."

Goods moving through the gray market are handled by three groups: questionable large distributors who mix stolen, counterfeited, or rejected parts with inventories acquired from the legitimate manufacturers; so called schlockers, who do much the same, and scrap metal reclaimers, who have "inside" men at semiconductor companies salt scrap chips with good ones, or who simply sell junked chips as good. Police officials say that payment to the assembly line employees who make the thefts is most often in the form of narcotics.

Whatever the point of entry into the gray market, the goods do not remain long. According to local police, some chips are stolen on order and have a paying customer waiting.

But the majority of gray market goods are sold back and forth among brokers looking for an edge, passing through a half dozen or more hands before they reach the customer.

The Jackson story is a case in point: According to statements by Mr. Jackson in police records, his independent distributing company,

Dyno Electronics of Santa Clara, sold the stolen chips to Space Age Metals, a metal reclaimer based in Gardenia, California. (Space Age, however, denies it bought chips from Dyno on that occasion, but admits it had done business with Mr. Jackson previously.) Further, Mr. Jackson said that Space Age sold the parts to neighboring Mormac Technology Inc. of Tarzana, California, and to Republic Electronics Inc. of Arlington, Virginia. (According to police records, Mr. Jackson also sold parts directly to Mormac.)

These two companies sold the parts to the same customer, E.D.V. Electronik, an electronics distributor in Munich, West Germany, which in turn sold them to A.G. Siemans, the West German electronics giant. Siemans, it turned out, had not been satisfied with Intel's 1,000 chip-per-month allotment. The case surfaced in November 1979 when Siemans began complaining to Intel, about faulty chips.

Such international chains are not unusual, law enforcement officials say. The channels enable the gray market to reach even the smallest company any place in the world. In addition, because the links are so loose, it allows even the most patriotic to start chips on a path that may eventually lead to the nose cone of a Russian intercontinental ballistic missile.

The Jackson case has a related angle. Charged with him was Patrick Ketchum, an officer of Mormac. Mr. Jackson claims that Mr. Ketchum sold some of his stolen chips to Anatoli Maluta, a Russian-born naturalized American, and Werner Bruchhausen, a West German. Both Mr. Maluta and Mr. Bruchhausen were indicted last year for illegally exporting semiconductor manufacturing equipment to the Soviet Union. Charges, however, against Mr. Ketchum, who was convicted in 1979 of selling counterfeit chips to the United States military, were eventually dropped because the government could not prove that Mr. Ketchum knew the chips he received from Mr. Jackson were counterfeit.

Over the years, a number of gray market trade routes have been established. The primary source of goods remains Silicon Valley, though the other electronics enclaves in this country, such as Boston and Phoenix, also are beginning to see a growing underground. In addition, the assembly plants of American electronics companies in Malaysia are also seeing an alarming number of truck hijackings and other thefts.

Many customers for the United States brokers are brokers themselves, operating out of countries not constrained by American embargo laws. Finland, France, Austria, and even Canada are pointed to by gray marketeers as key way-stations for moving electronic parts into the East bloc countries, Iran, and other unfriendly nations.

Who are the customers of the gray market? A current myth is that KGB agents are hiding behind every telephone pole in Silicon Valley waiting to steal the latest chip models.

In fact, the Soviet Union is said to have discovered what Japan and Hong Kong learned years ago—American gray marketeers will fight for the right to sell them whatever they need.

"The KGB would have to be crazy to come over here," said a former gray marketeer. "They aren't stupid people. They know they can get what they need by just staying at home and sending in orders."

For more than a decade the gray market has developed precisely to fill the orders of such customers. And succeeding generations of customers have tapped into the underground flow of parts. First the Japanese, whose current success depends in large part on their ability to acquire American chips and copy, or "reverse engineer" them; then the Taiwanese, Malaysians, and South Koreans, who needed chips for their consumer electronics factories; next the Eastern Bloc and the Chinese to skirt the United States embargoes, and now, increasingly, developing countries.

Not all sales are international. Much of the gray market business comes from small American original equipment makers, and in boom periods, when parts grow scarce, even some of the industry's largest and most respected companies have been known to dip into the gray market to keep manufacturing lines running.

Despite the claim that gray marketeers fulfill a necessary role, the indifference of the market to its customers can have dangerous results, such as the Southern California manufacturer of pacemakers that discovered it had a load of faulty chips. It is also impossible to quantify the damage to the nation's economic vitality and military security from the sales of advanced technology to foreign competitors or enemies.

And the prognosis, at least according to Mr. Borovoy of Intel, is not good for the immediate future. "It's going to get worse," he said. "We're beginning to see capacity problems in the industry again. Lead times are starting to climb. And when you can't get parts the legitimate way, you'll get them any way you can."

From the *New York Times,* May 30, 1982.

11

DAY OF THE JACKAL

In the world of high tech, where change is perpetual, today's hottest products will be obsolete and forgotten five years from now. The rate of failure is high. Few consider what happens to the ever-growing mountain of equipment that has served its purpose, or whose original owners have gone out of business even before their hardware goes out of style. Where does all that dispossessed paraphernalia go, and what can we learn from its fate?

Some of it, inevitably, goes to landfill. But each year thousands of pieces of electronic equipment find a second or third home back in industry, recycled by clever dealers who sell them to equally clever corporate buyers who appreciate that not everything in the digital revolution is instantly obsolete.

"It's the great American treasure hunt," says Lorin Bergman, opening the door to a garage that holds everything from modern process control equipment and diodes to a 1927 Lincoln. "You buy it for pennies on the pound and you turn around and sell it, if you're lucky, for hundreds, even thousands of dollars. And let me tell you, once you turn 75 bucks into 2,500, you're hooked for life."

Lorin Bergman is an information age junk man, "a scavenger," he says with a laugh as he cruises his Alfa Romeo sedan through the old industrial district of Mountain View, California, past the aging warehouses that were once the heart of Silicon Valley. He is an unlikely character in an equally unlikely profession. Raised in a wealthy south San Francisco Bay community, Bergman collects modern art, lives in an elegant apartment in downtown San Jose, and is part owner of an upscale Valley restaurant. His friends range from television producers to college professors.

But he's a scavenger nevertheless. Each morning Bergman visits his garage warehouse or one of several rented storage lockers, checks his inventory, then settles down to make calls before setting off to visit local contacts. "It's my own little virtual company," he says, and in recent years it has made him as much money as a lot of Silicon Valley senior executives.

What Bergman understands, and takes full advantage of, is that the secret strength of high technology is its potential to render gain from failure. Failed ideas, and the companies that died implementing them, are revised to be used again. Failed technologies are learned from and improved on. And the physical assets of these failed businesses, the detritus of the high-tech revolution, are also recycled to help power ongoing change.

Here's how the recycling process works: In whole or part, a company fails. It may go out of business or merely, in Bergman's phrase, "write off an entire product line with the stroke of an MBA's pencil." If it is a technology manufacturing company, this may mean auctioning thousands of parts, finished inventory, manufacturing, or test equipment. Even if the company isn't high tech, office computers and other infrastructure may go on the block.

Meanwhile, throughout the country and around the globe, hundreds of potential customers may vie for these castoffs. "Obsolescence is our greatest friend," says Bergman.

On this day he has driven up from San Jose to Mountain View to visit Test Lab Company, perhaps the world's leading independent reseller of used Hewlett-Packard test equipment. Test Lab was founded by Jim Trees, the dean of high-tech scavengers and a mentor to the current generation of junkmen like Bergman and Test Lab's longtime vice president Mike Megown.

For Bergman, business is always unpredictable. A typical scavenger usually works alone or with a handful of employees and deals regularly with a dozen or more "bird dogs" who help spot items for sale at auction. The bird dogs then notify the right scavenger, who fronts them money to make the purchase. Sometimes the scavenger may choose to attend an auction himself to nail down the best price.

The auctions may take place at a shiny new West Coast electronics plant that is selling off old inventory, or in a Rust Belt factory shut down after a century of hard use. Says Bergman, "New high-tech companies used to be embarrassed to hold auctions of discontinued lines—it was an admission of failure. But now the stigma is gone. They positively welcome us. It's at the old East Coast factories, where four or five generations have worked, where they really resent the hell out of scavengers. For them we signal the end of an era."

Scavengers become experts on how things end. "When you see a warehouse full of unsold goods, you know the company either misjudged its customers or its market." At a failed business filled with new, expensive furniture, a scavenger knows overhead was ignored in favor of impressing venture capitalists.

Auctions are the normal mode of acquisition, though a veteran scavenger may over time buy less from auctions and more from a collection of regular corporate suppliers and bird dogs. The other half of the process, finding customers, is more complicated. Many customers can be located through ads placed in such magazines as *Industrial Computing*. In the best scenario, a scavenger will have worked with a customer so long and know its needs so well that when he spots something at auction, he'll go ahead and take a flyer on the bidding.

Often, however, a scavenger will bid on something with no idea who will eventually want it, just because the price is too good to walk away from. That's what separates the pros from the pikers. Anybody can fill an order, but only the veterans—those who know more about their little corner of technology than anyone in the world—can make a market.

Lorin Bergman has been scavenging for about 14 years, and only now does he feel he has reached a point where he understands both his product line and the auction business. He believes he finally has a customer list extensive enough to support his ambitions. He now sits in Mike Megown's office, with its Corvette models, antique vacuum tubes, and old Hewlett-Packard test equipment catalogs, swapping gossip and retelling old stories of legendary scores.

Megown inhabits a different part of the scavenger world than Bergman. Test Lab operates out of a 20,000-square-foot building and employs 20 people, including 7 full-time technicians who work in the on-site testing and repair lab.

To tour the Test Lab facility is to pass through the history of modern electronics. In row upon row of shelves sit tens of thousands of old Hewlett-Packard oscilloscopes, wave analyzers, counters, and oscillators. Although most of the equipment is less than 20 years old, some, in beautiful wooden cases, dates back to the 1940s, a testament to HP's legendary durability.

If Bergman's overstuffed garage and lockers represent the hunter/gatherer level of scavenging market, Test Lab's warehouse is a few rungs up the evolutionary ladder. Each instrument has been cleaned, bar-coded, and stacked on the appropriate shelf. The result is less a junkyard than a convalescent home for aging electronics.

Though Megown and Bergman have prospered as scavengers, neither is immune to the same rapid changes in high tech that affect their suppliers and customers. Megown's scariest antagonist is Hewlett-Packard itself, which launched its multimillion-dollar used equipment business 20 years ago.

Bergman has always had plenty of competitors, but he's been able to hold his own and has little to fear from the big outfits because his field—industrial process control equipment—is so specialized and small. But in the long term, Bergman has one very big worry: the Internet.

"The Net scares me," Bergman admits. "My business is based on the reality of imperfect information. The seller and the customer don't know each other. And neither quite knows the value of the other. On top of that, nobody knows if there are other buyers and sellers out there. My business is to accumulate that information and use it. But when you can search the Net to find anything, anywhere, along with the best price, what happens to us scavengers?"

From *Forbes ASAP Magazine* © Forbes Inc., June 2, 1997. Reprinted by permission.

12

A GOOD DAY TO CONTEMPLATE THE REST OF LIFE

On a Friday morning in the spring of 1613, according to his notes, John Donne found himself on a horse riding toward Wales from the country estate of Sir "H.G." to an estate belonging to Sir Edward Herbert.

It was a seventeenth-century equivalent of a modern business trip: long hours in a saddle instead of business class seat, bad food in a smoky inn instead of airline food, and an anonymous Hyatt or Marriott, but in spirit the same.

Riding along, Donne, 41, no doubt resembled the businessman we see across the aisle from us as we wing over Nevada on our way to Comdex: a long, bony nose, a slightly receding hairline, hair a little too black to be natural, and tired eyes set behind parchment-thin lids. He had suffered a nearly fatal illness just a few years before, and that, along with the burden of providing for a wife and seven children (as well as the pain of losing five others) would have given him a ghostly pallor and an air of nervousness.

In 1613, though he did not yet know it, Donne was coming to the end-of a decade-long nightmare. As a young man, he had been the toast of English arts and letters. Beginning at Oxford, then at law school, young Jack Donne had lived high. He drank, chased women, traveled the Continent, followed the raffish Earl of Essex into battle—then writing about those exploits in brilliant "metaphysical" poems and essays full of wit and word play:

Go and catch a falling star . . .

Then it all collapsed. Caught in an affair with his patron's young ward (whom he would later happily marry), Donne had lost his position and his reputation. Having already burned through his father's legacy, marked by both past behavior and for being born a Catholic, Donne was reduced to taking odd jobs into survive.

Through the lens of twentieth century Silicon Valley, we can see in John Donne a kindred spirit, and in his travails a hint of an entrepreneurial mind in Stuart England. After all, there are no few of us, like that man across the aisle, who find ourselves washed up on the shores of middle-age wondering what happened to that bright promise, asking ourselves why we could never fit in the usual corporate slots, why we have always been our own worst enemies—and yet knowing, as we've always known, that we are destined to make our mark . . . somewhere.

Here in Silicon Valley we celebrate entrepreneurship. Rightly so; history may well call this place the greatest entrepreneurial explosion in human history. But in celebrating, we often forget the cost: the dark obsessions, the wrecked families, the career failures. Most of all the terror—the daily depressions and nightly sweats, wondering why, why, you can't fit into corporate life, why you have to shoot your mouth off and go and do the impolite just because you know its right; then wondering if you really have the courage to risk everything to go it on your own.

John Donne knew that darkness and fear. For years now he had subsisted on the largess of rich patrons he sucked up to—like Lady Herbert, to whom he was now riding—and on degrading writing jobs, such as authoring anti-Catholic pamphlets for the Protestant authorities even though his own brother had died in jail for his Catholic beliefs. In the process, his own writing had grown dark as well: His most recent work was an essay extolling suicide. Now his contemporaries, like the great Ben Jonson, were saying that he was past his prime, that he'd done his best work before he was 25.

If all that wasn't enough, John Donne was also suffering a crisis of faith. He had long left his Catholicism behind and felt himself increasingly drawn toward the Church of England. But hadn't he been raised to believe Anglicism a heresy? Years of theological research had only left him more confused and in anguish.

So now we find John Donne, at the end of his rope, believing that the best of his life is already behind him, riding through the Cotswold Hills that Spring morning in 1613. Then it hits him: It's Friday. Good Friday. He is riding to the West, away from everything he cares about, including himself and his God.

In pondering this, Donne begins to see himself as a tiny spot on the globe, tossed about by forces beyond his control, caught in the vortex of a new scientific world emerging about him. Today, our traveler might talk of quarks and quasars, mips and megahertz. But Donne is a seventeenth-century man. Isaac Newton is not yet born. Jamestown is less than a decade old, the Mayflower voyage seven years off. So his images are those of Copernicus and the growing debate about gravitation, and his yearning is to find a place within it; just as we struggle to understand where we fit in the emerging virtual world of the Internet and corporate downsizings.

Good Friday 1613: Riding Westward

Let man's soul be a sphere, and then in this,
The intelligence that movess devotion is,

And as the other spheres, by being grown
Subject to foreign motions, lose their own,
And being by others hurried every day,
Scarce in a year their natural form obey:
Pleasure or business, so, our souls admit
For their first mover, and are whirled by it.
Hence is it, that I am carried toward the West
This day, when my, soul's form bends toward the East.

Within a century, Donne's style of poetry was in disrepute, and he was nearly forgotten. Metaphysical poetry, with its wit and wordplay, and its sudden leaps from the personal to the cosmic, was seen as too facile and shallow to be taken as serious poetry. It is only in this century, beginning with a reappreciation by such influential figures as T.S. Eliot, that Donne's poetry has enjoyed a revival.

This isn't surprising. After all, we are the century of modernism and postmodernism where truth disappears into language and the words themselves are stripped of meaning. In this new reality, Donne seems right at home.

Ours is a world where radio telescopes and the Hubble spacecraft look out across 10 billion light years, and the submicron structures on the surface of an integrated circuit cut time into billionths of second. For our time, Donne's poetry is prescient.

So is his crisis of faith. In 1613, God was still alive, but hiding behind the murderous demands of different faiths for absolute adherence to their liturgy. Today, he's off beyond the Singularity at the beginning or the universe or behind the magicians screen of quantum physics . . . if he's still there at all.

Today on the radio, in the song "One of Us," Joan Osborne asked, "If God had a face, what would it look like?" Donne, riding his horse that Good Friday morning, asked the same question. He answered that we had seen it once before:

There I should see a sun, by rising, set,
And by that setting endless day beget;
But that Christ on this Cross, did rise and fall,
Sin had eternally benighted all.
Yet dare I almost be glad, I do not see
That spectacle of too much weight for me.
Who sees God's face, that is itself life, must die;
What a death were it then to see God die?
It made his own Lieutenant Nature shrink
It made his own footstool crack, and the Sun wink,
Could I behold those hands which span the Poles,
And turn all spheres at once, pierced with those holes?

John Donne also shared something else with us. He lived in a
violent time. The defeat of the Armada was as recent in time as
Vietnam is to us now. Plagues were at that moment killing thousands elsewhere in Europe, and in a few years would strike London
again. Galileo is ready to face the Inquisition and the Thirty Years
War is about to turn most of Europe into a charnel house. Donne
had seen war and murder and executions, just as we have watching
CNN in our even bloodier century.

Could I behold that endless height which is
Zenith to us, and our Antipodes
Humbled below us? Or that blood which is
The seat of all our souls, if not this,
Made dirt of dust, or that flesh which was worn
By God, for His apparel, ragged and torn?
If on these things I dare not look, dare I
Upon His miserable mother cast my eye,
Who was God's partner here, and furnished thus
Half of that sacrifice, which ransomed us?

Humbled now in the realization of his indifference to this day,
the truth comes to Donne; or more accurately, it emerges from

where it has always been, within him. He feels a fool, deserving to be punished like a schoolboy for his callousness toward both God and his own destiny. But at the same, time, John Donne feels liberated. He knows now what he must do, and this realization strips away the accumulated scars of the previous decade, and draws him upward, in the final couplets of the poem, to some of the most powerful imagery of his career:

> Though these things, as I ride, be from mine eye
> They are present yet unto my memory,
> For that looks toward them; and thou lookest Toward me
> O' Saviour, as thou hangest upon the tree;
> I turn my back to thee, but to receive
> Corrections, till thy mercies bid thee leave
> O think me worth thine anger, punish me
> Burn of my rusts, and my deformity
> Restore thine image, so much by thy grace
> Thou mayest know me, and I'll turn my face.

John Donne had found his place. He turned around and faced his destiny. Within months, he requested ordination in the Church of England. Two years later, the king approved. By 1615, Donne was giving his first sermons, and in 1621 he was named dean of St. Paul's—a post he held for the remaining 10 years of his life. During these years in the Anglican Church, Donne produced a body of sacred poems that rank at least with the secular poems that preceded them. His sermons are the finest in the English language.

The most disturbing and least admitted truth of Silicon Valley is that no one wins all of the time and most of us never win at all. That means someday, perhaps every day, each of us will be that tragic man in business class, like John Donne on that Good Friday morning in 1613, battered and tired and running away from our destiny, from what matters most to us.

A Good Day to Contemplate the Rest of Life

Just what that destiny is—starting our own company, changing our careers, devoting ourselves to our families, or, as with John Donne, turning our face back toward the East—only our hearts can tell us. A spring morning, like this Good Friday, with its hum of redemption and renewal, is a good time to start listening.

From the *San Jose Mercury News,* April 7, 1996.

13

HAS SILICON VALLEY GONE PUSSY?

A Silicon Valley veteran, a man whose career dates back to the Wild West days of Fairchild, sits at a mahogany Sheraton table across from a venture capitalist.

The Valley vet, his face seamed, his lungs tarred, and his liver half-rotted from too many late-night drinks with clients at the Wagon Wheel, too many 80-hour weeks trying to get a new product to market, too many stomach-churning 3 A.M.s worrying about meeting payroll, is a little seedy. His suit is of an obsolete cut, his tie stained, and he still smells like the cigarette he smoked in the parking lot before coming in. When he coughs, which is frequently, the sound is like a first death rattle.

By comparison, the VC across from him is half the vet's age—and looks even younger than that. With delicate, manicured fingers, he indifferently flicks his way through the vet's business plan. The young VC has an impeccable little beard and his Sea Island cotton shirt ends at the wrist with French cuffs and at the collar with the latest Armani cravat. His suspenders—"braces"—bear reproduction Victorian steel engravings of swooning nymphs. On one finger, the young VC wears a gold ring bearing the VERITAS emblem of Harvard. He doesn't drink (except for his collection of varietals) or smoke and he runs five miles each morning in Spandex tights. Though he was born in Belmont, when the young VC speaks, his words bear the inflections of Boston Brahmin and English boarding school.

The young VC looks up with a sort of tired disdain, "Aren't these projections incomplete?"

"Whaddyamean?" asks the vet, knowing from experience that all new company financials are bullshit.

But the young VC doesn't reply. He merely sighs loudly and continues flipping pages, "And where's your company's long-term strategy?"

The vet is taken aback, "Strategy? Hell, our strategy is to build and sell as many of these little bastards as we can."

The VC makes a little clicking sound with his voice, "Surely you don't expect us to seriously consider investing in such an enterprise before you've properly addressed such questions as channels, intellectual property protection, personnel policies, and equity distribution?"

The Valley vet swallows hard. His ass is starting to hurt. He leans across the table to the impeccable young man, "You know, I remember when business plans were written on cocktail napkins and venture deals were cut in an afternoon."

"Yes," replies the young VC, "and thank God those days are over." Closing the business plan, and without making eye contact, he adds, "Frankly, Mr. _____, your venture is far too speculative for our current fund strategy. Your product is just not enough like established products on the market for us to have any guarantees of its long-term success. But thank you for showing it to us." The young VC stands and gives the Valley vet a self-consciously firm handshake.

The Valley vet, standing in the parking lot and smoking a cigarette just 20 minutes after the last one, coughs and looks bloodily back at the Sand Hill Road office building. That does it, he decides, I'll get my money from the Japanese. At least they've still got balls . . .

Call it the Pussification of Silicon Valley. Somewhere along the line, just as the giant snarling predatory dinosaurs were replaced by sniveling little moles, the hard-living wildcatters of Silicon Valley legend were supplanted by a new breed of Valley executives: lean as a ferret, sensitive, obsessed with being politically correct at all times, ostensibly passive but secretly vicious and always devious. Silicon Valley has entered its Medici period, and the new knit-shirted courtiers are busily sharpening their dirks and mixing their poisons.

By 'pussy,' we mean neither the female nor the homosexual derogation. On the contrary, one has only to look at Valley executive women—Andrea Cunningham, Sandy Kurtzig, Brenna Bolger, Maryles Casto, Debi Coleman—to appreciate that they are among the last tough guys in the Valley. As for gays, have there been any braver or more heroic souls in our culture in recent years than young men quietly dying of AIDS?

No, our meaning for pussy harks back to the high school locker room and the dusty parade grounds of boot camp. It's the epithet spit on boys who won't stand for their rights, who won't carry their share of the load, who whine and suck up to the teacher for special favors, and cry for attention when hurt. It's the kid who throws a baseball like a girl. Later, it's the stigma awarded by the drill instructor on the recruit who burdens the squad by falling behind on the morning run and complaining that his rifle is too heavy. Among adults, it's the guy who provokes a fight with his smart mouth and then calls the cops when a punch is thrown; who allows his family to be insulted, who takes daily humiliations from his boss and who whimpers over such unimportant matters as secondary cigarette smoke. Most of all, it is the man who will compromise every-thing—pleasure, physical excitement, love, and friendship—in the hope of living a long, healthy, and hopelessly uneventful life.

Silicon Valley used to pulverize such pussies, now it lionizes them. Arguably, some companies are now organized so that being pussified is the only way to advance. The result is Iago as division general manager, Judas Iscariot as COO.

The change is obvious everywhere. In the early days of Fairchild, an emblematic employee party was Scotch and brownies in an empty room, followed by a hard night of further drinking and carousing (both male and female) at the Wagon Wheel. Now, the typical employee party is some kind of low-cholesterol, high-fiber nosh washed down with liberal tumblers of Evian water—followed by a jog, dinner on soybean curd at the Good Earth, then evening at home with the kids, educational toys, and "thirtysomething."

Sure, you may reply, many of those Valley pioneers soon suc-cumbed to alcoholism, lung cancer, and exploding aortic aneurysms while lying in strange beds—but so what? The whole point is that at one time in Silicon Valley, only a generation ago in fact, people un-derstood that there were better things than living to a weasely old age and, conversely, worse things than dying from one's vices. It was a time when betrayal was still a dirty word.

When did Silicon Valley suddenly go pussy? One can point to a number of contributing events, but ultimately the transformation came with the same sort of subtle deviousness exhibited by its principals. Even some of the legendary silicon sons-of-bitches who made this valley what it is have now succumbed. Guys who used to gnaw out the throats of subordinates just for sport have suddenly become "people-oriented." In these very pages, Don Valentine writes to explain that he is no longer the gilt-edged bastard he used to be. Well, why not? It used to be a badge of honor to be like

Valentine, now even he doesn't want to be like his former self. What he should be saying is, "Well, weenie, if you and your sensitive little startup don't want to play hardball, then why don't you go down the road and play patty-cake with Brentwood or Sierra?"

Valentine isn't alone. Jerry Sanders shaves off his mustache, Charlie Sporck professes to be embarrassed by National's old coarseness, and Wilf Corrigan—Wilf Corrigan for God's sake—now sponsors art shows. What's wrong with this picture?

On top of that, when an honest-to-goodness retro-hard guy, such as T.J. Rodgers, appears on the scene and starts popping off opinions that used to be the received view in Silicon Valley—like supporting entrepreneurs, trusting innovation, keeping the government off our backs—he's greeted about as warmly as an accused child molester.

No, the duty of every good Valleyite now is to follow our once-brave leaders and go mewling off to Washington in search of tariff protection, tax breaks and best of all, some kind of monopolistic consortium to defend market share. Anything but build better and cheaper products, start competitive new companies, take a lower salary, and just basically kick some offshore high-tech butt.

Is it any wonder the Japanese hold us in such contempt? They call us crybabies and who are we to disagree? Those guys play for keeps, just like we used to before we decided that surrender was infinitely preferable to sacrifice. That the way to personal satisfaction was to hold hands around the campfire. That a pose of sincerity was more important than either competence or experience.

History will record that the pussification of Silicon Valley began in the investment banking community and the consumer electronics industry.

The success of the local high-tech industry in the mid-1970s turned the Valley into a beacon for ambitious young plutocrats-in-training, their MBA diplomas still wet, from around the world. There were gobs of money to be made here, but how to get at it without an engineering degree, job experience, or an ounce of humanity?

One way was obvious, especially to the likes of young Harvard business Brahmins: If you can't be the famous person, at least be his banker. Soon, the investment banking industry was filled with lean, tortoise-framed pussies with the proper collar roll and a larynx full of dragged vowels. It was the perfect career for this rarefied species: judging other people's lives, doling out sums of money to the hoi polloi, and staying in regular touch with breeding companions in the canyons of Wall Street.

Why did the investment banking firms let these spores of pussification take root? Well, for one thing, many were in San Francisco, so were half-pussified already. Just as powerful, though, was the ever-present nouveau Valley need for respectability—the same driving force behind all the wine and art appreciation courses, ballet and symphony fund-raisers, and rents on Manhattan pied-à-terre that obsess the Valley's social climbers. Investment bankers wanted class, they wanted confirmation of their respectability, and what cheaper way to do it than to hire a few token Harvard, Stanford, and Wharton MBAs—especially if they'd done a stint polishing apples at, say, the Boston Consulting Group?

And so it was that the scourge of American industry at last infected Valley life, entering at its most delicate extremity. Soon the results were all too apparent: a disastrous triumph of style over substance. The lack of real-life, in-the-trenches, business experience soon told. No investment banking firm escaped uninfected, but those with the fewest anti-pussies were quickly overrun. Hambrecht & Quist, for example, was wounded but survived. By comparison, Robertson Stephens, once H&Q's biggest rival, was left nearly in extremis by acute pussiness. . . .

Pussyhood also attacked the law business in strength about this time. Here the damage wasn't so severe, if only because posturing, backstabbing, and manipulation were hardly novel to the profession.

If only the virus had been contained at this level, Silicon Valley might have endured. Unfortunately, since the mid-1970s the entire American culture has reinforced pussiness as an honorable way of life. Alda, Donahue, effeminate rock stars, and the guy at the bar professing to a woman his sensitivity while at the same time looking down her blouse—all provided a fertile ground for pussyhood's assault on American business, even at its toughest, here in Silicon Valley.

Venture capital, only one step removed from investment banking, was the next to go.

Venture capital used to be a fraternity of successful Valley veterans who felt a considerable kinship with the entrepreneurs with whom they worked. These VCs, and their names are now legend, understood what it was like to try to keep a new startup running, to meet the payroll while still getting the product to market on time. They knew, because they'd been there themselves and knew what made it work.

These VCs—Rock, Valentine, Perkins, et al.—were very successful. Too successful, because their very success attracted not only half-assed competitors, but, worse, mountains of investment money. This money had to be invested, and that meant more people managing the fund. Unfortunately, the VCs were no more resistant to the siren call of respectability than their investment banking counterparts. And soon, the extra offices all over 3000 Sand Hill Road were filling with venture pussies. By the mid-1980s, to visit a VC was to expect to be introduced to a parade of buttoned-down, horn-rimmed post-adolescents in pleated flannel trousers. The older VC would intone proudly, "Randolph here just joined the firm. He's Choate/Brown/Harvard MBA" as junior shook your hand firmly and tried to conceal a supercilious smirk under a dewy upper lip.

Here is an actual conversation, overheard at a dinner in San Francisco between two venture pussies:

"Capital wine."

"Quite."

Is it any wonder then that the venture capital industry soon found itself in trouble from which it has yet to emerge? Inexperienced children with good table manners now sit on the boards of powerful Silicon Valley companies, holding commanding stock positions, representing the next round of funding for the firm's survival. Having never run a company, met a payroll, or gone through the gut wrench of firing or being fired; in fact, having nothing to lose and riches to gain, these venture pussies make life a living hell for the management teams they ostensibly "advise." Most are callous and unsympathetic to the lives of employees, many are duplicitous and scheming, and some are downright evil.

As one Valley veteran of several new startups says, "The typical VCs today are into some kind of investment banker morality. Most of these dumb schmucks don't know their ass from a hole in the ground, but will lie, steal, and cheat to succeed.

"I sometimes feel like I'm in the middle of a Machiavellian nightmare."

Unfamiliarity also breeds contempt: for rules, clients, and customers. The breathtaking incompetence of many of the young venture pussies has put the VC industry into sad straits as round after round of good money chases bad investments. Shrewd pension funds and other investment sources are now demanding an accounting.

But the venture pussies are not deterred. According to another Valley vet, "The rules have changed here in the Valley. Return On Investment is now the new God. To qualify now with some major investors, you have to prove that you were in the top 5 percent in ROI among VCs in the 1980s. Now, say you're a venture firm, and one of your funds has a real dog company in its portfolio. If you let the dog die and take the write-off on it, you won't qualify for the 5 percent list. So what do you do? You merge it with another dog, promise the management team big future money that you have no intention of ever delivering, and then put a fictitious value for the new merged firm into your prospectus.

"And guess what? Your venture firm has now made the ROI top 5 percent club."

The other way pussiness entered Silicon Valley was through that festering wound of a company, Atari, in the early 1980s. Atari did so much for Valley life, including rotting children's brains, opening the Valley's first true executive dining room, robbing average people's hard-earned money in the company's financial collapse, and forcing on its employees the cruelest layoff in Valley history.

See a pattern here? That's right, in the two years before the collapse, you couldn't swing a cat in the executive offices of Atari without soiling an Armani suit here or crumpling an MBA diploma there. Literally in months under Warner ownership, Atari went from the stoned egalitarianism of the Bushnell era to the most stratified, schizoid, and self-destructive corporate environment imaginable. The young mandarins at the top despised the goofy game designers, and the designers got even by walking out.

Atari died, but the pussies survived, metastasizing and looking for a new vital organ to rot.

You've already guessed which one, haven't you? Of course— Apple Computer.

The terrible irony of this pussification of Silicon Valley is that it has had just the opposite of its intended effect. Driving a Volvo and declaring your city a nuclear-free zone and banning smoking in public places and always wearing your bicycle helmet and eating lots of fiber and calling your secretary an "area associate" and wearing jeans on Friday was supposed to make Silicon Valley a better place.

But just the reverse has occurred. The Valley is becoming increasingly conformist, intolerant of deviance from "correct" behaviors and ideologies, and appallingly self-righteous. It is no longer enough to work hard and not fuck up; now you must join the Noble Cause.

If, at its worst, the old Silicon Valley tended to authoritarianism—the CEO as warlord—at its best, this place also devised some of the most influential, empathic personnel policies American business has ever known. And for every screaming bully there were three or four Bill Hewletts and David Packards, Irwin Federmans, or Bob Noyces, Ken Oshmans, or Jimmy Treybigs—ambitious but honest, tough but kind-hearted.

The new Silicon Valley is a whole different animal. These days, the dark side is totalitarianism: the company as way of life. Goebbels and Himmler now run the Party. No one shouts anymore; rather, they patiently mix their poisons and wait for the proper moment. The Valley used to resolve its disputes with fistfights in the hallway or angry confrontations. But obvious violence is no longer politically correct—for that matter, neither is any extreme emotion—so power battles now resemble monarchial court intrigues, coups d'état and Renaissance papal successions. Peter Drucker is being replaced by Castiglione; Ouchi by Kafka.

What is most frightening is that the curse of pussyhood is now reaching out to every corner of the Valley. Having breached the barriers of consumer electronics and venture capital, it is now corrupting even the rank and file. By idolizing and imitating Valley heroes, Valley workers are now beginning to exhibit symptoms of the plague. The signs are everywhere—unless something is done we will be overrun by sensitive and thin men and women, sweaters tied around their narrow shoulders, crowding gelato shops, wearing bicycle clothing and helmets into bookstores, teaching their children to play soccer instead of baseball, sending their résumés to Japanese multinationals, pinching their faces with neo-Puritan rectitude at the sight of a Marlboro or an American car.

It is not too late to stop the disaster from occurring. There are still a few hopeful signs that Silicon Valley can be saved. For one thing, some of the old guard is showing new life; TJ is rampaging around Washington humiliating the electro-pussies begging Congress for protection, Grove is showing up uninvited at the nation's great newspapers to give them hell, and Al Shugart is taking out ads promising to geld securities lawyers. That's a start. So is the appearance on the scene of some Valley throwback characters, like Gordon Campbell, Paul Ely, Finis Conner, Gene Norrett, and Bob Miller.

But perhaps the real hope for the Valley lies with its outsiders: women and ethnic minorities. It is telling that in a valley where most executives now drive such pussymobiles as the Lexus or BMW 745, it takes a Sandy Kurtzig to own a fire-breathing Ferrari Testarossa.

Sometimes it seems that most of the lost testosterone in this Valley is being used by its women. Shunted off into staff positions, they have made those operations—PR, advertising, personnel, etc.—into some of the area's toughest, hardest-driving enterprises. One can only hope that the women, now that they are assaulting executive row, will teach their Y-chromosome counterparts a little something about fire-in-the-belly business dealings.

The same with minorities. These people know what losing is all about, and aren't going to let it happen again. Just ask a chain-smoking, hard-working Vietnamese man or woman whether surrender is a viable choice; or if some things might be worth dying for.

It is time to stop whining about overseas competition and to start throwing pitches at Japanese batters' heads. It is time to buck up and face our opponents in the office and in the world eye-to-eye. It is time to wipe the slobber from our chins and put up our dukes.

It is time for Silicon Valley to get hard again.

From *Upside Magazine,* June 1990.

14

SEDUCTION—FROM THE BITCH GODDESS, A NOVEL

Wright Cash kept both feet together and flat on the floor, his bottom forward on the chair seat, his back and head erect, and his fingers properly arched over the keyboard. His saint of a mother had told him when he was 10 to do that: "Good posture will always tell, young man. It will strengthen your mind and body and it is the mark of a gentleman."

She, as always, was correct. During those long nights in Stanford University's Artificial Intelligence Lab, fighting for processing time on the Cray supercomputer, Wright's precise posture and good nutritional habits—so different from the candy bar-gnawing and coffee-swilling drones around him—had been his edge. Here it was, 3 A.M., and while the rest were fading, Wright had found his second wind. It was all he needed for the final push on his doctoral project.

The others laughed at him, of course. But they'd always laughed at him, especially the girls. Now they also feared and hated him. His classmates and teachers knew Wright had the most extraordinary mind for computer design they had ever seen. So now they hated him too, but Wright could live with that.

On the color display before him, rotating in a 360-degree view, was Wright's defining achievement. It was the ultimate statement of his genius, his final gesture of contempt for the dim graduate students and professors with whom he'd been forced to spend his time. His would be the greatest student project in the history of the Stanford Engineering School. Long months of solitary, secretive work meant that generations of students would remember Wright Cash.

It had started that July day two years ago. He'd been contemplating a project on new algorithms to mimic the way humans established metaphors, and immersed himself in a database search. He'd plowed through all the familiar scientific articles by the famous names in brain science in search of a new wrinkle. But no luck. Bored and frustrated, for a rare moment he'd even contemplated going outside and sitting in the sun before forcing himself to go on. Then, in a minor article in an obscure journal on marsupial brain research, a tiny chart caught his eye. It was a relatively straightforward graph of how the electrical pattern of a lemur's brain changed with various visual and auditory inputs. The results were, as usual, what the researchers had expected.

But Wright noticed something else: The data on the graph suggested an interference pattern from some other source. What was it? He checked the actual tables of measurements from the test. There. The signals were actually pairs, the second no more than 1 or 2 percent of the main response and way over at the other end of the spectrum. The researchers had probably ignored these little companion signals as background noise or equipment inaccuracy. But they weren't, Wright realized, because the interference echoed across the measurements.

Twenty-four hours later, he still hadn't left the keyboard. He'd found traces of the same ghost frequency in 23 other tests on brain activity. Two in hummingbirds, one in nematodes, sixteen in fruit flies, three in flatworms, and one in a paranoid schizophrenic patient at a Huntsville, Alabama, mental asylum in 1949. Subsequent months of research found 62 other examples of phantom brain waves. All appeared in perfect symmetry to the primary brain function, but all could be found in a narrow, long-wave band of the electromagnetic spectrum. No one had noticed these waves before because no one was looking for them . . . and even if they had, the researchers never would have looked out the spectrum all the way to the edge of cosmic rays.

But they weren't Wright Cash, Wright said to himself. A dissertation on this alone would make him famous. But that wasn't enough. Wright wanted awe. How about, he asked himself with a mental chuckle, the ultimate controller? And now, eight months later, here it was, rotating on the screen in 125 colors. It was the size of an eyeglass case: just 16 components, including the 64-bit neural microprocessor with on-board DSP, A-to-D converter, and 64-Mbit RAM—Wright was proud of his integration skills—and a dime-sized receiver plate that needed only be 5 centimeters from the surface of the cranial vault to pick up the faint subdural waves. The device could recognize, in real time, four million different brain electrical configurations. Wright glanced at the sleepy faces around him: Given the quality of brains available, should be more than enough.

He looked at the image one more time with satisfaction, then, as always, transmitted it to the Sun SPARCstation in his apartment in Mountain View. Next, he shut down access to his home machine and purged the file in the Cray. Too many hackers around to take the risk. Then, for the first time in nine hours, he let his shoulders slump slightly. For fun, he hopped onto AOL, downloaded a freeware diagnostic tool for Apple PowerBooks. He stuck the diskette into the pocket of his neatly ironed plaid shirt. It was now nearly 4 A.M. Wright decided to pack it in. It had been a good night. He'd changed the world. Time to get some sleep.

He pulled on his corduroy jacket, picked up the Samsonite briefcase his mother gave him as a high-school graduation present, and headed for the door. Every face in the room turned with relief to watch him. Well, hell, the bleary faces said, if the Robot's hanging it up, so are we.

▼▲▼

The moon was like a silicon wafer vacuum-clamped to the night sky as Wright made the sharp right turn on the sidewalk—he never cut across on the dirt paths like the other students—and started down Palm Drive toward his car. The bright moonlight made the sandstone Quad look like an ancient Sumerian temple. The dewy lawn shone silver like the belly scales on a fish.

The C-permit parking lot was empty but for Wright's old Pacer and a brand-new automobile sitting at the far side of the lot. Wright noticed a figure sitting in the car. That was odd at this time of night. Probably some student sleeping one off, he decided with distaste. It took a few minutes to get the Pacer started. But finally it kicked over with a cloud of blue exhaust, and Wright made his way past the stadium and gas station to the wide boulevard of El Camino Real. The air was damp with a morning mist that dotted his windshield and made the streetlights blur. El Camino was empty, save for a couple of all-night liquor stores, 7-Elevens, and sweeper machines racing around empty parking lots. At the Arastadero intersection he saw a teenage boy sitting on the curb, deftly folding and rubber-banding newspapers in a single flick.

It was 4:26:32, according to his Casio calculator wristwatch, when Wright arrived home at a small apartment complex two blocks from Castro Street. Though the complex had 12 apartments flanking a central court and swimming pool, Wright knew none of his neighbors in three years had ever swam in the pool. Nor had he. Head down and lost in thought, Wright unlocked the wrought-iron gate and walked toward his ground-level apartment. He was already pushing the key into the doorknob when he noticed some things at his feet. He picked them up and held them to the light. To his amazement, he was holding women's clothing: a tube top, satin gym shorts, a pair of running shoes, and a very lacy pair of panties. That brought him out of his reverie. He dropped the clothing and checked the door. Locked. He heard a tiny splash. Wright leaned over the railing and peered into the darkness. Somebody was in the pool.

"Hello," whispered a very feminine voice. "Can you help me?"

Wright set down his briefcase and walked through the gate to the pool. He knelt at the edge, his eyes just beginning to register an amazing sight with long, blonde hair.

"What are you doing?" he asked in a halting voice.

"Well," said the woman, "It's sort of hard to explain. But every morning I jog by here and I see this pool. And I'm always so hot and sweaty that I just dream about jumping in and feeling all this nice, cool water all over my body." She splashed. "Well, this morning I couldn't resist. I wasn't expecting anybody to come home this late." A pause. "You must be quite the party animal."

"Look, miss," Wright's eyes had adjusted now and he was having trouble talking, "You can't stay here. It's against the rules."

"My," said the lady in the pool, "Somebody who comes home at 4 A.M. can't be too much of a stickler for rules."

"Your clothes are on my doorstep. I'll—"

"Really? That's an amazing coincidence. It's almost like fate."

"Well, perhaps. I'll go get your clothes and—"

"Actually, there is a small problem. You see, I forgot to bring a towel. Could I perhaps borrow one of yours to dry off?"

"Well, uh, certainly. But then you'll really have to—"

"Oh, thank you. You are a very nice person." The woman started to pull herself out of the pool.

Wright instinctively turned around, told himself to walk to his apartment and not look back. He found his last clean towel at the bottom of the closet. It had Marvel comic figures on it, but he didn't think the woman would notice. He started to trot back out to the pool but pulled up short when he found the woman standing in the middle of his living room, the long rivulets of water running down her torso and legs shining in the blue light of his computer screen.

"Oh, great," she said, taking the towel from his stricken hand and wrapping it around herself. "Thank you very much."

She looked around, "You have a very nice place here." The towel was too small for her and kept coming loose, forcing her to rewrap it. She glanced down at it, then up at him with surprise, "Are you a Marvel freak?"

"Well, I was."

"Really?" She pointed at the warty face of the Thing tattooed on her left breast. "Me too."

"Wow," said Wright.

The woman spotted something on the wall behind Wright and walked over beside him. He turned to look too: his diploma.

"Oh, my God," said the woman, taking Wright's arm and dropping the towel. "Did you go to Princeton?"

"Well . . . yes."

"So did I! I told you it was fate." She read the vellum sheet, "Computer Sciences. Hey, I took some computer science. Did you ever have Bockelmann? "

"Jim Bockelmann was my adviser," Wright said with a bit of swagger.

The woman shrieked and threw her arms around Wright. Before he realized it, their lips were pressed together. He could smell her hair, feel the soft skin of her back in his hands.

Then the woman pulled away, looking embarrassed, and again wrapped the towel around herself. "I'm sorry," she said, "It's just that it gets so lonely out here in Silicon Valley. It's so nice to see another Tiger again."

Wright smiled for the first time, "I know what you mean."

She smiled now too, a very sultry smile, "So, what are you up to these days, Tiger . . . besides partying all hours of the night?"

"Well," said Wright, attempting to return her leer, "I'm finishing up a doctorate at Stanford."

"Oh, really?" asked the woman, making a long, slow roll with her hips. "Let me guess: Your specialty is hard drives." She winked, "Or is it implantation?"

Wright felt the blood rise through him. No woman had ever talked to him like this, not even online. This was how he fantasized it would be. Amazing himself, he risked a response in kind: "Actually, my specialty is deep probes and sensors."

"Mmmm," said the woman appraisingly. "I'll bet your probe reaches all the buried substrates." Her towel opened again. This time Wright looked. She had nice TTLs and a very sexy waveform. He wanted her to yield. But what were the protocols? Would she flip-flop on him? Should he take the RISC? Yes, yes, he told himself, I've been a Unix too long.

She moved closer and began unbuttoning Wright's shirt. "I hope you're discrete. After all, I'm virtually naked."

Wright felt her touch all the way down to his power supply. He hadn't been this excited since the day his mother gave him a Commodore Pet. He was afraid his access time would be too quick. He didn't want her to think of him as a QuickDraw.

The woman unzipped the fly of Wright's Botany Bay chinos. "I hope this isn't a Microsoft or a floppy," she whispered huskily, then, "Oooh," she said, compressing his data. "Firmware."

For Wright, who had never known the touch of a woman other than his beloved mother, the moment was a revelation. In just 10 minutes, he and this strange woman had already progressed past the handshake, beyond Level One, and were entering the Seed Round. In a few moments they'd be docking. His head swam with the image of her cache. He felt faint, lost in the Ethernet. More than anything in the world now, he wanted to be the application for her toolbox. Her router. Her server.

She took Wright's hand and led him into the bedroom. They found the bed covered with twisted blankets, plates of food, and old issues of *Wired*. "No," she said, "too SCSI" and dragged him back into the living room. She licked his ear, then whispered, "Where would you like to do it?"

Wright hesitated and thought of his best fantasy. No, he thought, it's too bizarre. The woman saw his hesitation and assured him, "Don't worry, I'm user friendly. Configure me any way you want."

Wright nodded toward the Sun SPARCstation, until now the greatest love, after Mother, in his life. The woman chuckled, "You are ASIC character."

She skipped over and wiggled her bottom down on the workstation's keyboard. For the first time, Wright was glad the Sun had a large footprint. The woman looked around at her unlikely location. "My, aren't we the twisted pair." Then, giggling, she held her arms wide. "Come on, my little pixel. What you see is what you get!" she laughed lustily. "Hurry, Wright, let's plug and play. Let me be the socket for your card. The collector for your emitter."

The moment Wright had waited for all his life had finally arrived. No more fantasies about Deanna Troi and the female guests on "Computer Chronicles." This was the real thing. With a cry of "IEEE!" Wright launched into her gateway. The Herman Miller computer station squeaked and swayed; the keyboard beeped over and over. "RAM, baby, RAM!" she screamed in Wright's ear. "Do it 'til it MHz! Boot up!"

But Wright didn't hear her. He was now merely an actuator attached to a solid-state brain. His mind was doped; his body was hard as a crystal. "BitBlk. BitBlk," he panted incoherently.

"Oh Shottky! Oh Shottky!" she screamed, "I'm downloading!"

On the computer, the monitor announced over and over: "I/O ERROR I/O ERROR I/O ERROR I/O ERROR . . ."

▽▲▽

Wright awoke on the living-room floor, his current now a trickle. The afternoon sunlight burned through the curtains. He turned to reach for the woman, but she was gone. And, as he soon discovered after a frantic search of the apartment, every trace of her was gone as well. Then he heard splashing. Pulling on his trousers, he ran outside—only to find one of his neighbors playing in the pool with her two young children. They stared at the half-dressed man with the crazy, squinting eyes.

Wright retreated to his apartment. Only the flashing message on the computer screen gave any clue that anything had happened. Otherwise, it might have been a dream. But it wasn't a dream, damn it, Wright told himself. She loves me. I love her. Didn't I offer to marry her? And hadn't she laughed and said, "I don't need some Token Ring. You'll always be my Star."

She'll be back, Wright told himself. She's probably just gone off shopping. That's it. She went to the store for groceries to make us breakfast. But she didn't come back that afternoon. Or that night. Or on any of the next three days that Wright waited in his apartment, rushing outside with every sound. He kicked himself for never asking her name. Finally, he forced himself to accept that she was never coming back. It was only as he was getting dressed that he noticed the diskette that had been in his pocket was missing.

It all became clear. With this realization, something inside Wright Cash snapped. Hatred, like sour bile, rose in his throat.

Hatred for all of them: the professors who resented him, the class-mates who despised him, the women who laughed at him. And most of all, for the woman he loved . . . who betrayed him. Wright grabbed his glass Windows 95 paperweight and smashed it to the floor. She'd known his name. She had betrayed him. And for noth-ing but freeware.

He paced the apartment, kicking trade magazines and manuals out of his way. Betrayers! They only want what they can get from me. Well, no computer ever betrayed me. I'm just too good for people, Wright sobbed to himself. And they'll never use me again. Let them live their petty, greedy lives without me; I'll go where I can never be found.

By nightfall, he had packed his computer and clothes, moved out of the apartment and disappeared. The landlord kept the cleaning deposit and sold the furniture that remained, including a bent computer stand. At Stanford, they eventually tossed out the notes in his locker and closed down his access code (but only after a couple of teaching assistants peeked into the files). But Wright Cash wasn't forgotten. Instead, he entered into myth. Henceforth, whenever an especially brilliant computer student collapsed from overwork, the others said the student had "Cashed out."

From *Upside Magazine*, July 1996 (reprinted also in *Harpers Magazine*, 1996).

15

TECHNOFASCISM

With Silicon Valley going into supernova, eclipsing even Hollywood, New York, and Washington, D.C., the media—always acutely aware of where its next ad revenue is coming from—has embraced high tech and Silicon Valley with all the calculating passion of Bill Clinton sizing up a new intern. *Fortune* did it first and best, when it reportedly informed its advertisers that it intended to have either Bill Gates or Andy Grove in every damn one of its issues in 1997 (God bless editorial integrity!) and then did exactly that, adding legions of tech readers and advertisers.

Everybody else got the message. *Forbes* devoted several hundred pages of its 80th-anniversary issue to the technology revolution—then blew its credibility by misidentifying David Packard as Bill Hewlett on the cover. Not to be outdone, *Business Week* not only dedicated a special issue to Silicon Valley, it also gathered every Valley leader it could think of (well, no Jerry Sanders, Wilf Corrigan, or T. J. Rodgers—but, hey, ASICs are complicated) and turned them into BW Playmates of the Month with their own foldout cover.

Everywhere you look, tech coverage is ascendant. And it's not just business magazines, either. Every local newspaper seems to have a special computing and technology section, and tech coverage is taking over whole sections of *Newsweek* and *Time*—the latter even naming Grove Man of the Year about 10 years too late and for the wrong reason ("Intel is the world's largest producer of computer chips," its editor knowingly intoned).

And this is just the beginning. Entire networks, such as Ziff-Davis' ZDTV, are springing up to give us that dawn-to-dusk technology coverage we all crave. As if that weren't enough, there's always the Web, with its infinite supply of press releases, analysis, gossip masquerading as fact, and the endless ravings of the increasingly paranoid vox populi.

And now, in the final accreditation, literary carpetbaggers have descended on the Valley. You know you own the zeitgeist when New York publishers peer across the Hudson, decide there's something going on out here among us Indians, then send Manhattan writers out to do field studies. Thus, Silicon Valley is overrun with the likes of novelist Po Bronson, *Liar's Poker* (W.W. Norton & Co., 1989) authors Michael Lewis and John Heilemann (he of the dreary *New Yorker* profiles). These days, a daily part of any Valley CEO's job is to be interviewed by yet another book author. ("So I keep hearing about this company called Fairchild, but it's not in my American Electronics Association directory. Do you know any thing about it?")

In the works now are a feature-length documentary, at least one coffee table book, and a couple of multipart TV documentaries and, for all we know, a sitcom. The digital revolution is the story of the millennium (or at least millennium's turn). And the revolution's long-term impact will likely be as great, if not greater, than the most wild-eyed claims being made for it. It will undoubtedly change every human institution, tear down almost all our political models, annihilate the traditional nation-state and transform money, commerce, art, literature, entertainment, sports and even organized religion. The digital revolution will have an irrevocable impact on the neighborhood, the family, the self.

Nothing you haven't heard before, right? And somewhere on cable, someone is saying it again right now. This message has become our fin de siècle mantra, a phrase repeated so often we can mutter it without hearing ourselves speak or without pausing for even a millisecond to ponder its monstrous implications.

But wait a moment. If the electronics revolution is, and will be, as sweeping as we're all predicting, shouldn't we be *scared out of our minds?* And, just as important, shouldn't we be terrified by anyone who isn't frightened?

Why worry? Look at history. We pundits, myself included, like to blather about the many parallels between our current society and the first industrial revolution. We point to the rise of cities, modern science and medicine, mass production, high-speed transportation and communications, longer life expectancies and high literacy rates. All true. There's no question that the industrial revolution, in its first wave from 1795 to 1830 as well as in its second from 1876 to 1900, was one of the most beneficial events in human history.

But what human revolutions give, they also take away. It's polite to ignore the fact that the industrial revolution also killed the Enlightenment, set off the destructive and narcissistic counterforce called romanticism, buried us in soul-killing bureaucracies and, worst of all, gave us machine-age "total war." It's a single developmental thread that runs from Cold Harbor to Verdun to Stalingrad to Hue.

Here at the end of the most homicidal century in human history, the memory of millions of murdered innocents ought to be more than enough to make us wary of all the talk about the New Digital Man, *Homo computatis.*

People had their own absolutist dreams about the new and perfect human during the industrial revolution, too: Jean-Jacques

Rousseau with his divine primitive, Karl Marx with economic man and Friedrich Nietzsche with his Superman. The model was perfected most horribly in this century with the Aryan warrior and the New Soviet Man. Great revolutions seem to provoke absolutist fantasies and delusions of human perfectibility. And hidden behind all the talk of perfecting mankind are the screams of those deemed unworthy.

Here at the end of the millennium we're all so proud of our enlightenment. We walk out of "Amistad" and "Titanic" comforted in the knowledge that, unlike our lesser mortal predecessors—say, George Washington, Thomas Jefferson, and Mrs. John Jacob Astor—we would never consider owning slaves or treating the lower classes like subhumans.

But we have our own dirty little prejudice that, like slavery to a South Carolina tobacco grower in 1830, seems so much a part of the natural order that we scarcely notice it, much less feel the need to defend it. You hear it when Bill Gates, to general approbation, says Microsoft Corp. only hires the brightest people. You hear it in the words of the WestTech job fair recruiters, read it between the lines in every book about the new "learning" organization, watch it in the personnel policies of every hot tech company. It's a message that can be distilled into a single warning:

Don't be stupid.

That message is lost in all the brouhaha over Richard Herrnstein and Charles Murray's book *The Bell Curve: Intelligence and Class Structure in American Life* (Free Press, 1994). Everyone started shouting about the brief section on racial intelligence and somehow overlooked the book's larger theme: that our society is dividing along IQ lines. A hundred years ago when cognitive skills weren't as important in everyday small-town life, the local doctor might indeed have married the coffee shop waitress, and the schoolmarm might have wed the honest and hard-working—though slightly dim—automobile mechanic. Not anymore.

Today, electrical engineers marry electrical engineers, stock analysts shack up with venture capitalists and the demarcation between the worlds of the bright and the merely average is as rigid and impenetrable as the "white" and "colored" sections of a Memphis, Tennessee, movie theater were in 1935. The only difference is that in 1935, blacks at least had the hope of one day achieving equality. In an age when every organization's catchphrase is "smarter, faster, better," who's going to stand up for the millions—indeed, by definition, the majority—with average intelligence? Wouldn't any such leader automatically be outside the category?

And our IQ bigotry has yet to reach its most virulent form. Today we can only exclude the modestly intelligent from our companies, our neighborhoods, and our private schools. But a few years down the road when we have the right diagnostic tools—thank you, Human Genome Project—we'll be able to eliminate this burden altogether by liquidating the subbrilliant before they're born. And the sooner we get started, the better. After all, the demands of technology move the intelligence bar higher every year.

Heard this kind of absolutist talk before? Of course you have. It's the nightmare obsession of modern life. It pops up, captures our imaginations and our souls, then produces unimaginable horrors. Two million Kulaks, 6 million Jews, 30 million Chinese, half the population of Cambodia. Social Darwinism, Leninism, fascism, Stalinism, Maoism, the Khmer Rouge. Once you establish the perfect New Man, you can't help but stuff imperfect Real Man into him—even if you have to kill him in the process—or, in our more enlightened view at the end of the century, merely redesign him. Restructure his DNA, pop a few slivers of silicon into his cerebral cortex or just mainline his central nervous system right into the worldwide grid. Who needs neuromancy when you can hook right into the Net, become a human browser and act as your own software agent?

If this sounds outrageous, let me remind you of the kind of high-stakes game we're playing. You can't announce a complete, technology-driven revolution in human culture—as we regularly do in this magazine—and then duck the implications of such a profound historical discontinuity. If the industrial revolution gave us longer life expectancies and unprecedented material wealth while at the same time creating a global graveyard, are we so naïve as to believe that the digital revolution won't deliver a similar yin and yang?

Within a generation, there will likely be 5 billion people on the World Wide Web. There will also be perhaps 100 billion embedded controllers tucked away in every corner of the planet—all talking to one another. We'll be using 10-gigahertz PCs with a terabit of memory, 3D displays and 10Mbps modems. We'll consult many times each day with our personal software avatars, which will then race around the Net doing our bidding. We'll witness the arrival of the first biological interfaces to solid-state electronics. And we'll hurtle toward the first microprocessors that include as many transistors as there are neurons in the human brain. Does anybody still believe we will confine these awesome inventions to the office or the den? That we will merely add them to our lives, like cell phones and Walkmans, without profoundly changing everything about who we are and how we live? Most of all, does anyone believe that all these commercial, cultural, and personal changes will be strictly salutary?

In fact, a number of people (many of them my friends and colleagues in Silicon Valley) believe precisely that. To them, the electronics revolution is not only inevitable, it is the destiny of the race. Moore's Law is our new Invisible Hand—a market-driven theory of history leading us toward the Valhalla of cultural equilibrium, perpetual innovation, and general enlightenment and prosperity.

For this crowd, the great visionary is George Gilder and his defining work—his *Wealth of Nations, Road to Serfdom* and *Das Kapital* all rolled into one (no small irony for a legendary conservative)—is the book *Microcosm* (Simon & Schuster, 1989). Gilder is brilliant and passionate, and *Microcosm* is no different. Most of it is devoted to a superb history of the integrated circuit and the microprocessor, and how these devices changed institutions and the economy. But the last chapter is different. There, Gilder drops all pretense of narrative balance or subtlety and goes for it with everything he's got: Now the chip is not just a landmark invention but a transcendent vehicle for reordering human nature. This is no longer admiration but worship. And coming from a devout Christian, it approaches heresy.

At the time the book was first published, Valley leaders jokingly said, "Poor George stared so long at an IC that he saw the face of God." They don't joke about it anymore. In the intervening years, they, too, have been on the road to Damascus and been blinded by the light reflecting off a 12-inch wafer. Like George, they have found redemption in Moore's Law—and they aren't alone. Nobody is immune. Consider the following:

> The microprocessor is propelling humanity into an era of change the likes of which we have never known. It is not merely an invention, but a metainvention, an inventor of inventions . . . It is time to celebrate the microprocessor and the revolution it created, to appreciate what a miracle each one of those tiny silicon chips really is and to meditate on what it all means to our lives and those of our descendants . . . For thousands of years, mankind has searched for the philosopher's stone, the magical object that turns ordinary metal to gold. Who would have thought it would turn out to be a little sliver of glass with scratches on the surface? The microprocessor, in the

span of a single human generation, has evolved from a clever technical novelty to a tireless, almost invisible partner to mankind.

Know who penned that passage? Me. Like I said: No one es-
capes. I wrote the preceding for the new photography book *One
Digital Day* (Times Books/Random House, 1998), which *Fortune*
(in its zeal to cover more high tech than anybody else) recently
made into its cover story—as if it were a 31-page piece of independent reporting rather than a project underwritten by Intel
Corp. *One Digital Day* celebrates a day in the life of the microprocessor the same way its predecessors celebrated the United
States, Japan, and China. The book's theme is appropriate because
the microprocessor is a different country—and only a foolish
tourist believes it will be anything like home. Every era has its Big
Idea—and no idea has been bigger than that of the Digital World.
If you get too close (and who can resist), you will inevitably be
drawn into its vortex. Like Gilder, the longer you look at the integrated circuit or the Net or the PC, the more transcendental you
become, the more hyperbolic your musings. And these days, we're
all looking closely. Technology is the siren's call that just may dash
us all on the rocks.

Gilder's *Microcosm* gave the first public voice to the absolutism that has always been the dark shadow of high tech. But the
idea of perfectibility through high tech is as old as the vacuum
tube. Seventy-five years ago, Lee De Forest composed goofy mani-
festos claiming that messy mankind had sullied his invention by
using it to broadcast baseball games and "Fibber McGee and
Molly," when it was supposed to spread enlightenment and usher in
a golden age.

More sinister was William Shockley's involvement in racial pol-
itics. Shockley, co-inventor of the transistor, was one of the
smartest men who ever lived, but his brilliance only drove him
deeper into his obsession with eugenics, most famously with the

genius sperm bank. If only, Shockley believed, man could be made as pure and perfect as his technology.

But it was not from the top right but rather the bottom left that the vision of technological absolutism reached full flower. What's rarely mentioned about the Homebrew Computer Club—that mid-1970s phenomenon that gave birth to the PC and the personal computer nerd—is its messianic streak. Steve Wozniak may only have been trying to build a cheap minicomputer, but almost everybody else at the meetings was trying to change the world, not the least of them Steve Jobs. The University of California, Berkeley contingent, in particular, was forever looking at ways to deliver free hardware and software to the masses, to tear down the old order and bring about the New Age. And when Woz and Jobs weren't Homebrewing, they were hanging out with Captain Crunch, the phone hacker who believed the first step to utopia lay in undermining Ma Bell.

The whole history of Apple Computer Inc., in fact, is one of undying belief—in the face of all kinds of evidence to the contrary (including Apple itself)—in the perfectibility of man through computers. Hence Macolytes' hatred for Gates for cynically destroying that dream. But in his own cold-blooded way, Gates is an absolutist, too. After all, what is his book *The Road Ahead* (Viking, 1995) other than a paean to the edifying promise of technology? The only difference is that Gates believes paradise will have a Microsoft logo on the door.

But Gates scares us in ways that more frightening personalities like Jobs and Larry Ellison do not. Gates offers us a glimpse of something we all secretly know but are afraid to admit: If a giant global commune of digital men and women is what the absolutists want, Microsoft is an early warning of what they will likely get—technototalitarianism. Not the Eloi but the Morlocks, not the Federation but the Borg. When the Big Brother of the famous 1984 Macintosh ad morphed into Gates on the big screen at Macworld in

1997, a cold wind blew through the computer industry. It was an early warning of the storm to come.

At the 1996 Progress & Freedom Foundation summit in Aspen, Colorado, technology pundits—from wild-eyed radicals to sci-fi dreamers, self-proclaimed futurists and cool-eyed capitalists—gathered to discuss the Digital World. In addition to the obligatory preening (and partly because of it), a number of debates ricocheted around the room regarding government's role in the new digital world, personal freedom vs. community needs, profits vs. freeware, etc.—the usual debates between left and right and libertarian that have gone on for generations.

But astute viewers would have noticed something more, something amazing. Beneath the sectarian differences, everybody fundamentally agreed. From conservative free marketers to liberal social activists, everyone in that Aspen hall accepted that the technology revolution was inevitable, irresistible and—once we got past our pesky sectarian differences—promised to be the greatest transformation mankind had ever witnessed. Having accepted that position, it was easy to take it one step further. And although it was Esther Dyson who made the actual proclamation, nearly everyone in attendance shared her attitude. When asked what should be done about the millions of people who refused to join this Brave New Digital World—those silly souls who refuse to buy PCs or surf the Net—Dyson simply replied that they must be made to join us, the enlightened.

Although Dyson may have been half-joking (with Esther, it can be hard to tell), her remark was ghastly nevertheless. Among that crowd, however, the enormity of her utterance went largely unremarked. After all, why would anyone object? If tech is indeed the greatest thing ever, won't it then carry us across the river to the Promised Land? Surely anyone who refuses such a trip would have to be considered confused or delusional—and not to be left to his or her own devices. For their own good, the unbelievers must be forced onto the boat; resistance must be made futile. That, at least, was the message Gates delivered to the federal judge and the Senate committee and, more recently, directly to the Department of Justice: *How dare you challenge me?! I'm on the side of the angels, on the train of history. You in government are merely an impediment, an anachronism that doesn't know enough to go off and die.*

Dyson's comment has given us a preview of what the future may hold. In recent years, there has been much talk about the fact that traditional political alignments of Republican and Democratic, left and right, are no longer tenable—that some new bipolar alignment will emerge that will more accurately reflect the fears and desires of people living in the new Digital World. You can see the disintegration of traditional boundaries as common cause transforms old enemies into allies.

Thus, under the sheet of technological absolutism we are seeing some strange bedfellows. On the right, among what might be called the technoreactionaries, are Gilder and *Forbes* publisher Rich Karlgaard, whose *Wall Street Journal* editorials epitomize the belief that technology will set us free. On the left, among the technoutopians, are Vice President Al Gore, with his obsession to drive every school kid down the information superhighway; *Fast Company,* the fantasy magazine for middle managers waiting to man the ramparts of the tech revolution and overrun executive row; and *Slate,* which brings the moral arrogance (and good writing) of the old left to the new media.

To leftists, the tech revolution is the great equalizer, tearing down institutions and giving voice to the dispossessed. Among libertarians there is Virginia Postrel, the estimable editor of *Reason* magazine, who is working on a book with the absolutist title *The Future and Its Enemies.* The book, to be published by Free Press this year, divides the world into the technologically allegiant and everybody else. Libertarians are perfect candidates for technoabsolutism because mass customization and PC proliferation play to their love of anarchy, and the billions of hiding places on the Net fulfill their dream of a playground without grown-up authority.

These different camps may squabble amongst themselves, like Mensheviks and Bolsheviks, but in the end they always find common cause against anyone—politicians, thinkers, religious leaders, publishers—who doesn't share their digital dream. They are more alike than different, and their dislike of one another pales next to their contempt for anyone who would suggest that the coming paradise may instead turn out to be perdition.com.

Of all the participants in the technoabsolutist movement, none is more emblematic than *Wired* magazine. Although detractors dismiss it, no publication can be this successful and influential without having tapped into something essential in our culture.

In fact, the closer you study *Wired* the more you realize it espouses a new synthesis. On its pages you can find a buttoned-down blue-blood conservative like Gilder bumping up against a hippie rancher agrarian-anarchist like John Perry Barlow. There's also the mix of a radical posturing about personal freedom crossed with an old-left celebration of communalism, distilled through hypercapitalistic entrepreneurialism and then poured into the flask of Generation X alienation and anomie. It's a heady—perhaps lethal—mix that at any other time would simply explode. However, these aren't other times.

And on top of it all is attitude. Code words are an insider's argot; a sense of not just moral but also genetic superiority. You're supposed to feel as if you've entered midway a conversation in which the participants are speaking with arched eyebrows and ellipses, code words and euphemisms—all the while secretly laughing at you. Only the true believers—the illuminati—can really understand.

A defining moment for *Wired*, though perversely not in the way the magazine had hoped, came in its fifth-anniversary issue. On the cover was the manifesto of the movement in its purest form:

"Change Is Good." Inside, the usual players—Barlow, Bronson, Gilder, Postrel, and Nicholas Negroponte—all weighed forth. Julian Simon of the libertarian think tank the Cato Institute modestly declared that the past five years had been the greatest humanity has known; London-based technology writer John Browning once more declared the death of government; *Wired* contributing editor Oliver Morton extolled the advantages of genetic engineering; and Barlow happily reported from Africa that people in underdeveloped countries may offer less resistance to "becoming digital" (Negroponte's alluring and terrifying phrase) because they don't have to forget all that worthless stuff about the industrial revolution. Apparently, unlike we rich Westerners who will likely thrash about under the process, the world's poor will merely lay back and submit to their digital transformation—and no doubt their leaders will be happy to help.

Although *Wired* wraps these predictions in bright ribbons of optimistic layout graphics and talk of the "long boom," you can't help but get a cold feeling in the pit of your stomach when reading this stuff. There's something monstrous about such happy certainty over that which is unknowable—namely, the future. Perhaps Moore's Law is the path to paradise, but what historical precedent do we have for believing so? Does any reader of this article intuitively sense that everything is getting better thanks to the technology revolution? More likely the most you can claim is ambivalence: Thanks for the fetal monitors and anti-lock brakes, but can you please take back the alienation and the porn spam mail? And thanks for letting me work at home and adding a couple of years to my life expectancy, but could you also let me keep a few scraps of privacy? Impenetrable optimism in the face of something as profound as social revolution is its own type of immorality.

Yet it may not be enough. Mainstream publications such as *Wired* carry with them the seeds of their own inconsequence. To reach out to the hundreds of thousands of readers you need to land those big IBM Corp. ads (not to mention to snag a big-media patron such as S.I. Newhouse's *Condé Nast* Publications Ltd.), you must compromise. And absolutism, by its very nature, abhors compromise. You can't lead the revolution when you're busy handing out ad-rate cards. And thus having drawn the masses together for revolution, *Wired* is becoming one of its first victims.

For true believers, the only path is deeper—out onto the Internet, into obscure alternative sites that bear an uncanny resemblance to the old Algerian revolutionary cells. There, under cover of anonymity, you can utter your dark thoughts to the like-minded, achieve intellectual climax in the affirmation of your wildest conspiracies, circle-jerk your dreams of infinite bandwidth and infinitesimal human interference, and imagine yourself in intimate congress with the Web itself. In cyberspace, you can be immortal, infinite and infinitesimal, and move at the speed of light. You can be perfect.

One can laugh at the so obviously imperfect—the perverse, the genderless, the nose-ring brigades, the feral, and the agoraphobic—trying to lead us to perfection. But similar claims have been made, with consistently misguided failure, against closet totalitarians for the past 200 years. People dismissed the bloodless Robespierre, too, as they did a strange Austrian corporal and a wild-haired guy in the British Museum Reading Room. Yet it is precisely these people who lead totalitarian revolutions: Only fringe folks have the time, the intensity, and so little to lose.

Somewhere out there, right now, sitting at the next table at Starbucks or repairing the server at a porn site or pounding a PC keyboard with sweaty fingers, is the man or woman who will one day lead the real digital revolution. And that person won't arrive on a sealed train from Berlin or at a failed beer hall putsch but on e-mail, in Salon, or on CNBC—or he might just mail bombs from a Montana shack.

But wait a minute: What, you ask, does the Unabomber—Ted Kaczynski—have to do with all this? Doesn't he oppose technology? The answer to this question takes us to the most demonic corner of technology absolutism: Mass movements become murderous when they absorb their own contradictions. The descendants of Bavarian tree-huggers, after all, built the slick, mechanistic killing machine of the Third Reich. The atheistic Soviet called on the deity of Mother Russia to justify the liquidation of internal enemies. And it was the coffee-drinking intellectuals of the Sorbonne who ended up creating the peasant-run charnel houses of Vietnam and Cambodia.

Kaczynski, then, is only the latest incarnation, a foul-smelling prophet. And he's not antitechnology. On the contrary, like a good engineer, he was intent on making each of his bombs a technological improvement over the one that preceded it . . . version 1.0, 1.1, 2.0 . . . Each one a more lethal killing toy than the last. He even used the latest media to disseminate his psychotic manifesto—eerily reminiscent in tone to that of the futurists.

No, in the end, Kaczynski is a technoabsolutionist, too. Like everyone else, he accepts the inevitability of Moore's Law and the triumph of technology. He just doesn't like it—not, as he claimed, because it's inherently evil but, as he showed with his lifestyle, because he wasn't running it.

Kaczynski offers us the first glimpse of yet another faction beginning to emerge: the technofailures. Their numbers are legion, but their voices are small. They are the millions, even billions, that the technology revolution is leaving behind. In their paler form, they mutter about conspiracies and vote for Ross Perot. In their darker iterations, they join militias or hide in Montana cabins. In the Third World, they sign up with the Shining Path or the Hezbollah and slit throats in the name of antiprogress. And they all await the leader who will take them back into the future and restore the power they believe was once theirs. In the meantime, they e-mail each other angry notes about their hatred for technology and use word processors to compose fliers demanding the destruction of machines.

In his now-famous essay of two years ago for the Big Issue of *Forbes ASAP,* Tom Wolfe harkened back to the prescient writings of Nietzsche, who predicted a century ago that after we killed God, we would search for him everywhere, especially in science and technology. It was Wolfe's guess that we would eventually destroy everything we believed in making that search, tearing down one institution at a time until we were left with nothing—and only then would we again feel God's presence.

Perhaps Wolfe is right. But in the meantime, the absolutists are hardly ready to admit defeat. Having had one god that failed (Marxism), they have now found a new one on which to pin their hopes and energies: the digital revolution.

And these true believers in the digital deity will be accompanied on their long march to perfection by the hypercapitalists, chasing their own will to power up the sweeping curve of Moore's Law, tossing out the weak and wounded along the way. They will be joined by a third group, this one of outriders—the digital anarchists, who will burn and loot and hack away at every institution along the march's path. And at the front of this vast combined column will be a figure we as yet don't even know, who will be the most famous (and notorious) face of the age—the mandatory screen saver on every display. This warlord will be the smug voice of technofailures everywhere, calling on his armies of the dispossessed and disenfranchised to purge the state of the sinful, to ignite a new cultural revolution. The real Big Brother will have finally arrived, a few decades late, in Oceania.

Two years ago—to enormous controversy in Europe—six historians published *The Black Book of Communism.* Its thesis was simple but devastating: that the two great totalitarian systems of the twentieth century, Leninism/Stalinism/Maoism and fascism/ Nazism, were essentially the same. They arose from the same absolutist impulses; they were underpinned by the same pseudoscientific models; they both quickly collapsed into oligarchies; they used the same techniques to brainwash their subjects; and, ultimately, they implemented the same modes of state terror to remain in power.

It has all been said before by political philosopher Hannah Arendt and, most powerfully, in Vasily Grossman's novel *Life and Fate*, where the commissars and the death camp guards are all but indistinguishable. But *The Black Book* was the first to tackle the subject in nonfiction after the collapse of the Soviet Union and the brief opening of its state files. As the book showed in devastating detail, beneath those black shirts and SS insignias, the Order of Lenin medals and the Mao jackets, beats the same cold heart.

French communists and intellectuals howled: After all, their totalitarianism had been of the enlightened kind, bent on improving mankind rather than succumbing to the debased racial hatred that underpinned Hitler's national socialism. But *The Black Book of Communism* effectively destroyed that argument by showing how Stalin and his successors spent 40 years—literally from the day German panzers crossed the Vistula—convincing the world that Nazism and Stalinism were not only different but antithetical to each other. Henceforth, Nazism would be known as the reactionary culmination of evil capitalism (though it had declared itself anticapitalist), while communism would be the ultimate (if, for now, too pure) achievement of good liberal socialism.

It was an exercise in re-education that has proved wildly effective. We still teach this Stalinist rationalization to our schoolchildren as fact. And thus, while former Nazi leaders took turns dangling from ropes in a Nuremberg gymnasium, unrepentant old Soviet functionaries today drive their Volgas past Lubyanka prison on the way to lunch at the Moscow Mickey D's.

So history isn't fair. Big surprise. Those good Germans marching in the 1871 Hermann Festival in their Visigoth outfits had no idea their parade would end at the gates of Auschwitz. So, too, those Victorian intellectuals sitting around someone's parlor singing "The International" could hardly have foreseen the Gulag Archipelago. And those Italian futurist painters in the first years of this century, with their worship of machinery, couldn't have guessed that the first use of that machinery would be to kill defenseless Ethiopian tribesman.

None of them could have predicted the horrors they were unleashing. But that doesn't spare them the blame. Their fantasies became our nightmares. The sea of blood washes back in time to splash their hands. They refused to let any practical understanding of human nature intrude on their perfect dreams; they refused to consider that, to paraphrase British newspaperman and novelist Malcolm Muggeridge, the only true human perfection—equality and peace—is found in the graveyard. In that respect, their dreams came true.

What then of today's technoabsolutists? Good intentions may one day prove their greatest crime. After all we've been through in the twentieth century, can there be any excuse for yet another quest for human perfection in the twenty-first? Sure, the spit and sperm and sweat of real human existence is messy and troublesome, especially when compared with the clean, orderly ranks of integrated circuits on a motherboard. And, compared with the sweep of Moore's Law, human "progress" seems like a bad joke, an oxymoron. Yet in the end, it's all we've got. We're doomed to be the toolmaker and never the tool. And the further we stray from a healthy appreciation of our contradictory selves, the more we stretch toward the latest grail of perfection, the more likely we are to leave the back door open to the darker, Dionysian part of our nature.

They're out there waiting: the stepchildren of technoreactionaries such as Gilder, of technoimperialists such as Barlow and Dyson, of technoanarchists such as Postrel, of legions of technofailures, and of technoutopians like Gore and, God help me, myself. All those happy children are now good technofascists, genetically pure technojugen in their chip-embedded brown shirts, marching in lockstep on the Sudetenland of the computer illiterate, the unbrilliant and the imperfect. Singing songs of freedom through technology. Joyfully building the 1,000-year Digital Reich.

From *Upside Magazine,* August 1998.

PART IV

SILICON WORLD

16

THE FRONTIER OF THE HEART

Nineteen years old and the soda fountain girl at Downs Pharmacy, Micky Unruh prepares my malt as conscientiously as her male predecessors did for my mother 60 years ago, my grandparents 20 years before that, and my great-grandparents at the beginning of this century.

But for her Nikes and digital watch, Micky could be in one of those lost worlds. Past the chrome-rimmed stools and zigzagged Formica counter, none of the appliances she uses to make lime rickeys or BLTs is less than 30 years old. There isn't an electronic display or keyboard to be seen. Here in the heart of the heartland, she seems to embody that part of American life still untouched by the electronics revolution.

"Do you have a computer?" I ask. "No," she replies. Of course not. Here at Downs Pharmacy, amid the napkin dispensers and ketchup bottles, lies a tiny oasis, a respite from one of the greatest social transformations in human history.

Micky pauses for a moment to wipe away an invisible wet spot with her towel. "Course I could use a computer in the lab at school to e-mail all of my relatives."

The digital age has fallen on Enid, Oklahoma, a prairie metropolis of 46,000 souls, as quietly and as uneventfully as the red plume of dust settles to the road behind a passing pickup truck,

Two doors from Downs Pharmacy, past a sewing shop, and sharing an equally splendid view of the art deco WPA-era courthouse with its statue of a doughboy to honor the World War I dead, sits the Computer Connection store. The Computer Connection must struggle to survive—not because there is no market, but because Enid currently has at least seven computer stores. And that doesn't include the stereo stores and superstores in town selling PCs as well. In fact, until recently, there were three computer stores on the main square alone. Now, to the relief of the others, the biggest of the stores has moved to the new side of town.

On this day the Computer Connection is having a sale: software, CD-ROMs, a few peripherals. It seems that these few dozen disks, which combined carry the equivalent of most of the printed books in the Enid Public Library a block away, are already so obsolete to the computer owners in town that their prices must be slashed to sell.

The Computer Connection is also offering special package prices for new multimedia computer system—Pentium computers with color displays, a billion bytes of disk memory, CD-ROM drives, and stereo speakers. Two thousand dollars for more computing power than an entire squadron of the T-37 jet trainers that regularly fly overhead from nearby Vance Air Force Base.

Keith Winter, 16 years old and a junior at Enid High, is managing the store today. His brother-in-law, who owns this store and one in Dodge City, Kansas, is off selling a program the two of them customized for use in livestock auctions. "It makes running an auction a lot easier," he says. "You just put in the tag number for each animal and it does the rest, like keep track of bids."

Keith himself is a Dodge City transplant. He describes Enid as "okay, but not the most exciting place," and he dreams of studying law at OSU. In the meantime, he works afternoons in the store after putting in a day at school. He uses computers at Enid High, he adds, but admits, "I'm not as hardcore about it as some of the guys."

The store does okay, says Keith, but the real profits lie in the sales of its custom software, as well as large-volume computer hardware, software, and network equipment purchases by local school districts. These days, however, all the computer stores are getting ready for the next big thing: the Internet. There are already three service providers in the area, and it's rumored that the phone company will be running the first ISDN lines into Enid next year.

"There's a *lot* of people in Enid who want to go on the Net," says Keith with a teenager's emphasis. "I bet I get six phone calls about it a *day*."

In the square sits the Enid Public Library, its 1960s architecture a sad successor to the classical stone Carnegie library it replaced.

Even on a Monday afternoon in August, the place is busy with pensioners reading newspapers, children studying picture books, and young men and women searching the want ads.

On the second-floor mezzanine sit the computers: PCs, an Infotrac Magazine Index, and CD-ROM players, as well as a programmable Xerox machine. All of this hardware and software gives the Enid Public Library more books and magazines (though many are now virtual) than the best big-city libraries of 50 years ago.

The computers were set up by Mike Murray, a Michigan native. Trained as a computer scientist, he found work in Enid as the reference librarian and moved here with his wife and four children. "I like it here," he says. "It's quiet."

Near all the electronics is the historical reference collection, called the Marquis James Room after the Enid resident who left for New York and a measure of literary fame in the 1930s. He was Enid's most famous son, before Apollo astronaut Owen Garriott. James's two Pulitzers are on the wall in the room, as are pictures of old Enid, including ones of my grandmother's old elementary school, long since demolished. There are also numerous images from the turn of the century, when Enid was a boomtown—a wild combination of Dodge City and Silicon Valley, burning through fortunes as fast as the rest of the country burned through gasoline in their new flivvers.

But the real story of Enid, told over and over in the books and images in the collection, is that of the Cherokee Strip Land Rush. It began a dozen miles south of town as thousands of land-hungry pioneers swept up to and around what is now the city limits in their race to stake out free 160-acre plots of prime farmland.

In the collection are, of course, numerous copies of the famous photograph of the start of the rush, one of the few great images of action of the nineteenth century. It is straight-up noon on September 16, 1893, the pistol has just fired, the rope falls, and scores of settlers, on horseback and in wagons and buggies, race forward in a blur of dust, wheels, and hooves.

In the middle of the photograph is a rider hunched astride a dappled gray horse as it bursts into a gallop. That man may well be my great-grandfather, Charles Hasbrook.

According to family legend, Charlie's father, Abraham Hasbrook, was a child on a wagon train to Oregon when Indians attacked and murdered his parents. As was often done, Abraham was taken up by another family in the wagon train, the Hasbrooks, and raised as their own.

Charlie was born in 1868 in Sheridan, Oregon. When he was 12, the family moved to Concordia, Kansas, then four years later back to Oregon, leaving Charlie behind to finish school. By 1890, young Charles was working on a surveying team for the Rock Island Railroad laying out the grade for the new line that would run from the Black Hills of South Dakota to a terminus at Darlington, in the Oklahoma Territory. Not coincidentally, this was the same route, the Cimarron Trail, used for 20 years by Texas cowboys bringing cattle to market. Rock Island wanted that business, and Charles Hasbrook was one of those assigned to find a way to do it.

One hundred fifty miles south of Wichita, the crew stopped to rest at a small, spring-fed lake. The spot had sustained the local Indians for centuries, often serving as a campground, not just for the water but because tribal legend claimed that no tornado had ever touched down there (nor has one to this day). Cowboys also regularly stopped there to water their cattle and horses.

Sick of drinking muddy red water, Charles and his crew took an old barrel and sank it in the pond as a skim filter for clear water. On the prairie, even as late as the last decade of the nineteenth century, the technology of a water barrel could still change history. Soon travelers and stagecoaches were stopping at the pond, as did trains traveling the tracks Charlie had surveyed.

Enid was founded there, but Charles Hasbrook had long since moved on. Eleven miles to the south he had forded a tributary of the Cimarron River in the shade of a stand of cottonwood trees— and decided that if ever this region were opened to settlers he'd return to claim this land.

That's why, three years later, at noon on September 16, 1893, he joined the hundred thousand other settlers at the starting line of the Cherokee Strip Land Rush. He was in the saddle of the gray racehorse which he'd shipped by train to the site. He needed a fast horse because, of all the 6.3 million acres, his dreamland was very close by. That night, two miles north of the starting line, he slept beneath the cottonwood trees on his new 160-acre quarter section of red dirt farmland. A few days later he lined up with thousands of others to file his claim at the land office located almost exactly at the site of the Enid library, where I now stand.

It is 96 degrees and thunderheads are building up to the west in the Texas Panhandle as my rental car throws up red dust on the road to the old Hasbrook farm. My car, a new Chevrolet, contains five or six microprocessors and microcontrollers, in everything from the engine computer to the cassette deck, each of them performing more calculations in my 15-minute race down this road than all the scribes and bookkeepers in the world performed for the entire year of 1895.

I drive down this road at 50 miles an hour, tiny microcomputers adjusting the advance on engine timing, changing the mix in the fuel injectors, keeping the filtered air around me at 68 degrees and holding the radio in tune on a AAA baseball game being transmitted into the atmosphere 400 miles away. I am wearing tennis shoes designed on computer and sewn together half a world away, jeans that were cut and sewn by robots, and a T-shirt with the corporate logo of a software company that has just gone public on a stock exchange that itself exists only on computer.

As I drive the 15 minutes down a road it took the Hasbrooks a half-day to traverse by wagon, I pass farmers who are Charlie's spiritual descendants, just as I am his genetic one, driving trucks with comparable processing power to my car's, or riding combines and harvesters, which, with their cell phones, desktop computers with wireless modems, and CD players, have even more.

Charles Hasbrook lived in a dugout, a cave he'd dug into the riverbank with a wooden door on the front. It was to this literal hole in the ground that he brought his wife, Mary. And it was here my grandmother, Theresa, spent her infancy. Standing at that door, I can imagine my grandmother's hungry cries joining the sound of wild turkeys and magpies in the air.

Looking up from the bank, I see the house my great-grandfather built by hand with the help of a bachelor neighbor, a onetime carpenter named Hayes. Hayes was happy to help: Just a few months before, a prairie fire had come sweeping down from the north and threatened Hayes's new house. Charlie Hasbrook had jumped on his racehorse, ridden around the fire and found Hayes cutting green fodder as a firebreak. "It won't work!" Charlie yelled as he rode up.

He convinced Hayes instead to build a backfire literally at the front porch of his house.

As the wildfire approached, the two men soaked every blanket, piece of bedding, and burlap bag they could find and hung them on the walls of the house and outbuildings. The fire burned through. The house and the men survived.

Time did to the Hayes house what the fire couldn't. But the Hasbrook house still stands. The porches have collapsed, the architectural details have long since been torn off by people desperate for a bit of handcraft in a world of mass-produced goods. But the structure itself, with its adzed frame and handjoined joists and stairs, is still sturdy enough, 30 years after it was abandoned, to bear up under the occasional curious cow that wanders upstairs.

The generation of five children who lived in this house, the children of the last century's turn, may have known more change than any in human history. Theresa Madora Hasbrook, my grandmother, a beautiful but solemn girl, began her life staring at the dirt walls of the cave and lived long enough to watch men shuffle in the dust of the moon. Her first ride was in a wagon, drawn by Charlie's old racehorse; her last, as a frail body in a casket, was in a 737 bringing her home from Florida.

The tiny front room of the farmhouse, now ruled by a giant garden spider and a consortium of hornets, was my great aunt Hazel's, the baby of the family. Now nearing 90 and fading slowly into forgetfulness, she lives in a retirement home in Enid a few blocks from stereo stores and computerized gas stations, her own condo guarded by electronic alarms. She spends much of her time watching cable television.

Charles and Mary Hasbrook spent 45 years on the farm, which quickly grew to 320 acres, before old age drove them into town. In the intervening years, they had watched as each piece of farm equipment was transformed in its turn. By the early years of the century, many of the horse-drawn harvesters and threshers had been replaced by giant steam machines. The first automobiles could be heard coming from miles away down the road. And a suddenly irreplaceable new machine, the tractor, appeared in one field after another.

This new technology changed the rules of farming and rewarded those forward-looking individuals who mastered them. One of the new breed of farmers, a man from Texas named Collins, moved in next door in 1910 and proceeded to make himself a small but tidy bankroll. A man with a big mustache and an even bigger stomach, Sylvester Collins had five strapping sons, all of them six feet or taller.

As was not unusual in that hermetic world, the boy and girl next door fell in love, and Theresa Hasbrook married the oldest Collins boy, Arthur, in 1917. That year the same technology boom that made Sylvester Collins wealthy took its payment. In France his second son, John, died of pneumonia after being gassed at the front. He is one of the dead honored by that doughboy statue.

Art and Theresa had five children, the first four of them daughters and the first two born at the Collins farmhouse, now marked only by a pair of trees in the middle of a plowed field. The second daughter was my mother, Lela Nadiene. She still remembers her excitement as a child when she returned to the simple world of the Hasbrook house, with its gas lamps and privy, and the gray horse, now ancient and spavined, calmly chewing hay by the barn.

The newlyweds stayed on the Collins farm for three years, then moved to town. The lights of the big city, visible now on the horizon, drew them. In those 30 years since the land rush, Enid had become, in the words of one historian, "the most wide-open town in America." Oil had done to Enid what gold had done to San Francisco, silver to Denver, and what silicon would, one day, to San Jose. Electrified by 1902, Enid became a town of saloons and hotels, wildcatters and salesmen, where a man claiming to be John

Wilkes Booth came to die and where Clyde Cessna's first airplane was born.

My grandparents found a new house in a new neighborhood just south of downtown, and as the 1925 Enid commercial directory attests, Art Collins took work as a delivery truck driver for C. E. Loomis Furniture. He and Theresa kept an impeccable house, the flowers on the porch well tended, the lawn always clipped.

It was a good life. The kids were healthy. Jobs were plentiful, thanks to the oil boom, and Phillips Petroleum was pouring money into the local economy.

Then the Great Depression rolled over the town with the darkness and fury of one of the great Dust Bowl storms that hit the town a few years later. And like the fine red dust, no matter how tightly Art and Theresa sealed the windows of their house, the hard times seeped in and piled on the sills and thresholds.

By 1930, Art was holding several jobs at a time, and even then the family would have gone hungry were it not for fresh vegetables and eggs coming from the two farms. My grandmother, driving the eggs into town one day, ran the car off a bridge, broke the eggs, and was so stricken with guilt she never drove again. The daughters passed down clothes, saved a nickel for the movies, and gave sandwiches to the growing army of hoboes who strolled down the street in front of the house, from the railroad tracks to downtown.

Disaster, always waiting, struck in 1934. Progress again took payment. Art, working as night clerk at the Youngblood Hotel, was checking the upstairs floors when he stepped into an elevator shaft, which had not been properly lighted—its cage door left open. He fell three stories, like a living pinball that missed all the flippers. He was saved only by crashing into the rubber bumper at the bottom of the shaft. He crushed his right shoulder and broke his left leg in two places. He took a year to recover; the family was saved only by the regular deliveries from the farms.

In 1939, Charlie and Mary Hasbrook moved to town, following the Collinses by almost a decade. Both couples moved just a block from their children, and their grandchildren often visited on the way to and from school. The economy was nearly restored now, though Enid was still recovering from the shock. The girls were now at Enid High School.

The four-story brick school, looking almost like the stage set of a traditional Midwest high school, has changed little on the outside. Inside much is the same as well. Display cases show trophies as old as 1925 and as new as last term. The floors are still linoleum, the classrooms still have ceiling fans and doors with transoms and window curtains. And on one wall I find a picture of my mother, class of 1939. But when I stop a student to ask where the computer lab is, she replies, "Which one?" Indeed, I find three: Beyond the oak wainscoting and closets and the ancient pencil sharpener stand rows of tables bearing two dozen 486 PCs.

There are other signs of the revolution here as well: VCRs, an electronic security keypad on the door to the athletic director's office, a computerized message display near the front entrance. As I pass a roomful of teachers in summer training, I hear one say, "I gotta check my e-mail."

Nine hundred one South Washington is now an old house in a tired section of Enid. As I ring the doorbell, I note that the porch is now gone and there isn't a flower in sight. I can hear a television inside. As I wait I notice the drainage ditch out front. My mother stood right where I am and caught her first glimpse of my father, a blind date, as he and his future father-in-law knelt in the ditch trying to spot in the culvert under the driveway "the biggest damn raccoon I ever saw."

My father, one of a long line of slightly dangerous, ever-moving, recklessly charming, and often self-destructive Irishmen, had just returned from the war. Now he would take my mother away from this doorway to the great cities of the world, first as the wife of an

intelligence agent, then as a perpetual tourist. He would finally settle her in Sunnyvale, California, in Silicon Valley, in the heartland
of a new era, and he would learn computers in middle age with
some of the young men down the street who would start the personal computer revolution.

But the other daughters and the only son stayed either in Enid
or in smaller towns a few hours' drive away. My Aunt Aliene, the
eldest, married my Uncle Delbert and they opened an appliance
store. In late 1949, they bought the first television set in Enid.
Mary Hasbrook had died that summer and Charlie was hospital-
ized. Aliene and Delbert wanted the TV set for Charlie when he
came home, so that he could watch his favorite radio show, the Friday night fights, for the first time. But Charlie never came home.
He died peacefully in the hospital, surrounded by his family. His
name, with Mary's, is on a tile at the Cherokee Strip Museum.

Aliene and Delbert soon became well-off selling TVs and installing aerials all over Enid. Now retired, they live in an air-
conditioned double-wide trailer at Keystone Lake on the road to
Tulsa. Delbert plays his electronic organ sometimes, but mostly he
channel-surfs the 200 TV stations available on his dual satellite
dishes. In the autumn, he loads another dish on the trailer, and he
and Aliene head for northern Oklahoma, where he watches the
world and hunts with crossbow or black powder.

Late one night, back home, Delbert uses his computer ground
stations to race across the spectrum, showing me the raw news
feeds that give him more inside information than I ever had sitting
in a newspaper newsroom. Then Delbert confides to me that he is
thinking of adding a third dish to pick up the KU band. "That's a
hundred more stations," he says with a grin.

The door to my grandparents' house finally opens, to an oversized TV screen and the loud music of a Christian revival station.
Olga Padilla, who lives there now, warily keeps the screen door
closed. I see three children.

Olga and her husband took over the South Washington house after my grandparents died as part of an urban homesteading program designed to revivify old housing districts by making financing available to low-income buyers. The sole condition was that they keep up the home, something the Padillas have largely done, if not with the care that my grandparents did.

I ask Ms. Padilla if she has anything electronic in her house. She can't quite think of anything—not because she doesn't know, I learn, but because like most people she's never thought about it. In time we come up with a list: VCR, cable TV, digital watches, a microwave oven, an electronic stove, air-conditioning, Super Nintendo. No computer? "I wish," says Ms. Padilla. Mariana Padilla, 13, joins her mother in the doorway to add that she uses computers in class at Emerson Junior High.

My grandparents' house now has more computing power than NASA did that day my grandparents sat on the mohair sofa with the doily antimacassars and watched Neil Armstrong step out on the moon.

As I drive away, I see a freight train passing a few blocks away. Instead of hoboes, it bears a three-foot-tall bar code on its side to be read by computer-driven optical character readers along the way to its destination.

"The downtown is pure Norman Rockwell, man," says Jim Ferree, Enid's city manager since 1990. He laughs at the comment with Chris Henderson, the city's director of community development. Both men have the cocky, jokey manner, the "I'll buy the first round tonight at the country club" style of big men in small towns everywhere.

Ferree once had Henderson's job. He arrived in Enid just in time to oversee the most economically explosive time in Enid in decades. For 30 years after the war, Enid had been prosperous, happy—and dying. It gained things that didn't matter—more tall buildings downtown, new shops and stores, and the signature giant grain elevators on the North Side. And it missed things—an interstate by 28 miles, a major university—that did. As the city became momentarily famous for turning on all of its lights on an August night in 1973 to be seen by Owen Garriott Jr. as his space capsule flew overhead, it had already ceded its economic power to upstarts like Tulsa, Stillwater, and Norman.

Then, like a miracle, the oil boom hit. "We were processing 400 building permits per year," says Ferree, "and we still ran out of places for people to live. Folks were in tents in the park. Unemployment fell to almost zero, the lowest in the entire nation."

It was as if the exciting old days had come back at last. Then as quickly as it came, the boom collapsed. By 1983, Enid was in free fall. "We lost 10 percent of our population, 5,000 people, in the following decade," says Ferree. "We're still coming out of it."

What saved the town, Ferree admits, was a retail mall, the first in the region. But it was a devil's pact. "When you're hungry you take what you can get," says Ferree. The Oakwood Mall and its new neighbors—Wal-Mart, Kmart, Hardee's, and Homeland—tore the guts out of Enid's downtown, as they did to downtowns across America. Enid's town square became a ghost town of empty storefronts and locked doors.

Walking the Oakwood Mall, it is obvious why it triumphed. The classic shopping mall of the 1980s was a nexus of all of the latest mass technologies: ample, well-lit parking lots, climate-controlled promenades, the color and glitter of food and gifts in walkway kiosks, the cacophony and flash of a thousand TV screens and stereos. Every morning for years, as blizzards blew or the sun scorched outside the tinted windows, my great-aunts and great-uncles, the children of Charlie and Mary, Sylvester and Allie, walked these promenades for their morning exercise, passing their children, grandchildren, and great-grandchildren as they shopped, flirted, or stared out of baby carriages.

But what technology first offers the collective it then takes back to give to the individual. Despite the dire predictions of their eventual commercial hegemony, the big malls and megastores aren't doing quite as well these days, while more cars drive through the city center today than have been seen there in years.

Standing in Oakwood Mall, clues to the sudden reversal are as obvious as the Macintoshes that peek out between the air conditioners at Rex TV & Appliances. A few doors away, at Waldenbooks, manager A. J. Shorter says, "Oh yeah, we've got a lot of computer books—though not as many as I'd like. We get a lot of people coming in for that first text on Windows 95."

Nearby, Bill Diedrich, retired as a petty officer first class after 20 years in the navy, is searching the rack for past copies of *Dr. Dobbs and Mac Home* and for this month's *Windows 95* magazine. He and his wife live nearby in Marshall, population 288—the closest town to where Charlie Hasbrook staked his claim, and the town name on my mother's birth certificate. Diedrich says his wife, the town postmaster, wants to use their new Packard Bell Pentium PC for mailing labels, "but me, I definitely want to use it to go on the Net."

There may be 5,000 computers in Enid, if you include the many at Vance Air Force Base. Not a vast number, but enough to support those seven retailers. And to buy all of those computer magazines and books sold in bookstores and supermarkets all over town. And enough to create enough hard-core computer sophisticates to understand the big electronic sign on the Computers & More store that reads: "SIMMS . . . Twenty-four Pin Printer . . . Memory Blowout." And it is enough that you notice computers everywhere you go, from the laptop in city manager Ferree's office to the one used for reservations at the Ramada Inn. In Enid's promotional brochure, a local print shop prominently displays its Internet address, while the course catalog for little, now age-worn Phillips University lists numerous computer courses.

It is also enough computers to counterattack the forces of homogenization wrought by the previous generation of computers. Back at the town square, in almost every shop, even the Olden Daze Antiques Mall, one can see PC screens glowing amid the discount furniture and Fenton glass. At Downs Pharmacy, owner Ray Downs has kept his 92-year-old business alive against the depredations of the big supermarket pharmacies by combining computerized records with personal service. "Service is our edge over the Wal-Marts," he says. "I'll come down here on weekends or at night to fill an order." That was enough to keep Downs open when the other two drugstores on the square failed—and he inherited their clients.

"I was a computer operator in the army," he says. "Worked on the old IBM 407." He laughs, "I remember that it could store a cool 20 characters." Now he has two computers, one for ordering pharmaceuticals and storing prescription records, the other for keeping the books.

But, he adds, it isn't getting any easier. Against the relentless pace of technological innovation, there can be no rest. Just as the downtown is coming back, small pharmacies are under assault from a new collectivizing force in computers: the giant databases of HMOs and their hunger for data links with the large drugstore chains.

He smiles a sad smile, "I tell myself that if I can hold out for just eight more years, this store will be a hundred years old. Then I can retire."

Chris Henderson, the city's director of community development, knows most of the numbers by heart. Enid has 22,000 residential houses, 1,800 commercial and industrial buildings, and 15 municipal buildings, including the Martin Luther King Jr. municipal complex where we now sit. City residents also own 53,000 automobiles. There are nearly 3,000 students at Phillips University and at the town's rapidly growing vocational schools. And two hospitals with a total of 429 beds. There is also a cable television system that carries a local public-access station.

Buried within these figures is the real electronic revolution transforming Enid, Oklahoma, the one you don't see. Though there are an amazing 187.2 million personal computers in the world, there are a staggering twelve *billion* microprocessors and microcontrollers in use. These computers-on-chips, often as powerful as their desktop counterparts (which they also run), are embedded everywhere in modern life. And it is in these tiny, almost uncountable electronic brains where the real transformation of society has begun to occur.

How great is the impact of this invisible revolution? Consider Enid. In as unassuming a house as my grandparents' on a tired street in a poor part of town, the Padillas own perhaps 20 microprocessors and controllers. Even if these are simple four-bit devices, that is still about 10 million instructions per second of processing power, more than the largest computer in the world had 20 years ago.

Now extrapolate out to all of Enid's homes and businesses and cars, and don't forget to add in all the computerized appliances in the hundred new homes built every year, and the new $100,000 intranet system going in at Town Hall, and the Link trainer fighters over at Vance AFB, and the sensors out at the Phillips Petroleum refinery on the edge of town, and the streetlights, and stoplights, and air conditioners, and patient-monitoring systems at the hospitals, and the ATMs and automatic gas pumps and the lottery machines at the gas station minimarts, and the videogame arcades, and the cash registers, and credit card readers . . . and on and on in a blinding dust storm of applications. And when you are done you come up with a raw estimate of Enid's total computer power: nearly a trillion instructions per second. That is equal to all the computing power in the world just 12 years ago, the year the Apple Macintosh was introduced. It is enough computing power, if fully tapped, to completely change every single event in Enid forever, and yet it will double and double again by the end of the century.

Edward Tenner, in his book *Why Things Bite Back,* has written about what he calls "revenge effects"—how technological advances create small changes that over time have huge effects. Every day someone in Santa Clara or Austin or Jakarta sinks the digital equivalent of a barrel into a pond and sends a corner of the world racing off on a new historical trajectory.

We are all on that rocket. And even a place like Enid, Oklahoma, is no longer immune. Once isolated and secure, Enid is now as much the center of the world's information grid as is downtown Manhattan, but it is also far less secure. There is now a dialysis center in a local strip mall and lithotripsy equipment passes regularly through town in the back of a semi. The world's greatest medical experts can be brought in on a patient's case through computer networks and teleconferencing. But there are also drug overdoses and rapes, and a month before I arrived a retarded man got an idea from network news and burned down a local black church.

Both opportunities and threats now come from unexpected directions. My surviving great-aunts and great-uncles, in their nineties, are healthier today than 50-year-olds at the time of the land rush, thanks to the miracles of lasers, computer diagnostic tools, and microsurgery. From his trailer this winter, Delbert will not only see the world on his television, but also hunt game in his eightieth year because of new techniques that saved his vision. The budding Marquis James of 2005, now sitting before a computer screen in the Enid library, will not have to leave town to become a nationally recognized author.

But my grandfather, Art Collins, the onetime truck driver, at 84 caught in a world moving faster than he could understand, pulled out of one of those new shopping center parking lots and never saw the oncoming truck that killed him. And 2,000 miles away, the most sophisticated medical tools on earth couldn't save his great-granddaughter—my prematurely born daughter—after another modern diagnostic technology, amniocentesis, went awry. The technology revolution, as we now know too well, won't save us.

Instead, it reshuffles the deck, creating new oppositions, new dialectics, and ultimately, new winners and losers.

Will the new electronic tools for mass marketing and inventory management enable the big retail chains on the edge of town to triumph, or will the enhanced personal services brought by the PC to the shops on the town square reverse that victory? Will access to the outside world be so fulfilling as to keep the children of Enid from leaving for the big city, or will they find the difference between what they see, the bright lights of the biggest city of all, and how they live so frustrating that they'll move away as soon as they can? Will the lives of the elderly be not only longer and healthier, but also more fulfilling? Or will they find themselves electronically barricaded in rest homes from the predators that roam the streets outside? Will families come to Enid because it offers all the qualities of small-town life without sacrificing the benefits of the outside world? Or will they arrive only to discover the town now indistinguishable from that world?

Jerry Pittman, managing editor of the *Enid News & Eagle,* sits hunched over his computer screen in his newsroom office, working out details in his proposal to fully integrate news and advertising in the computer composition of the newspaper. Born in Arkansas, he started out "in the hot-metal days" of newspapering as a sportswriter, "lugging a typewriter and a portable telecopier" from one game to the next. These days he sends his young reporters out armed with laptops.

Eleven years ago, he worked for *USA Today* at its headquarters in Roslyn, Virginia. He hated it. "You just felt so isolated from the reader," he says. So, when Gannett offered, he took a job as deputy managing editor in Shreveport, Louisiana. But it was a rough town. And in 1991, when he and his wife adopted a baby, Pittman began looking for a way out. "I wanted to do a community paper. The kind of paper where you are deeply involved in the life of the town," he says.

He found it in an *Editor & Publisher* ad for the *News & Eagle*, circulation 23,000 on weekdays, 25,000 on Sunday, and he seems a happy man. He talks enthusiastically about the new composing scheme and how he intends to establish a Web page for the paper next year. Then, with an apology, he cuts the interview short. He has an appointment at home with his computer supplier.

Pittman found the small-town life he was looking for in Enid. So too has Mike Murray, around the comer at the library. But will the delicate balance hold, shored up by the new technologies—or are these two men, with their computer dreams, unwittingly helping to topple it?

I drive out of Enid, away from the homes and tombstones of my ancestors. The tape deck is playing, with seeming appropriateness, Bruce Springsteen's *The Ghost of Tom Joad*. But that's wrong. The people of Enid, the Hasbrooks and Collinses and the thousands of others, aren't the people who gave up and left, but those who fought to stay.

If current trends continue, as the great aquifer dries up beneath the Midwest, the drier regions of the Great Plains will largely become uninhabited, abandoned to the wildflowers and prairie grass Charlie Hasbrook saw to the west from his claim. If that happens, Enid will have come full circle again, to becoming a frontier town.

That is, a frontier town by geography. It is already a town on a different frontier. I surf the digital radio dial, past the numerous Christian stations to an alternative rock station out of Tulsa. Trent Reznor is shrieking, "I want to f____k you like an animal! I want to feel you from the inside!" The music of Nine Inch Nails and the reality of MTV is now as much a part of Enid as it is of Inglewood or East Hampton.

For more than a century, the Midwest has been the moral center of the United States, and thus, to some degree, of much of the world. This morality was taught in school all week and in Enid's 90 churches every Sunday. It was carried across the decades in the stern Christian rectitude of people like my grandmother.

But part of propriety's strength lies in its isolation. The more difficult the vice is to obtain, the fewer the people who will take on those obstacles to get it. As long as Enid was a dry town, it was hard to be a drunk. If you never saw drugs it was tough to be an addict. But now any form of pornography can be found on the Net with a few keystrokes. And so will every other image and experience the human mind can devise. They will be within reach of Micky Unruh and Keith Winter and Mariana Padilla. They will be out there too in the airwaves on my Uncle Delbert's satellite dish. Thanks to new, fast forms of transportation, illegal drugs can now be brought cheaply to your door—or you can use inexpensive chemistry equipment to make your own. And instead of three television stations, there will be one thousand, and five thousand radio stations, and ten thousand movies on demand.

When the obstacles to our weaknesses, addictions, and perversions are lowered, even removed, how many of us will be able to resist? In a great nation like the United States, the periphery can perhaps go crazy—as it has—and the body politic still survive. But what if the center goes mad as well? The extremities may become diseased, but what happens when the infection reaches the heart? Will the people of Enid again use the flames that approach them to build a backfire in time to save their homes and families?

Riding our buggies, wagons, bicycles, or even a racehorse, we are all caught up in our own land rush. It is noon, the pistol has fired, and we race into our unknowable technological future in hopes of staking a claim and building a good life.

May we be as fortunate as Charlie Hasbrook.

From *Forbes ASAP Magazine* © Forbes Inc., "The Big Issue," December 2, 1996.

17

BANDON BEACH

Seas of pixels. Oceans of bits . . .

The small coastal Oregon resort town of Bandon-by-the-Sea has seen most of the changes the digital revolution has brought to the rest of America. Bandon used to be defined by the sweet smell of the local lumber mill and the morning fleet of fishing boats that chugged their way out the mouth of the Coquille River, past the busy lighthouse and out to a long day and night on the Pacific Ocean.

Today, the mill is closed, the fishing boats fewer and the lighthouse used only for postcards and screensavers. Bandon now is a tourist town. The houses along the cliff, looking down on the rocks and beach made famous by Jeep Cherokee commercials, are filled with wealthy retired Californians. Locals drive by in pick-ups chatting on their cell phones. And the local paper is filled with letters complaining about the quality of the cable television service and the local Internet Service Provider.

Bandon these days lives on e-mails and FedEx, eBay, and the WWF. But when you climb down the cliff to the beach, with its pounding breakers and looming off-shore monoliths, Bandon Beach is the same as it was a million years ago.

Or a century-and-half ago. Back then, when the beach was more likely to be walked by Coquille Indians than American settlers, elsewhere in the world great, troubling poems were being written about places like this. The great Victorian poets of England and America were obsessed with the ocean. Perhaps they saw in its power and fury the last great, untamable, force on earth. Or just as likely, they saw in the sea a metaphor for the great waves of industrialization and scientific discover rolling over them, shattering the world they knew, scattering the pieces all over the planet. The result was poems that haunt us still: Coleridge's "Rime of the Ancient Mariner," Poe's "Annabel Lee," Whitman's "Oh Captain, My Captain," Robinson's chilling "Eros Tyrannos" (". . . like a stairway to the sea/Where down the blind are driven").

We haven't thought much about the ocean lately. It too has been largely conquered. The age of exploration is over. Container ships haven't the romance of clippers. The global positioning systems on the local fishing boats are infinitely safer, but far less awesome than the old Bandon lighthouse. Civilization has evolved; the age of sail has become the age of the microprocessor. And, as the giant fiberoptic trunk line that comes out of the woods and dives into the Pacific a few miles north of here reminds us, we have now entered the century of the World Wide Web.

Yet, through it all, the ocean hasn't changed. The waves still break against Face Rock, and the gulls still wheel overhead. And as I walk alone down a mile-long stretch of empty beach, the debris beneath my feet—severed crab limbs, broken sand dollars, stranded jellyfish, dead sand crabs—reminds me of yet another Victorian ocean poem. It is perhaps the most disturbing poem of the nineteenth century.

Matthew Arnold, the son of England's most prominent educator, was on his honeymoon at a coastal resort on the English Channel.

Walking the beach one evening, he was stunned with a vision of the world to come. Some say he was merely panicking at the prospect of marriage, but I don't think so. Walking this beach, I am two decades past my own honeymoon—ironically, spent right here—yet I think I know what he felt.

The final stanza of "Dover Beach" is chilling:

> Ah, love, let us be true
> To one another! for the world, which seems
> To lie before us like a land of dreams,
> So various, so beautiful, so new
> Hath really neither joy, nor love, nor light,
> Nor certitude, nor peace, nor help for pain;
> And we are here as a on a darkling plain
> Swept with confused alarms of struggle and flight,
> Where ignorant armies clash by night.

A new world was coming, of machinery and factories, blitzkriegs and civil servants. And in a few years, Arnold would abandon poetry and become a good bureaucrat.

I said that the ocean has been almost forgotten. But in the last couple years it has made an unexpected reappearance in our literature. Books such as *The Perfect Storm* and *Lost at Sea* restore the sea to its almost-forgotten role as metaphor. We find ourselves suddenly curious about the unsinkable Titanic, and the Galveston hurricane and even cannibalism among those adrift. Like Arnold, we too may be sensing something immense and terrible rising up beneath the surface, a distant undersea quake already springing a tsunami toward us.

Ours is not an age of poetry, but technology. And it is there, in technology magazines and books where we may find what is about to emerge. Bill Joy, chief technologist for Sun Microsystems, recently played Cassandra in an epic, Unabomber-like, essay in *Wired* magazine. In it, he warned against the next era of digital technology—that of self-monitoring, self-reproducing, self-aware machines. Meanwhile, the Human Genome project nears completion, opening that Pandora's Box of bioengineering triumphs and horrors.

But even they pale before the scenario presented by scientist Ray Kurzweill in his new book, *The Age of Spiritual Machines.* In its pages, he posits a time, less than a generation hence, when we will port the map of neurons in our brain onto computer disk—and from there, migrate our consciousness out onto the Web itself.

It is the most tantalizing appeal of all. Who can resist the lure of immortality? Of infinite scope and near-omniscience? To live forever; to know everything; and to race about the earth at the speed of light? It is a dream destined to gain millions of followers in the years to come.

And yet, walking along Bandon Beach I find myself thinking that the Internet itself is a kind of ocean. And should we become one with it, we too may become ocean-like: vast, dark, and cold, indifferent to the struggles of life and death beneath us; deaf to the clash of ignorant armies in our midst.

Finding himself on the darkling plain of his era, Matthew Arnold fell back on the one thing he knew could save him: love, and the fidelity that was its truest form.

But when we choose to become the darkling plain itself, will love still be there to save us?

From *ABCNEWS.com,* June 6, 2000.

18

PRESSING THEIR CASES
COAST TO COAST

Imagine: You spend years building a high-tech company and establishing your self as one of its most powerful executives—and then one day you're forced to ingratiate yourself with an inevitably bored kid in a New Jersey storefront who holds your reputation in his hands.

That's the lot of every West Coast high-tech executive stuck with promoting a new product or company to the East Coast trade publications on a whirlwind press tour.

"It's one of the most intense business experiences I've ever been on," said Karen Milne, vice president of marketing for the JSB Corporation, a computer software maker in Scotts Valley, California.

Begun in the early 1970s by West Coast companies seeking publicity, press tours typically involve visiting as many as 20 magazines and newspapers in three East Coast metropolises—Boston, New York, and Washington—all in just three or four days. They start with a flourish as summer ends each year and companies scurry to introduce new products for the fall trade shows.

Ms. Milne recently spent five days in the three big cities promoting a new software interfacing product to magazines as diverse as *PC, Windows, Client/Server Today,* and *Federal Computing Week.* A typical day, she said, included "interviews all day, even one during dinner."

"You're always late and lost," she said. "I think in Boston I broke more traffic laws than in my entire driving career. I'm convinced cars should be made to carry one of three signs: student driver, pizza delivery, and press tour."

A public relations account executive usually tags along to keep the high-tech executive moving, and for Ms. Milne that was Paul Franson of Franson, Hagerty & Associates. Mr. Franson estimated he'd been on 50 such tours as a publicist.

"Something always goes wrong"—like magazines that have moved without notice—he said, "so you just have to be prepared."

Every Silicon Valley public relations executive has a press-tour horror story. One remembered being trapped with a client in New Jersey on a 95-degree day in a rental car in which all the power windows were stuck. Another recalled the time one of his account executives had a flat tire on a Massachusetts highway and, because her clients were asleep in the car, had to change the tire herself, in her business suit, as truckers honked and whistled. And yet a third watched in horror as Steve Jobs, then running Apple, simply removed the cassette from the reporter's tape recorder when he didn't like a question.

Fred Hoar, president and chief executive of Miller Communications West and one of the originators of the press tour 25 years ago at Fairchild Semiconductor, has developed a list of executive and reporter types. The trade-press reporter types, who are typically young and ambitious, include: the Prober, who is always challenging everything said; the Machine Gunner, who doesn't wait for an answer before asking the next question; the Mike Wallace type, who revels in being aggressive, the Bob Woodward, who prefers an analytical approach, and the Columbo, who lands the sneaky rabbit-punch question when it's least expected.

Mr. Hoar's executive types include the Preacher, the Explainer ("if you ask him the time, he'll tell you how to build a watch") and the Patient Misunderstander ("polite but never understands the question"). To prepare them for the first group and help them avoid acting like the second, Mr. Hoar puts his clients through a half-day of training.

Michael L. Joseph, vice president for strategic marketing at Iomega Inc. of Roy, Utah, which makes instant removable memory for PCs, goes on as many as 10 tours each year. He, too, has had his rough moments on the tours, but still, he said, "I actually think they are a lot of fun. They're a grind, but you talk to a lot of smart people who challenge you on every possible thing that could go wrong with your product and your company."

Dirk I. Gates, president and chief executive of Xircom Inc., a mobile networking equipment maker in Calabasas, California, has found that being just 33 years old helps his cause. "I'm not that much older than many of these reporters, so I try to talk their language. But you have to be careful about knowing your audience. Talk to an older financial reporter about bits and bytes and his eyes glaze over, but 22-year-old tech reporters can't get enough."

William Krause, by comparison, is a 20-year press-tour veteran. He has gone on tours as an executive at the giant Hewlett-Packard Company; as chairman and president of a midsize network equipment maker, 3Com, and now as president and chief executive of Storm Software Inc., a startup based in Mountain View, California, that makes software to transmit photographs and sound.

"When you tour for somebody like HP," he said, "you always get in the door at magazines because whatever HP does is important. But with 3Com, especially in the beginning, you end up sitting in the back room with some kid. He has no idea who you are or what your product is, and he's never heard of your company. That experience teaches you patience.

"Now, with my new company, we've got a hot market—consumer, multimedia—so we're out talking to entertainment magazines. These are dream tours, a real break from technology magazines. But it's still being in a rock band: you have to be up for each concert."

After nearly a week of touring, executive and publicist drag themselves home, usually "quite sick of each other," Mr. Franson said. But high-tech products generally have short lifecycles, and so within six months the same team could easily be on a new tour.

Not Karen Milne, however: "I don't ever want to again find myself in high heels carrying that much paper and two computers through strange airports. Next time I'm going to delegate the tour to someone who works for me."

From the *New York Times*, September 18, 1994.

19

NOTES FROM A DISTANT NODE

Dinner tonight will be zebra filets with South African merlot. And at dawn, peering in from the high grass beyond the fence, will be kudu, with their great corkscrew horns, or even cheetah.

This is Namibia, once known as South-West Africa, and it lies on the Atlantic Coast just north of South Africa and just south of forever-troubled Angola. Namibia itself is an uneasy mixture of Africa and Europe, where the 1.5 million sons and daughters of Bushmen, Germans, and Brits try to live side by side.

Our hosts are Diethelm and Kailja Metzger. Diethelm is a third-generation Namibian. His grandfather arrived in the country from Germany more than a half-century ago. The Metzgers, in their 30s, run a 50,000-acre ranch 75 miles down dirt roads from the capital. They make their living raising championship cattle and running hunting and photographic safaris for visitors.

This is not to suggest that the Metzgers' life is a primitive one. On the contrary, I am filing this story from Diethelm's business office, which sits between one of the guest rooms and the bar. There may be a zebra rug on the floor, but sitting here beside my laptop is a Pentium-based PC, a Hewlett-Packard inkjet printer, and a scanner/fax machine.

Taljana, the Metzgers' daughter, surfs the Net for her reports when she's home from boarding school on the weekends. Every morning Katja listens as each of her neighbors checks in on the CB in the living room. On the road, she uses a cell phone to call stores in Windhoek. Whenever Diethelm is out in the bush, he carries on his hip a walkie-talkie that quickly links him both with the house and the driver in the Land Rover.

But Africa always defies expectations. You walk a hundred yards off the track, passing through a landscape that looks just like northern Nevada, when suddenly you find yourself face-to-face with a wildebeest, 500 springbok, or a giraffe.

By the same token, Europeans and Americans for centuries have approached Africa with stereotyped expectations—the Dark Continent, jungle, lions and crocodiles, savage tribes—and lately, grinding poverty, racism, and a land ravaged by AIDS—only to find those stereotypes both true and utterly wrong.

Africa is too complex, too diverse, to be reduced to a handful of phrases. The newest of these African myths has been promulgated by some of the self-proclaimed visionaries of the Internet Age. In this theory, Africa has an advantage over both West and East precisely because it is so wretched and backward.

Because it has such little infrastructure in place—dirt roads, old copper telephone lines, etc.—Africa doesn't face the legacy issue of replacing costly, but obsolete, systems already in place. Thus, Africa should be able to leapfrog the rest of the world, putting in place a wireless/fiber telecommunications network that will put the rest of us to shame and thrust the continent into leadership of the Internet Age.

Implicit in this vision is the Utopian fantasy that underlies most high-tech futurism: Once Africa puts this infrastructure in place, all of its problems—tribalism, racism, poverty, and disease will disappear in the purifying light of a fiberoptic cable.

We in high tech love this myth because it puts us on the side of the angels—as much as the idea of bringing the True Faith to the heathens swelled the hearts of our Victorian ancestors as they happily bore the White Man's Burden.

But, as always in Africa, the truth is more complicated—and much harder to swallow. These days, the order to hack your neighbor to death comes over the radio. The homicidal young soldier pointing the AK-47 at a terrified family has a cell phone on his hip and a GameBoy in his pocket.

Even in Namibia, peaceful now for a decade, the ranchers— most of them white nervously watch as the government restricts their ownership of rifles and diesel fuel and wonder if life wouldn't be so bad in Germany or the United States. They keep touch with reality by surfing the Internet.

Meanwhile, the working class—mostly black—can't afford computers and is reduced to reading the government newspaper or watching the government-owned TV station (CNN being blacked-out because it is too "biased").

This is the real Africa, where a small part of the population quietly suffers the terror of knowledge, while the large majority unknowingly awaits the call to arms.

In the West, protected by laws and rights, we think of the technology revolution as a race—into an ever more prosperous and dynamic future. Here in Africa, and in all of the other explosive places of the world, it is a race, too—but of a different kind. Here, those who want to save Africa from another century of horror are, literally, in a dead heat against those who derive their power from misery and chaos. Frighteningly, both are armed with the latest technologies, the winner is far from predictable.

This, not some Silicon Valley fantasy, is the real techno-future. This is the real world of the twenty-first century. And as Diethelm Metzger will tell you, out here, behind that next tree may be a docile little steenbuck . . . or a very big leopard. Death still crouches in the tall grass of cyberspace.

From *ABCNEWS.com*, August 6, 2000.

20

CHILDREN OF THE [ONCE] FUTURE

Call it the Summer of SOMA. And it is going to be long and hot.

I've been thinking a lot lately about 1967, and the Summer of Love. I was 13 years old, a suburban kid from the as-yet unnamed Silicon Valley, walking through the Haight-Ashbury, looking at all the freaks. It was supposed to be the dawn of the Age of Aquarius; tens of thousands of 20-something baby boomers had hitched their way to San Francisco in search of Owsley's acid, good music, and, of course, Utopia. Some of these tie-dyed wonders were my neighbors, the older brothers and sisters of my friends. No more talented, dangerous, and narcissistic group ever lived. I'd never trusted them; and as I looked out on this landscape of merry pranksters, space cowboys, and cinnamon girls, I could already smell the self-delusion and hysteria.

Everybody was so busy performing that no one noticed that the curtain was already falling. By fall and fog, the crowds had gone home to college and jobs, the runaways were eating dog food and

the smack junkies had taken over the Hashbury. Then came Alta-
mont. Now a new summer is upon us in San Francisco, and I can't
help feeling the ache of déjà vu. There is a new set of young dreamers now, and their spiritual home is on the other side of town, in
the old district of winos and auto shops South of Market (SOMA).
They don't survive on handouts in the Golden Gate Park panhandle, but lunch on sushi and macchiatos on the green lawn of South
Park. It is hard to recognize these young dot-com entrepreneurs in
all-black mufti and nose rings as the spiritual descendents of the
hippies.

But make no mistake. The dream is still the same, only the
path has changed. In Search of the Perfect Life Where the Haight-
Ashbury generation tried to find paradise through neolithic tribal
communalism, two-hour jams, and massive quantities of pharmaceuticals, the SOMA crowd, perhaps made cynical by their long-
haired parents, has instead embraced capitalism with all the ardor
a cynical Gen-Xer can muster. Term sheets, stock options, and red
herrings are the lingua franca of this crowd. They aren't working
those 100-hour weeks for a perfect world, but only a perfect life: a
couple years of hard work in a startup, then a killer IPO, then
sweat through the lock-out . . . then walk away with $100 million
before their 30th birthday.

It is the old narcissism in a new bottle. And it is just as doomed
to end badly. Even now, as I stroll through South Park, or wander
about one of the networking-frenzied "salons," or sit in an Aeron
chair in the Gymboree-like headquarters of one of these startups,
I can smell that old hysteria again.

A Second Youthquake

It started four years ago, with all the thrill of a New Wave crashing
onto the scene. Amazon, E Trade, Yahoo!, and the rest. It was the

Acid Test of the cyber age. There was that sense of the illicit, of being part of something so new and so immense that you could hardly breathe. The old Valley guard predicted it would all come to nothing—that too was part of the fun. And then it hit. It hit so big it was like a dream, like an hallucination. It was off the wackiest spreadsheet of the most unrealistic startup in town.

Overnight, the Valley veterans faded into history. It was like 45 years of the electronics revolution had never happened. Everything was e-business now. It was a second youthquake: the media, the markets, the whole damn society suddenly fell in love with dot-coms. And the postadolescent stars of this new wave, nobodies a few weeks before, became stars—and billionaires. With *Wired* singing "If You're Going to San Francisco, Be Sure to Carry a Business Plan in Your Hand," Xers all over America, then the world, fell in love with the idea of becoming cyber-millionaires.

The E-Tycoons

It was easy: the market was wide open, venture capitalists were rolling in cash from investors who also wanted to play the I-game, and apparently all the rules of business (profits, market share, normal price-earnings ratios) had been suspended to greet the newcomers.

The business and tech press, secretly starting Web sites and plotting their own IPOs, were more than happy to play cheerleaders at the rave. Even as these thousands of budding entrepreneurs were spell checking their business plans, one e-commerce company after another public—to billion-dollar market caps and newly tycooned 29-year-olds.

Soon they were arriving in droves, with their graduate degrees and teeth turning brown with Ecstasy, their BMW Z3s, a willingness to work 24/7, and their talk of eyeballs and branding. The plan was to put in a couple years of hard work, then walk away with a hundred million or so to start phase two of their well-planned "perfect lifetime" strategy.

But life doesn't work that way. Just ask all those Patchouli Patch Kids now selling real estate in Sacramento and Bullhead City. It all started out so well too; but then, it always does. It was fun in the SOMA playpens. You could act like a 9-year-old yet still believe you were Jack Welch Jr., buy your latté with the coins in your glove compartment, then look at brochures for your future Gulfstream V.

And the money kept rolling in—not from customers, of course, you didn't have any of those yet, but from new rounds of venture capital. It was a lovely asymptote: $2 million for the A round, $10 million for B, then $50 million for C. And since it cost less to run an e-commerce company than to buy a house in Sunnyvale, all that money was to be spent on marketing and brand building. That was even more fun. It was one thing to give your company a stupid name to get attention; now you could devise a stupid, rude, or incoherent television commercial and spend $10 million for a Super Bowl halftime slot.

All in the name of branding! But the commercials didn't take, nor did the idiotic billboards and radio slots and sky-writers and bus banners. Even if the ad registered a reaction, the company name never did. There was just too much noise; too many hundreds of dot-coms all with the same idea; too many scores of competitors jammed into each and every market niche.

Technology "Dethroned"

Now it is spring. The fog has returned to the Bay and they've switched on the lights at the new Pac Bell Park a few blocks away from the children of SOMA. No doubt they see the glow; they're working long hours these nights. But last week, uber-analyst

Christine Callies told her clients to reduce tech stocks in their scenarios. "Technology has been dethroned," she said.

Nasdaq, meanwhile, has been plummeting. Perhaps it will bounce back once again, but there are fewer props these days to hold it up. And the next time a month or two hence? No Nasdaq boom means no IPOs. And that means the dot-coms will have to do like traditional companies always did during hard times: buckle down and hold out for good times again. Somehow I don't think that rule of business has been suspended.

But in recent days both *Red Herring* and the *San Jose Mercury-News* have reported that hundreds of dot-coms, having shot their powder on six months of wasted advertising, are rapidly running out of money. Some have already died or suffered crippling layoffs. Others, like DrKoop.com, CDNow, and PeaPod are reportedly almost out of money. Many more will be broke by the end of summer. Few will last the year. Most will try to go back to the well for more, but VCs are the fairest of fair-weather friends.

The Death of Dot-Coms

Being an entrepreneur is all about believing your fantasy. But in the playpens South of Market it's getting harder and harder these days to drink the Kool-Aid. It's rumored that one dot-com just sent around a memo to its staff asking if anybody had an idea for a new business the company could enter. There's always the "Next Big Thing," b-to-b commerce, but that's for people who read *Industry Week,* not *Industry Standard.* And even as the prematurely aged children of the Blair.com Project huddle together and whisper that everything will be okay, new fresh-faced and greedy kids are rolling into SFO with dreams of overnight riches.

The curtain has begun to fall, even as the music reaches a crescendo. At my magazine, I'm deluged with frantic calls from dot-com flacks offering interviews, parties, salons, anything to get attention. The hysteria is rising, the end will be brutal, and the trauma—like the death of the Age of Aquarius—will last a generation.

The Summer of SOMA is upon us. When the music's over, turn out the lights.

From *ABCNEWS.com*, April 4, 2000.

21

THE GILDERED AGE

"Oh, my God. We're rich." My wife began to cry. Twenty years of being broke, of fights and fears, ducking bill collectors, and borrowing from family were instantly, bodily lifted from our backs and flung into the blue Silicon Valley sky. The vacuum left by the departure of our former life was so shocking it was hard to breathe.

My family plunged into the Internet Age on a blistering Silicon Valley summer day in 1997. We never felt it coming—and now, three years on, we are still trying to understand what happened. I am now wealthier (though I'm not sure I deserve it) and wiser (if only because I'm now convinced I don't understand anything anymore).

I grew up in Silicon Valley. I live four blocks from my junior high school, five blocks from the shopping center where I watched young Steve Wozniak and Steve Jobs buy the parts for the Apple I, and two blocks from the house Ted Hoff lived in when he was designing the first microprocessor. So, perhaps more than most business journalists, I feel the deep rhythms of Valley life.

None had been stronger than the five-year cycle, that ebb and flow of high-tech boom and bust that defined our lives. As a teenager, I watched the great downturn of 1970 cast one neighborhood father after another into unemployment.

Five years later, after finishing at Santa Clara University, I graduated to yet another downturn so miserable I scrambled back to the sanctuary of business school. In the early 1980s, I was at the *San Jose Mercury News,* part of a great media tidal surge in which the endless run of economic-misery stories suddenly inflected, seemingly overnight, into a parade of ain't-the-economy-great features.

So, as 1997 dawned, five years into the latest boom, I was again preparing for hard times in the Valley. I'd actually begun the year before. As a freelance writer for 15 years, I knew that lean times in the industry could mean good times for me, doing the work of now-departed company flacks and magazine editors. But it would be hard money: hard to earn and even harder to get paid. And this time around, I had an added handicap: We had purchased a historic house, the oldest American home in Silicon Valley, that was well beyond our means—especially when we discovered the roof, plumbing, wiring, and foundation had to be replaced.

So, like a good Valley squirrel facing the return of an economic El Nino, I scrambled to build my bank account by gathering up every gig I could find. One of those jobs came with a call from a forceful entrepreneur who talked like a wise guy and had the coiled energy of a middleweight college wrestler. Would I be interested in writing a book with him? He had been a vice president of sales for Oracle, then made a fortune turning around and selling Gain Technology to Sybase. Now he was sitting in a rented office in Menlo Park, with a partner, a receptionist, and two staffers. He was going to build software to attack an industry, sales force automation, that was both balkanized and dusty, and he wanted to write a book about "virtual selling" to kick off the whole venture.

As an aside, the entrepreneur asked if I'd be willing to take my share of the advance in stock options. Sure, I said, ignoring my own plan, rationalizing that the advance wouldn't be that much anyway.

At about the same time, I got a call from two young men at another startup, also in a rented office, this time in San Jose. They wanted to talk about positioning and branding their new venture, one of the first in the new field of Internet commerce.

I didn't know much more about the Net than a few forays on America Online, and what I'd seen hadn't impressed me. Nor did this little company. It had a lot in common with the first: four people, rented office furniture, folding tables, red licorice whips instead of M&Ms, and the same belief in the invincibility of their cause.

But unlike the software startup, these founders weren't sure where they were going (that's why I was there to help), only that they were onto something big. Most of us were short of cash, so we'd pool our money to buy Chinese food and hold extended lunch meetings—long, freewheeling conversations about the new frontier of the Web and their place in it. It was fun, a slightly guilty break from my race for money, my one long shot on a table of sure things. And I knew that when the company crashed, as so many like it had before, that my heart would break a little for these two young men and their virtual pipe dream.

Then something extraordinary occurred. More precisely, didn't occur. In 1997, winter never came, the Valley never crashed. All the traditional signs were there: Semiconductor book-to-bill ratios fell; bankruptcies increased; the outrageous real estate prices began to fall; and the personal computer industry, led by a dying Apple, watched orders slip. Everything said it was time to hunker down, update your résumé, and get ready for hard times. But hard times never hit. Just as the exhausted runner was about to stumble and fall, he handed off the baton to a brand-new sprinter, rested and ready to run. Unbelievably, magnificently, at the very moment it should have collapsed, the Valley went through one of its most important transformations.

It seemed to come out of nowhere. I'd heard about the Arpanet for years. And the Well, which was getting pumped by the old *Whole Earth Catalog* crowd. Then, about the time I began work on the book with the first entrepreneur, a lot of the heads-up guys I knew started talking about the Web and a new kind of software called the Mosaic search engine. The Web is still a mess, they'd say, but some of it is very cool. And if they ever figure out how to index and move around on this thing, the Internet is going to be huge.

Over the next several months, it began to dawn on me that the Internet wasn't just an intriguing invention but something far rarer: an invention of inventions. I'd seen it just twice before: first with the microprocessor in 1971, then five years later with the personal computer. Certainly I'd seen staggering success stories, from mini-computers and calculators to video games and cell phones. But when I first heard about the Intel 8080 microprocessor, and when I saw the Apple II being introduced at a computer show in San Francisco, it was like doors being flung open to new worlds.

There was an epiphany—"Wait a minute. Now you can do this, and this, and this. Holy shit!"—that made you want to reel out of your chair and start companies, reorganize society, change the direction of your life.

Now it was the Internet. All of Silicon Valley seemed to wake up to the realization at the same time. Everywhere I went, I found myself talking about the Web, increasingly using that new term, *e-commerce.* And I wasn't just talking to VCs and analysts: Corporate types, even journalists and people with no contact with tech, could hardly wait to swap names of cool new sites with me. And more than one quietly took me aside and whispered his idea for a new company. Would I like to get involved? Did I know any angles? Any VCs?

The media were turning, too. In three months' time, my assignments suddenly shifted from computers and semiconductors to the cyberworld. My old standbys, *Forbes ASAP, Upside,* and the *San Jose Mercury News,* were now asking me to fly to Seattle to interview executives at Starwave or write about the Band of Angels. *Wired* suddenly showed up on the checkout racks of both my video store and my local supermarket. And a strange new magazine, *Fast Company,* which seemed to be about everything and nothing at all, was asking me to contribute a story with a Web angle to every issue.

There is a moment in a technology revolution when you sense the swell building beneath you. Being in California, with Santa Cruz just over the hill, Valley companies as far back as Advanced Micro Devices in the 1970s have used surfing as a metaphor for success. "Catch the Wave," said the famous AMD commercial of a man in a business suit racing his short board across an 8-foot curl, an image that has defined the Valley ever since.

As 1996 turned to 1997, we could sense that wave mounting. All of us, as one, turned and started paddling, trying to pick up enough speed to catch the roller. And just like at Lighthouse Point on a summer day, it was crowded out there: amateurs and veterans alike, jostling for position, pushing one another out of the way, desperate to catch the biggest ride of our lives. Thousands caught it, more than ever before—and almost from that instant we wondered what we had done.

I finished the book, as always, broke and desperate for money. This time I was doubly desperate, having no final advance check waiting for me because I had taken the stock options instead. So anxious was I to get on with making money, I never even took the time to carefully write down either the option price or the number of shares. I figured the shares were worth 10 or 20 grand—a number that wouldn't matter for at least six months anyway, when the company, named after my coauthor, Tom Siebel, planned to go public. A few months later, when I received the prospectus in the mail, I didn't even notice my name printed inside.

Meanwhile, I took the two young entrepreneurs in to see a venture capitalist I knew. After a series of meetings, he made them what I thought was a pretty amazing offer: $40 million for the firm. They turned him down. Afterward, over lunch in the Fountain Restaurant at the San Jose Fairmont Hotel, the two young men, Pierre Omidyar and Jeff Skoll, said they wanted to thank me for all my help over the previous year by awarding me some stock. I was to be a founding shareholder in eBay.

I rarely saw Tom Siebel again over the next six months. I did stop by eBay a few times, to find it had moved from a single office suite to the entire floor of the same building. There were 40 employees now—and an equal number of full-sized *Star Wars* cutouts. Meanwhile, as these two fledgling startups exploded into supernovas, I hit the road, writing stories and hustling speeches wherever I could. One evening, in Fort Worth, Texas, I addressed John Roach and the board of Tandy over dinner at the quarterly directors meeting. A wild-eyed new convert to the Internet revolution, I lectured the distracted group on how e-commerce would change the world. They looked at me as if I had just landed from Neptune.

That summer I traveled to São Paulo and found a business world still trying to cope with the personal computing revolution, never mind the Internet. After returning to California, the combined effect of winter in Brazil and summer in Silicon Valley overpowered my immune system, and on the hottest day of the year, I found myself in bed with a temperature higher than the 103 degrees outside. Soon my entire family was infected, my wife and two young sons covered with spots, and all of us lying half-delirious on the unfinished floor of the downstairs library, surrounded by blowing fans and the sound of workmen's hammers. I was vaguely aware that

Siebel Systems had successfully gone public, but it was more than a week later when I decided to call and check my options.

Already Siebel's stock had raced up to $50 per share, with no ceiling in sight. I sat in my half-demolished office—and it looked to remain that way forever because we had run out of money for the contractor—at my desk made of a door and two file cabinets, and talked on the phone to one of the scores of new Siebel employees I had never seen.

"Lessee," he said. I could hear his fingers clicking keys. "Okay, here it is, Mr. Malone." He quoted me my total shares. I dropped the pen. "How many?" I didn't hear his answer. Later I remembered writing something down, but within hours I lost the note and had to call the company twice over the next few days to hear the numbers again and again—as if on one of the calls they would suddenly tell me there'd been a recording error and that I didn't own any options after all and that I should stop bothering them. I held my crying, still-sick wife. We'd done it. It wasn't a huge sum—a mere rounding error to the Siebel entrepreneurs, who would soon be billionaires, then multibillionaires—but more than we ever thought we'd see in our lifetimes. With some smart investments, we'd pay for our children's education and perhaps guarantee a comfortable retirement. Not bad for a hack. Not bad at all.

Yet even as I was floating above the world, I also felt myself tethered, then reeled back down to earth. I thought of my late father. One Saturday, sitting over beers in my folks' kitchen, he chuckled, "Son, let me tell you something amazing. You know we just had all of our property appraised? Turns out the houses and properties altogether are worth a million bucks. Can you believe it? Me? A millionaire? Incredible!"

It had taken him 60 years. He had bled for every penny of that million dollars, and in the end it killed him. Now I had traversed the same rugged path as if in an airplane, a distracted traveler thumbing through a magazine, rarely glancing at the landscape below. I hadn't even kept track of my portfolio.

Six months later, the airplane turned into a rocket. Now it was eBay's turn to go public. Everyone on earth knows the story of that stock. And once again, I had forgotten how many shares I owned. There were no tears this time, only stunned disbelief. This was a number almost beyond imagining, several times the value of our Siebel holdings.

I once spent two years immersed 80 hours a week in a startup, a true believer, convinced I was part of a great crusade that would create a new world and make me a titan of it. That company went nowhere, and I was left holding 40,000 shares of air. Now, through no strategy whatsoever, I had serendipitously become a founding shareholder of two public companies, one the fastest-growing firm in America in the 1990s, the other one of the greatest business phenomena of the century.

Unexpectedly, unaccountably, I had struck gold in the Gildered Age.

In 1873, Mark Twain coauthored his first novel and gave a name to the era. The *Gilded Age* satirized the opening round of the second Industrial Revolution as it transformed America. As his lifetime of disastrous investments proved, Twain's understanding of business was pretty lousy. So he missed most of the story—of the rise of mass-production factories, the bureaucratic corporation, and large-scale investment capital. But what he did understand was people, in all their foolish obsessions and follies. So in the novel, he poked fun at the indefatigable optimism of a nation just emerging from a brutal Civil War and finding itself with peace, a continental reach, and a host of new technologies.

One of those new technologies was consumer credit, and that subject gave Twain the most famous lines of the novel: "Beautiful credit! The foundation of modern society. Who shall say that this is not the golden age of mutual trust, of unlimited reliance upon human promises . . . [In the words of] a distinguished speculator of lands and mines: 'I wasn't worth a cent a year ago, and now I owe two million dollars.'"

Historian David McCullough goes on television to talk about how we are living in a new Gilded Age, a time of incredible wealth creation and economic expansion. But why? There has been no war to set off a flurry of rebuilding, new babies, and ambitious veterans racing to make up for lost time. Instead, this economic explosion has been touched off by a collision of technologies. Moore's Law of integrated circuits has linked up with Metcalfe's Law of networks and a half dozen as yet unnamed laws of technological innovation to create a gigantic ratchet mechanism on society. Every few months the lever is pulled down, the ratchet teeth connect, and the economy is impelled upward just a little bit higher. When the only dynamic was Moore's Law, there was always the sneaking fear that one morning Intel, HP, IBM, and Motorola would hold a joint press conference and announce they had at last hit an insurmountable physical wall in the design of microprocessor chips. And that would be it; the digital revolution would be over—leaving us to clear the wreckage from the battlefield, nurse the wounded, adapt to the new world, and begin writing legends for our grandchildren.

But now there are too many laws for it all to stall if a single one fails. There are so many different floor jacks under the Body Electric that the levitation won't slow even if some of them snap under the burden. What's more, with the Internet, the innovation has shifted largely from hardware to software—which opens the game to millions of imaginations without electrical engineering degrees. And finally, if all else fails, biotech is waiting in the wings, promising changes for which the digital revolution may prove only a rehearsal. The speed at which the Human Genome Project is outrunning all of its schedules gives a glimpse of what is to come. So it's not going to stop. Not for a generation or more. That's the message the technology world is sending us. More of us are hearing and believing that message these days. But even five years ago, those of us in the business of decoding high tech's pronouncements had our doubts.

Except George Gilder. The John the Baptist of the Digital Age, Gilder always believed. I remember at the beginning of the 1990s, reading *Microcosm's* penultimate, mystical chapter, and thinking George had lost his mind. But Gilder was right. We are all a little messianic these days about technology. And with good reason: It offers us life and it takes it away, it extends our sight to the end of the universe and our voice around the world, and it blesses us with riches. Riches at the turn of an idea or the flash of an e-trade.

Gilder had that right—and more. He not only understood that the new laws of technology were going to create a perpetual revolution but that they were going to intersect with a second revolution taking place in society, that of venture capital and entrepreneurship—and when the two finally teamed up and hit their stride, the whole world would be a track meet. This new age would hold the potential for perpetual prosperity for all who pursued it. It would reorder the world, heal the sick, and bring forth realities once only imagined in science fiction. No one really believed him. Andy Grove certainly didn't. And Bill Gates doesn't believe him yet.

Perhaps the disbelief stems from the nature of the messenger. Gilder is a pale, nervous Yankee with abrupt, combative opinions about everything. Early on, he was so distracted that he sometimes forgot the audience he was talking to, sometimes so obtuse and tangential that listeners came away convinced he was drunk, and so absentminded he would wear a sport coat with running shorts or have to be fetched from down blind hallways and wrong turns.

Yet this is his time—it's the Gildered Age. George jets around the world now, often dazed from jet lag, talking to government leaders, giving three speeches on three continents in the same number of days. At his conferences, true believers rush the stage while corporate CEOs mill around outside like Metallica fans, trying to score tickets. Most of all, George moves markets. He points out in his newsletter a couple of hot companies—and those stocks take off. Is he that accurate at appraising the near-time potential of startups, the most volatile of all companies, or are his predictions self-fulfilling as investors rush off in any direction he points? Does it matter?

If Gilder is our messenger, there are many other wise, intelligent, aggressive entrepreneurs who are confused and disoriented. As am I. Everything around me has the pretzel logic of absurdity. During a meeting between a well-known Sand Hill Road VC and a startup team, I watch the VC listen patiently to the presentation and then drop the bomb: "My one real concern is with your company's name." The team looks confused.

"See," says the VC, "my feeling is that in e-commerce it pays to have the stupidest name possible. People remember it."

"We're very flexible on the name thing," says the team leader anxiously.

In November 1999, I filmed a new interview series with some of high tech's most famous entrepreneurs. These are the founders of the Silicon Valley I know, not the one I currently live in. They built great companies in crazy, dangerous times, but not so crazy or dangerous as now. They are very smart people. Some—like Intel's Gordon Moore, Apple's Steve Wozniak, and Bob Metcalfe, founder of 3Com—are among the most creative thinkers of the twentieth century. Others—like Jerry Sanders of Advanced Micro Devices and Oracle's Larry Ellison—are among the shrewdest wheeler-dealers America has ever known.

It is with relief, and then fear, that I find they are as stunned and confused by the Gildered Age as the rest of us. "I really don't get it," says Carol Bartz of Autodesk, who always seems to get it. Metcalfe, who wrote the defining rule of this game, predicts the bubble will burst any day, any hour. Even Woz, the Mozart of the digital age, admits that the e-world is passing him by.

Jerry Sanders announces that the day Advanced Micro Devices went public was the proudest of his life—then adds, of course, that was back when going public meant you weren't going bankrupt soon.

Only the founder of Atari, Nolan Bushnell, with the heart of the carnival hustler he once was, feels at home. Having lost everything—the mansion, the money, the power—he is starting over as a hungry entrepreneur. "I've got a great idea for a dot-com," he says. "It's so good I can't even tell you about it."

On the cold January morning when the lockout ends on my eBay stock, I'm in Washington, D.C., on business. Like everyone with founders' stock, I've died a thousand deaths in the last month.

The nightmare is always the same: I turn on cable news to see the market in complete Black Thursday collapse, my shares leading the way to oblivion.

But the nightmare is not to be. By the time I am ready to sell, the shares are doing well, and I find myself allowing the idea that we just may make it.

Being on the East Coast, I'm in the unique position of being on the road by the time the market opens. I call my broker on the cell phone and place the order to sell as much as I can. Not for an instant do I consider holding them. Even now that I'm about to become one of its beneficiaries, I still don't believe in this bubble. My broker quotes me the price, pauses, taps some keys, then says, "Okay, the shares are sold." I can feel my heart pounding.

I have some time before my meeting and make an unscheduled stop at National Cathedral. As we tour past the statues and carvings, something pulls at me. I excuse myself from the group, and almost before I know it, I find myself doing something I haven't done in a very long time: in a pew, kneeling in prayer.

Lately, the critics have been preparing us for the coming bust: a devastating wound that will once more bathe Silicon Valley in blood. "You can smell the shakeout in the air," says a fellow reporter. Most of us know intuitively that these young Web companies, minted by the hour, will not all survive and prosper. In the coming reckoning, investors will lose money, retirement funds will be erased, and the valuations that rule the stock market will again become rational.

Perhaps the critics are right. We have become selfish and self-absorbed, more interested in money than achievement, caring now only for possessions and not for our souls. Some days you sense the madness can't go on much longer. Driving up Foothill Expressway, I watch two new Ferrari 355 Spiders pass each other, each driver giving the other a crisp wave. At the coffee place, a real estate salesman tells me he is starting to hate his job: Fifteen minutes after he opens the lockbox on a house early on Saturday morning, it has sold for 50 grand over its half-million dollar listing—a house all reason says is only worth half that. "What's the problem?" I ask. "You're getting rich, aren't you?" "Yeah," he replies, "but I can't stand the crying, the weeping couples that have lost out on their sixth straight offer and have no place to live. It makes me feel like crap."

Late at night, as I walk through my neighborhood, I can see the glow of one neighbor's computer screen as he works on the spreadsheet of his new business plan, and the bright lights of another neighbor's garage office as he debugs code for a client.

It will all end. The madness, the impossible valuations, and the absurd business models will all fall away—sooner, rather than later. That is, unless something else comes along to goose the Valley forward into yet another boom. But even if everything goes to hell, those glowing lights in my neighbors' windows tell me that the Silicon Valley dream will still survive.

From *Forbes ASAP* © Forbes, Inc., February 21, 2000. Reprinted with permission.

PART

V

SILICON HOME

22

THE PACKARD WAY

David Packard, who died Tuesday at age 83, is the greatest figure of the electronics age, its most admired entrepreneur, and, history may well record, the most important businessman of the twentieth century.

Justly so, because in many ways Packard epitomized that century. A child of the Depression, he built a gigantic corporation, dominated the increasingly international world of business, watched his company begin to fade, then restored it to even greater glory. He fit the part, too: a tall, rangy outdoorsman, who for all his experience in public settings, remained a little shy and even taciturn.

Most of all, David Packard exhibited a trait once synonymous with Americans: an absolute, rock-hard integrity. He had it in Pueblo, Colorado, as a teenager, he had it in the Emerson Street garage when he and Bill Hewlett took a borrowed $538 and started Hewlett-Packard Co., and he had it on the day he died 60 years later. It is that integrity that made David Packard who he was. You could trust him to do what was right, whether you were a newly hired clerk at an HP division in Boise or the president of the United States.

Great lives are always moral lessons. The lesson of David Packard's life is that a man or woman of honor can change the world, improve the lives of millions, and die with the satisfaction of a life well-lived. It is the oldest lesson and the hardest to learn. You can only stand in awe of a man like David Packard who, despite the distractions of power and unbelievable wealth, still set out each day to do the right thing . . . and did it.

Famous men don't really die. Rather, they turn into the myth awaiting them.

We all know that myth. It starts in Fred Terman's electronics class at Stanford. Then the garage and the first sale of audio oscillators (priced at $54.40 because it sounded like "54–40 or Fight!") to the Disney Studios to help make "Fantasia." Then the sudden burst of growth created by the war, the struggle to keep the company together afterward, and then the great success of the 1950s. In there as well is the Stanford Industrial Park, the ideal for every industrial park since.

Most of all, there is the HP Way, probably the most celebrated business philosophy of all time, and Packard's greatest legacy. To encounter it in print, after years of hearing all of the hoopla attached to it, is to be disappointed. Its precepts—such as, "Be a good corporate citizen"—are depressingly banal. Every company in the world has a comparable statement of philosophy, usually ignored.

That's the point. Before HP, such statements did not exist. And if its tenets seem prosaic, they are in fact beliefs distilled to their essence through years of use. The HP Way changes about as often as the Constitution. The comparison is not out of place: Just as the Founding Fathers devised the chief executive on the figure of George Washington sitting at the desk in front of them, so too it is obvious that the HP Way is the corporate reflection of David

Packard in the 1950s, the man handing out profit-sharing checks to every employee at the Christmas party, who sat beside them on a bench in the corporate cafeteria, who knew each of them by name.

The printed HP Way is also a disappointment because it was never meant to stand on its own. Rather, it serves as an organizing principle, a table of contents to a vast corpus of legends, anecdotes, quotes, and standards of behavior that define every day life within HP.

Ask an HPer to explain the Way and he will be hard-pressed to do so, but work inside the company's walls and you know it intuitively without having to reference it. It's just the way you do things, the way Bill and Dave would have done it.

▼▲▼

How did they do it? Here's an example: In 1960, a team of scientists out of Sylvania approached Packard about getting HP into the integrated circuit business. Packard agreed to back these individuals by creating a new company division, HP Associates, which the founders and HP would each half-own. As part of the agreement, in five years HP would have the option to buy out HP Associates at a price based on its sales, profits, and contribution to the parent company.

And that is precisely what HP did, creating an operation that ultimately completely transformed the company's product line, made it competitive in the digital age, and led to billions of dollars in revenues.

So far, so good. We have a story of a company making a brilliant investment thanks to the founder's vision and business acumen. Every successful company has one or two of these tales in its scrapbook. But, as always, the Packard story has an added twist:

At the end of the five years, Packard called the Associates on a Friday night and told them he was prepared to exercise the option on Monday, and for them to spend the weekend coming up with a price.

The team members worked night and day, and on Monday morning they sat across the table with a 40-page, flip-chart presentation to justify the price. The presentation included both a high-end estimate that the team thought too greedy and a low-end estimate they were prepared to live with.

As they sat down, Packard saw the booklet. "Hey, what's this?"

"This is our presentation," one of them replied.

Packard frowned, "What do you need a presentation for? I just need a price."

"Well, this is to justify the price."

"Oh," said Packard, "I see. But look, I don't want to have to listen to this entire presentation. How's this? Let me make my offer, and if you don't like it, I'll listen."

The associates swallowed hard and nodded. Then Packard offered them 20 percent more than their high-end estimate. After all, he appreciated even more than they did the value of their work. So, of course, it was the right thing to do.

The HP Way means technologically progressive, but financially conservative, of the highest quality (and sometimes the highest price), with dignity toward customers, peers, and even competitors, and a sense that you are part of a very large, but very close, family.

Once you have experienced the HP Way you never really leave it or Hewlett-Packard. No matter where your life and career lead you, there is always the sense that you left a special place and are now arcing outward in a long circle that may last decades, but will someday bring you home.

Read that before? Of course you have. The combination of innovation, financial stability, and high quality was precisely what

American industry used in the last decade to regain world leadership. The model of linkages between employees, suppliers, distributors, and customers is the same one used in every modern book of business theory.

That's not surprising either. Look in the indexes of the most influential business books of the last 20 years, from "Theory Z" to "The Virtual Corporation," "In Search of Excellence" to "Reengineering the Corporation" to "Built to Last." In almost every case, Hewlett-Packard has served as the model of where to go next, and the HP Way has always been there, waiting for each of us to rediscover its application to a changed world.

Profit-sharing, flex-time, management by walking around, sales force automation, global customer service systems, new employee health programs, reduced workweeks instead of layoffs—HP has always been there first. As such, it has always taken the risks for which the rest of us have eventually enjoyed the benefits.

HP did so because, as always with Packard, it was the right thing to do. HPers weren't employees, they were family; you trusted in them, you protected them, and you expected from them your best. It has taken most of us 60 years to come around to what Packard knew the first day he and Hewlett walked into the garage. And some of us aren't there yet.

There was something else Packard always knew that most entrepreneurs never understand: He allowed others to be smarter than him. Packard was a brilliant man, but even at Stanford, he was surrounded by brighter intellects. Hewlett was a far superior engineer, and Barney Oliver and Russ Varian were authentic geniuses. Packard found a way to befriend all of them, and in the case of the first two, work with them the rest of his life.

Packard would do the same with the long parade of stellar young scientists and managers that followed. If most were too entrepreneurial themselves to stay at HP, all left changed for the better for their contact with Packard. Most—their names read like the Silicon Valley Hall of Fame: McCracken, Ely, Treybig, Krause, Hawkins, Wozniak—remained in touch thereafter.

This ability to remain in command while yet accepting the sometimes greater talents of others, enabled Packard, more than any entrepreneur before or since, to grow through all the stages of leadership. It is hard to imagine how difficult it is for the founding entrepreneur of a new start-up company to evolve into the president of an established mid-sized firm . . . yet look how few make it. And fewer still can progress on to be the CEO of a Fortune 500 corporation.

Those who then become an industry spokesman you can count on two hands; you need only one to list those businessmen who then go on to become national figures. Add to that great philanthropy and you are down to just Bill and Dave. Finally, to reach that pinnacle where you assume the role of industry patriarch, there is only Packard. He wore it easily, as he did everything else.

In 1983, when the queen of England toured Silicon Valley, there was no question that her host was David Packard. At the reception that night, Jerry Sanders of Advanced Micro Devices, himself a Valley pioneer, the CEO of a company racing toward a billion dollars, and a man accustomed to recognition and fame, was stunned to see Packard wave to him from across the room and say, "Hi Jerry!" A week later, as he recounted the story, Sanders beamed, "I mean, David Packard knew who I was!"

▼▲▼

In the end, Packard's greatest legacy is his own life and how he conducted it. It is no coincidence that the best local companies adopt HP-like traits, or that the most ambitious high-tech executives seem to be following the paths he first cut, to Washington, to the creation of charitable foundations and to public service. In death now, as in life, David Packard is the yardstick by which we in Silicon Valley measure ourselves.

On the day he died, one local radical Democrat said, "Packard was the only Republican I ever respected."

Packard returned this respect with loyalty, which, after all, is one form of integrity. Loyalty comes in many shapes, all of which he exhibited in spades.

One type of loyalty is friendship. The partnership of David Packard and Bill Hewlett is one of the most famous friendships of our time, and is nearly unique in business history. Bill and Dave weren't just business partners, they were best friends. They not only worked together, but played together as well. For six decades, through hard times and great times, there is no record of them having a single major dust-up. Not one. This isn't just a miracle; it is a testament to nearly infinite trust.

But that wasn't the only example of such loyalty. The friends Packard made in the early years of HP, from his vice presidents to secretaries, he kept for the rest of his life. When they needed help, he was there for them. As another ex-HPer, Bill Krause of Storm Tech has noted, when it came to work, Packard was hard-hearted, demanding perfection from everyone in the company, but when it came to his employee's lives, he was the most soft-hearted of men.

And it is emblematic of the loyalty of both Packard and Hewlett that when they made an immense donation to build a new engineering center at Stanford (an act of loyalty in itself to their alma mater), they chose not to put their own names on the facility, but that of their old teacher, Fred Terman.

Another type of loyalty is fidelity. Much has been written about David Packard's half-century marriage to Lucile Salter and their extraordinary charitable work together, most notably the Children's Hospital at Stanford. But what is less remarked upon is his extraordinary dedication to his children. When you walk into the Monterey Bay Aquarium you see only the most famous but least important part of the story; what really mattered was David Packard the father, in his overalls, helping build some of the aquarium's exhibits with his own hands.

Finally, loyalty is patriotism. Packard's patriotism was made famous (or notorious) by his self-imposed pay cut in World War II, his willingness to take a thankless job in Washington at the height of the Vietnam War, and his outspoken conservatism. But it was much more complicated than that. Few Pentagon insiders have ever been so tough on the military or its contractors. For Packard, the man who could not be trusted could not claim to be an American patriot, no matter how hard he waved the flag. And if that meant a break from at least one president of the United States, so be it.

If there is a flaw in the HP Way it is complacency. A company, as it grows old and fat and rich, can become content in its superiority. That is the sure path to oblivion, especially today, in our fast-moving, hypercompetitive world.

In the late 1980s, as if reflecting the growing age of its founders, Hewlett-Packard began to slowly rot from the inside. The world was changing fast, entire product categories such as the once dominant minicomputers, seemed to evaporate overnight. Only the most nimble firms managed to survive by dancing ahead of events. Meanwhile, sclerotic, flat-footed giants like Wang, Data General and DEC—HP's toughest old competitors—were sunk or left crippled in the water.

The clock was now ticking on Hewlett-Packard, and HP acted as if it didn't care. The entire company seemed bloated and out of touch, its employees buried in endless meetings. Products were late or inconsequential, marketing programs were half-hearted or misdirected and the best talent was bailing out for more exciting opportunities elsewhere. Even suppliers seemed to have caught HP's disease, consistently delivering components late or incongruent with the original orders. Bill and Dave, each now approaching 80, had long since pulled away from the day-to-day activities of the firm, and were on the brink of full retirement.

Hewlett-Packard Co. was dying.

What saved the firm was the HP Way, or, more precisely, the relationship of trust the two founders had created with their employees. It was a note to Packard from a longtime HPer, a note that would never have been sent to the chairman of any other company, a note that never would have been read and believed by any other corporate chairman, that turned Hewlett-Packard around.

The note was simply a complaint by this HPer that she was wasting all of her time in meetings instead of getting anything productive done, and that this problem seemed endemic to the entire company. Packard, and Hewlett with him, saw much more.

Thus, at an age when rich old men retire to their country homes and resist any threat of change, Packard and Hewlett set off a revolution in the giant company they had once built. It was their last hurrah, and one of the most heroic acts in modern business.

Before they were done, Hewlett-Packard had been all but turned upside down. Decision making had been streamlined, recalcitrant managers retired, customer service improved, relationships with suppliers revitalized (the problems there turned out to be HP's own fault), and the company had been turned again into an aggressive force.

The result, as we know, was historic. By the mid-1990s, HP was the fastest growing, and most profitable large company in America. It again dominated entire markets, such as printers, and was making huge in-roads in everything from graphical workstations to PCs.

No one knows just how close HP came to disaster, but it is very likely the difference was Packard's willingness to trust the judgment of one HPer he barely knew. Had the truth taken traditional channels to emerge in another year or two, it might have been too late for the company or for the old men who saved it just in time.

The first time I met David Packard was in 1976. I was a 22-year-old rookie employee in HP's corporate PR department. He had agreed to write a letter of recommendation for me to graduate school (you can imagine how Stanford reacted to that letterhead) and, in typical manner, Packard had wanted to meet me.

In those days, HP's main building was in the old facility on the hilltop above its current headquarters. As was HP's practice, since imitated by everyone else, the entire floor was wide open, and it was easy to see Bill and Dave and all the vice presidents standing around during coffee break each morning at one of the ubiquitous coffee and doughnut stations. I had even once spent a very nervous lunch sitting next to Bill and Dave on a bench in the HP cafeteria.

But this time was different. I was going into Packard's office itself. And I was terrified. I remember standing with my boss, PR director Dave Kirby, outside the closed office door as Packard's lifelong gatekeeper and executive assistant Margaret Paull, called in.

Then the door opened and a giant appeared. David Packard, all 6 feet 5 inches of him, was at the height of his powers, a silver-haired titan of industry who looked to me, at that moment, like God himself.

I remember a giant hand enveloping mine and then we were in the room. It was big and filled with photographs and flags and awards. I managed to say something stupid to the effect that it was a very impressive office. Packard chuckled in a deep rumble and pointed at the floor over by the window, "I don't know about that. See over there? The linoleum's starting to come up. I'd have it fixed but I'm going to retire soon anyway."

Then he ushered me to a sofa. Under the glass top of the coffee table at my knee was his folded Defense Department flag.

David Packard sat on the couch beside me and started to ask me questions.

I had expected to be drilled on my knowledge of the philosophy of science to see if I was worthy of his recommendation. But just the opposite occurred. Dazed as I was, it dawned on me that a David Packard, the David Packard, appreciated my nervousness and was taking great pains to make me feel comfortable. He was concerned about me. Like many before and after me, I left his office grateful to have met such a man.

▼▲▼

The last time I met David Packard was three years ago. It was to talk about my participation in a book, "The HP Way," that would in the end be written without me. In a kind of strange autumnal symmetry, the cast of players, albeit nearly 20 years older, the same. Kirby, now retired, again walked me up to Margaret Paull. This time, however, Packard had not yet arrived, so we both were escorted into the boardroom.

While we waited, Kirby told me a recent story about how Packard had asked to join the board of a major biotech firm. Wanting to bone up on genetic engineering in preparation for his first quarterly meeting, Packard had sent his handyman off to Stanford's bookstore with a long list of books on genetic engineering.

The result was that a few weeks later at the meeting Packard asked such penetrating questions about recombinant DNA that the company's executives had to call in their top scientists for answers.

It was vintage Packard, a new late chapter for the legend. David Packard was once more larger than life. It was enough to make me believe that the years hadn't passed; that the same man I knew would enter the room.

But then the door opened. At 80, David Packard was shockingly old, as very tall men seem to be. His voice was an even deeper rumble, like thunder, and having just recovered from an infection, he moved carefully and with great fragility. It would have been heartbreaking, but for his mind. There, he hadn't lost a step.

He was still gracious, but tougher now, almost curt, as if there wasn't much time left to waste on delicacies. The legendary David Packard and the real man now seemed detached from one another, as if the myth was ready to break free and take wing.

The last I saw of him was out the boardroom window. He was outside now, hunched in a cold wind, taking instructions as always from Margaret Paull. Then, an ancient king in his blessed kingdom, he set off alone to face his last challenge.

As always, he did it right and he did it well.

From the *San Jose Mercury News,* March 31, 1996.

23

PIXIE'S LAST LESSONS

Appropriately, Pixie died while I was at a meeting discussing the future of the Internet. I missed her departure from this world by minutes. She was stretched out on the bathroom floor next to her bowl of water and untouched plate of food. Her body was still limp and warm.

Thankfully, it hadn't been a lonely death. My wife and youngest son had spent the morning holding and petting and talking softly to her. They had left briefly to pick up my oldest son from school when I returned and found her. Even in death, Pixie looked beautiful. At 18, she was an old cat but looked half her age—and the bath at the vet, which had probably given her the fatal heart attack, made her look even younger.

I picked her up and cradled her in my arms, the way I had every night of her life, and carried her around the house. Six thousand nights. Since she was a kitten named Scoundrel. Since she had moved in with us from the house next door, with its endless parties and drug dealers. Since she had played with a black widow spider and had been left to lie near death for a week.

Now, almost two decades later, long after she'd outlived most of the creatures and even some of the people who had bedeviled her, death came for Pixie after just four days of illness. It was the kind of gentle departure that often comes to the very old. Our 96-year-old neighbor, at whose house Pixie was known as Lady, had time to say goodbye to her friends before slipping away. My grandmother, visiting one of my aunts, went to bed early, and in the morning my cousin found her lying in bed, her clothes neatly folded on a chair, her arms carefully folded across her chest.

Even while Pixie was ill, I was editing an essay by a technology futurist. In it, he predicted that, thanks to the relentless pace of technological innovation, people would soon begin loading the electrical grid of their own brains onto computer disks. Encoded literally as ghosts in the machine, their brains could be upgraded quickly with new languages and libraries of knowledge, linked directly to the world via the Internet, and, of course, regularly copied and debugged. As stunning as this prediction was, what made it even more disquieting was the futurist's absolute confidence that human beings would happily surrender their corporeal selves for a chance at digital immortality.

He wasn't alone in hearing the faint echo of living heartbeats emanating from the silvery surface of a silicon chip. Others are looking at the Internet, with its hundreds of millions of networked personal computers and servers, and seeing a digital leviathan, a metaorganism about to shake itself to awareness. At MIT, they are debating whether turning off a new robot constitutes an act of murder. Onscreen, as the new *Star Wars* draws millions to a technocatechism, director George Lucas expresses real regret that, for now, he still has to work with human actors.

On the wall above my oldest son's bed is a poster of all the Pokémon characters—a menagerie of 150 creatures, some mutations of others, all designed by Japanese animators. Pokémon isn't just a comic book but a trading card set, stuffed animals, a video game, and a television show whose throbbing graphics were once accused of causing seizures. And if that weren't enough, you can buy a special cable and link your Pokémon-playing Game Boy to your friend's and discover additional "pocket monsters" together.

In this alternative consumer universe, little Pikachu and its horde of confederates aren't just cartoons but the first multimedia creatures, rounded out not by flesh and bone but by multiple formats. And that makes them infinitely more intriguing than any real animal. Perhaps that was why I often saw my oldest son, 8, reach out and absently stroke Pixie's ears but then turn and focus on the figures gamboling across the little LCD screen of his Game Boy.

Today we are all dreaming the ultimate dream—immortality. No doubt it is because science has entered the game, and for 400 years now, wherever science has played, it has won. Disease, time, space, even God himself, have retreated before the relentless march of the scientific method. Physicists now speak triumphantly of the Theory of Everything, the imminent empirical proof of superstring theory and the knitting together of the five basic forces into the pentagram of all existence. So when biologists confidently announce that human beings will soon live to 150, who are we to doubt? One hundred fifty isn't immortality, but you might be able to see it from there.

Moreover, we already have, literally at our fingertips, proof that technology can do just what it claims. Medusa conferred a form of immortality by turning passersby into undying stone. Solid-state physics, the most influential science of this closing century, does much the same thing, and its unruly stepchild, semiconductor technology, grows 100 million tiny crystalline statues every day. The integrated circuit, especially its evolved form, the microprocessor, is as close to an immortal creature as God or man has yet devised. Left literally to its own devices, and barring a power surge, a chip will outlive the oldest bristlecone pine. Only cosmic rays, hurtling across the universe, can really harm it. Encase it in diamond (which we will), adapt it to derive power from the stars (which we will), and fling it into space (which we already do), and it will likely still be muttering its Boolean thoughts, a billion a second, as the cosmos goes black.

The chip is immortal because it is magnificently elemental. It was Gordon Moore, the man who helped invent the chip, who first pointed out that the integrated circuit is made from the most plentiful and enduring things on earth: silicon sand, oxygen, water, and heat. Fire, water, earth, and air; Anaximenes redux—the theories of the Greek scientist-philosophers made manifest by immigrant vestals of the Gorgon, dressed in cleanroom bunny suits.

We can't help but look at these tiny wonders and feel both admiration and fear. We are in awe of the microprocessor because it presents an impossible balance between complexity of design and singleness of purpose. Set before it a vast problem and it will chase the solution, at an unimaginable speed, until the end of time. We console ourselves with the conclusion that this makes chips mere idiot savants, but at 400 million calculations per second for thousands of years, this is a kind of divine idiocy before which we can only stand in wonderment.

That wonderment is also why we fear the chip. We sense that it is leaving us behind. A gigahertz processor experiences in less than a second the equivalent of all the thoughts we have in a lifetime. And there will soon be 100 billion such processors. And a trillion other chips—more than all of the mammals, including man, on earth. And chips are social creatures. Take a few hundred microprocessors, add a few thousand support chips for memory and communications, hook them together, and you have a supercomputer capable of sophisticated speech recognition, robotic control, even the building of other chips. In 20 more years there will be as many silicon gates in one of these computers as there are neurons in the human brain. Link a computer via a broadband Internet to millions of other computers, large and small, around the world, and the great cyberhomunculus rears its silicon and fiber head.

But you have only to look at the empty heart of a computer to realize that terra incognita will be a cold, empty place. Chase immortality down an optical fiber and you may find endless existence—at the cost of everything else.

It's not that we haven't been warned many times. The first warning came 400 years ago, literally on the morning the modern world was created. Tucked into the pages of the book that gave us the scientific revolution, *The Advancement of Learning*, there is a tiny phrase that may prove the most important and enduring admonition ever given. This revolution, Francis Bacon said, must be "for the uses of life." Since he was also a consummate politician and one of the greatest of all essayists, we can assume this was not a throwaway line. The Lord Chancellor meant what he said, and he meant it both ways: Science must always work to improve life and always be at the service of living things.

Bacon wasn't alone. Two hundred years ago, Mary Shelley tried to warn us again. The real monster in *Frankenstein* is not the poor, tragic creature—though, tellingly, here in this century we've convinced ourselves it is—but the doctor himself. He is a man of science and genius who sets out to find the secret of life so that, a Modern Prometheus, he can bestow the gift of immortality on mankind. How fitting that the story should reach its climax in the frozen Arctic.

The third, and perhaps final, warning about technology and immortality came from the anthropologist Loren Eiseley. Eiseley is (or was) justly celebrated for the powerful imagery in his essays: the snout rising up from the primordial ooze to sniff fresh air, the Neanderthal man walking down a crowded city street, the cave filled with millions of daddy longlegs—and most famously, the "star thrower," the solitary figure flinging beached and stranded starfish back into the waves.

But in Eiseley's greatest essay, the opposite is true: The images are unforgettable precisely because they are unexceptional. Eiseley finds himself on a beach, sitting under a beached boat. There, his thoughts cast back 30 years to the death of his father, a once powerful, vital man reduced at the end to little more than a shadow. Eiseley is paralyzed with his sorrow. Just then, he discovers he is not alone. He sees the tiny, excited face of a fox pup—"alone in a dread universe" but not afraid.

"He innocently selected what I think was a chicken bone from an untidy pile of splintered rubbish and shook it at me invitingly. There was a vast and playful humor in his face . . . the wide-eyed innocent fox inviting me to play, with the innate courtesy of its two forepaws placed appealingly together, along with a mock shake of the head. The universe was swinging in some fantastic fashion around to present its face, and the face was so small that the universe itself was laughing."

Deciding it is "not a time for human dignity," Eiseley arranges his own forepaws together, then leans forward, picks up a bone in his teeth and shakes it. The "puppy whimpered with ill-concealed excitement." Soon they are rolling around together, laughing and barking.

It is that gesture by the fox, the two cinnabar paws poised together in expectation, that redeems and saves Eiseley's life. The middle-aged scientist knows he can now go on. He can accept his father's death and ultimately his own. Life has once again closed the circle. The Innocent Fox, at the start of its own brief arc, is ready to play.

The message of all of Eiseley's essays is that nature is surpassingly strange. That this strangeness is our link with all living things. And that buried at the heart of this strangeness, perhaps forever unknowable, is our purpose.

Strangeness colors all of life, across the panorama of species, from beginning to end. It was there when I closed my father's eyes and when I watched my infant sons open theirs. It's there in the movements of the raccoon who rules my yard by night, and the Cooper's hawk who hunts the same yard by day. It's there in the indifferent brutality of the scorpion in my oldest son's terrarium. And in the endless wakefulness of the goldfish who tirelessly circles in a glass tank nearby.

Most of all, it was there in Pixie. The same cat who always kept a careful distance from the mischievous hands of our boys also managed to appear within the frame of every photograph we took of them. The same creature who would meet me at night with the wild look of a killer and who would torture a mouse until it finally succumbed to trauma and shock, also stayed on the bed with my wife during her second, horrifying pregnancy—creakily limping outside only when forced to do so.

Thanks to technology, we can pretend the animals are still around, only safely packaged, controlled, and edited. We can turn on the Discovery Channel and watch, in the comfort of the living room, exotic animals we would never normally encounter. We can see them at the zoo. Or dissect them on the computer. Better yet, we can invent our own, like the legions of Pokémon, all of them odd but never strange. Always anthropomorphic, they can never live their lives without us. Only our pets remain, and in my son's absentminded gesture of patting Pixie's head, then turning back to the computer screen, I fear I saw the future all too well.

Once we lived embedded in the world of living things different from us. It was scary and exhilarating and instructional. In the animals around us, we found a definition of life and even, if only for an instant, thought we caught a glimpse of God passing by. We were within life, if only because we had no choice.

We now have that choice. And despite the warnings, we are turning away to a new partner. A partner that is perfectly knowable, perfectly predictable, and never dies. R2-D2 has already replaced Lassie. The sexiest woman on television is a Borg. And as we are now turning, soon we will be running, then racing with our arms outstretched toward that distant point of convergence with our machines, that frozen place where thoughts are singular and forever.

But we are not there yet. If we are lucky, we may never get there. And if and when we realize the futility of the chase, we will find ourselves alone . . . and rediscover that we are the strangest creatures of all.

We buried Pixie beneath the holly tree. It may be the oldest holly tree in California, probably brought as a seedling from Maryland during the Civil War. I dug the hole alone. Then my little family gathered as I lowered Pixie's tiny, blanket-wrapped body. My wife and children cried. My voice caught as I said a few words. Then we went back to our cell phones and computers and video games.

Unselfconsciously, through a precise combination of claws and purrs, flirtation and denial, Pixie taught my boys to be better human beings—and me a better parent. No video game and no intelligent agent/expert will ever do that. Those are the most important lessons of all, and those are the ones we are about to lose.

We cannot learn the big things from our machines, from our special effects, because they are not strange. At best, they are merely very precise mirrors.

When all that is left is reflections of ourselves, who will tell us what matters? Who will teach us how to live? And most of all, who will show us how to die?

From *Forbes ASAP* © Forbes, Inc., "The Big Issue," October 4, 1999. Reprinted with permission.

24

SECOND SIGHT

I bought it on eBay as a lark, in the days when we all felt rich enough to do such flippant things. I don't even remember my winning bid, which says something as well.

It came in a three-foot square cardboard box, which I opened on the driveway to minimize the mess, as workmen behind me sanded and hammered away while restoring my house. It was wrapped in a black foam sheet encased in wadded pages of the *Connecticut Post*. One headline read: "Gates Tells Congress to Trust High Tech."

I knew what I'd find when I pulled away the sheet: a Norden bombsight. But I was still taken aback by its presence.

It was black as anthracite, with dust in every corner and curve. The dust of an English runway, perhaps? Or sand from North Africa? Perhaps just the cobwebs of the garage in which it had sat for the past half century.

It seemed less menacing than coldly malign, in the way only a relic weapon could. Twenty pounds, not much bigger than a football, with a cylinder at one end, a sphere at the other. It was seeded with knurled knobs and toothed gears and dials. From one side hung an old cloth-insulated wire terminating in a plug. Underneath, it held a small pane of glass the size of a cigarette pack. On top, a second pane opened like a porthole into the sphere. And at the center, covered with a rotting rubber eye protector, was a lens.

I set the contraption atop the recycling bin and stepped back to regard it. On that bright Northern California day, my prize seemed like a dark emissary from a forgotten time. From one angle it looked like a clock mechanism, from another an automobile transmission, from yet another a bomb.

It was, in fact, all three. Mounted in the nose of a B-17 bomber, attached with gyroscopes and rotating mirrors and cables to the airplane around it, and manipulated by a deft bombardier, the Norden was the most dangerous weapon in the world in the early years of World War II. Once it was set on a target and adjusted for airspeed and other variables, the Norden literally took over for the pilot, flying the plane on a strict approach path and telling the bombardier when to push the button to release the ton of bombs or incendiaries from their racks 10 feet behind him.

So technologically innovative and important was the Norden— neither the Germans nor the Japanese had anything close—that bombardiers were sworn to do whatever was necessary to keep one from falling into enemy hands. If the bomber was going down, they were to pull out their .45-caliber automatic and shoot it, pull a switch that ignited an explosive mounted inside the device. Or, if all else failed, they were to obey orders to ride the plane right down into oblivion in the German soil.

My father sat at just such a Norden bombsight on a rickety seat in the Plexiglas nose of the "Badland Bat," a B-17 in the 615th Squadron of the 401st Bomb Group of the 8th Air Force. As the barrels of the twin .50-caliber machine guns cooled from his futile attempts to shoot attacking German fighters, as flak burst just beyond the glass and dying men in planes around him screamed into his headsets, and as his heart pounded and his hands shook from the fear and the adrenaline, he would bow his head as though in prayer and bring his eye against the frozen eyepiece. Twisting one knob, then another, he would align the reticulated crosshairs on the target. Then, so frightened with helplessness and horror that the passing seconds seemed like days, he would hit the switch that surrendered control of his life and those of the seven men around him to that little black machine.

The target itself had been identified that morning at a predawn briefing in a Quonset hut thick with the smell of cigarettes and coffee. The target always had a name—Schweinfurt, Cologne, Berlin—and a title: ball bearing factory, pillboxes, industrial district. But on the map and in the crosshairs, it was merely an image of a bridge or a crossroads, or the shape of a building. There were no people in sight; just the abstract shapes of targets and then the sudden blooming of explosions as the "Badland Bat" left a swath of fire across a hundred miles of German farms, villages, and towns.

Thirty times over Germany and France between January and June 1944, my father bowed to his bombsight. Looking back, he would tell me that for all the terrors of being fired on by antiaircraft guns and being strafed by German fighters as his bomber flew into and out of target zones, the worst moments were always those seconds when he handed his life over to the Norden—the long moments as he waited for it to tell him to rain death over the countryside.

My father was a young man of intelligence and imagination, and those combat experiences made him brazen. He sneaked off the base the night before D-day to meet a girl in a local pub. They also made him cold-hearted. When a rookie crew arrived to replace his hut mates who had died in an earlier raid, my father teased them, saying they'd taken the doomed side of the shelter; they died the next day on their very first mission. But, after four months and 25 missions, the experience began to break his mind.

In letters home, the cocky young man who'd circumvented the censors by disguising his number of raids as his birthday ("I am 21 years old today.") found himself toward the end struggling to compose a single coherent sentence ("I can't seem to keep my mind on one thought anymore.").

Unlike every second man in the 8th Air Force, my father made it home alive and unhurt. Five years later, he was back overseas, this time—on a Pacific island and with a new job in Air Force intelligence. Through another lens this one shielding his eye with a smoky black filter—he watched purple lightning crackle across the mushroom clouds born from nuclear tests being conducted on barren atolls.

I was a Cold War baby, born in Munich, then a city of vacant lots scraped smooth of the rubble of a once thriving metropolis. It had become a Norden world, with all of us hurtling forward on autopilot over a menacing landscape. Only a few people, like my father as he took the .32-caliber automatic out of the closet and headed for the Czech border, still felt they had some control of their fate.

But soon he lost even that. At the end of the decade we came home. My father found himself closing his military career in Washington, D.C., shuttling back and forth as liaison officer between the war rooms of the Pentagon and the White House, and between the CIA and the FBI. It was a position of enormous responsibility but little control. My father began to sit alone at lunch in the garden of the Hirshhorn Museum to calm himself; on Friday nights he would drink to fend off his sense of the inevitable.

He reached its nadir in October 1962. On duty nights, my mother would awaken me at midnight and we would drive from Falls Church, Virginia, into D.C., me in pajamas and wrapped in a blanket in the back seat. It was usually so lonely and dark that I would sleep the whole way. But this night was unlike any other.

Every light in every building on Pennsylvania Avenue and along the Capitol Mall seemed to be on. Yet, the streets were eerily empty.

We picked up my father. He usually drove us home, but on this night he was incapable of holding the steering wheel. His voice had a tone I'd never heard before—a tone it probably hadn't taken in almost 20 years. The Cuban Missile Crisis had begun. Earlier, during the day, my father had sat alone, in the basement of the Office of Special Investigations (OSI) headquarters before a bank of Teletype code machines, reading with growing horror as they spit out the beginning of the end of the world. The ICBMs armed, Strategic Air Command (SAC) at fail-safe, airborne divisions kneeling beside runways. He had known as much as anybody on earth about what was unfolding, but he could do nothing about it. The bombsight had taken over. And for hours he sat helpless at ground zero, waiting to die, knowing his family would die as well.

Suddenly, it was over. Everything seemed to change. Although it was still a Norden world, the target had receded for the moment. My father had almost been a victim. A heart attack a few weeks later nearly killed him. But he survived, retired from the military with honor and took a job with NASA, heading west with his family to California.

We arrived in Silicon Valley just in time to join the illusion. The Valley had been born of war. Military contracts had built Hewlett-Packard and Varian; the nuclear age had given birth to the Valley's largest employer, Lockheed Missile and Space. So too had defense orders underwritten the success of the Valley's first modern company, Fairchild Semiconductor. All had grown rich building successive generations of weaponry; they would grow richer yet.

About the time we arrived, in an event all but forgotten even by historians of technology, the Federal Communications Commission announced that all future televisions would offer not only VHF tuners but UHF tuners as well. It was a little event of immeasurable consequences. Chasing million-unit orders, the chip industry for the first time turned away from the bombsight business and toward the department store.

It has never turned back. I remember the day my father brought home a Hewlett-Packard 35 calculator and pronounced it a miracle. I remember standing in line, with the boys who would later create the personal computer revolution, in the lobby of a NASA building waiting my turn to play Lunar Lander on a computer terminal. I saw the first Atari video game in the hallway of a comedy club down the street from my house. And I walked with my father through a trade show in San Francisco and saw the Apple I, built by two of my neighbors.

America no longer seemed a Norden nation. Our fate was no longer on autopilot. Sometimes we even imagined we were flying the plane. My father cheated death for a quarter century. Each time his heart would fail, some new technology appeared on the scene to save him. He traveled the world, programmed his computer, drank beer, and gave his time to charitable work, acting as though death couldn't catch him. And when he did die—from a fall off a ladder, not from his scarred old heart—even his death seemed an act of will, not helplessness.

It was now a willful world, as though an alchemy of technology and desire would deliver to us all of our dreams. Our enemies were less defeated than enlisted into a cybernetic common cause. The autopilot retreated so far into memory that two generations forgot it. We replaced it with nostalgia for the future: the aching desire for that distant, more perfect place we could already imagine, promised to us by our technologies. Our perpetual unhappiness was that we were not there yet, a there that raced ahead from calculators and PCs to bioengineering and nanomachines. Somewhere, no doubt just ahead, lay the fulfillment of all our desires. The beauty of it was that now, it seemed, anyone could plot his own flight path and pilot his own life.

Second Sight

It was in that prelapsarian time, just ended yet long ago, that I carried the Norden bombsight out to the sunny driveway, past the workmen and the new Jaguar, all of them paid for with overvalued stock options. I set it atop the recycling bin, filled with newspaper headlines about the latest stock market record high: "eBay's Whitman America's Richest Woman CEO." I looked through the eyepiece . . . and saw nothing. Nothing except a mirror reflection of the brilliant day before me.

Disappointed, I put the device back in its box, another bauble from the bubble, and returned it to the garage, between the old, unread art books and the new, unused porcelain—an evil old black toad forgotten in the shadows.

Then late on a mid-September afternoon I took the box out again. Our family had just returned from church, where we had, with other Silicon Valleyites in the pews around us, wept and prayed for the thousands murdered by terrorists. As I bowed my head, I felt the distant mechanical shudder of the autopilot kicking in once more. Driving home, I could see my neighbors putting out American flags and glancing up nervously at any sound overhead. We put out a flag of our own. Then, without thinking, I went into the garage and brought out the Norden.

I did the same as before, though the day was overcast, and the papers in the new recycling bin carried headlines proclaiming "WAR." The Norden was dustier and darker than ever. The eyepiece seemed harder and more brittle. Once again, I bowed and put my face to it. Looking through the lens I saw this time what I had missed before. What my father had seen before me.

I saw my family and home caught squarely in the bombsight's crosshairs.

ABOUT THE AUTHOR

Michael S. Malone has been called "the Boswell of Silicon Valley" by the *San Jose Mercury News*. He was raised in Silicon Valley and holds a bachelor's degree in combined sciences and an MBA from Santa Clara University. He hosted *Malone*, a half-hour interview program that ran for nine seasons and was seen on PBS stations nationwide. His current 16-part TV series, *Betting It All: The Entrepreneurs,* an in-depth look at some of America's most famous entrepreneurs, will appear on PBS stations beginning May 3, 2001.

Beyond the television programs, Malone is best known as an author. His first book, *The Big Score: The Billion Dollar Story of Silicon Valley* (Doubleday), was named one of the top 10 business books of 1985 by *Business Week*.

The book grew out of Malone's years at the *San Jose Mercury News* as the nation's first daily high-tech reporter, where he co-authored the first investigative stories on toxic waste contamination, workplace drug abuse, and espionage in Silicon Valley. *The Big Score* went on to become the basis for the KTEH documentary series *Silicon Valley,* which aired on PBS in 1987. Another documentary hosted and written by Malone, *Future Tense*, earned a 1996 cable television Telly award.

In the past decade, Malone's articles and editorials have appeared in such publications as the *New York Times* (where he was a columnist for two years), the *Wall Street Journal,* the *Economist, Forbes ASAP,* and *Fortune.* He was featured as a lead essayist (with Tom Wolfe and Mark Helprin) in the celebrated *Forbes ASAP Big Issue* (1996).

About his book, *Going Public* (HarperCollins), published in 1991, *Inc.* magazine wrote that it "contains all the suspense and intrigue of a Robert Ludlum thriller." In 1992, Malone co-authored (with William H. Davidow) *The Virtual Corporation* (Harper-Collins), which became the subject of a cover story in *Business Week* and was one of the most influential business books of the decade. *The Microprocessor: A Biography* (Telos/Springer-Verlag) was published in September 1995 and was the winner of a Critic's Choice Award. *Virtual Selling* (Free Press), co-authored with Tom Siebel, was published in February 1996. *Intellectual Capital,* co-authored with Leif Edvinsson, was published in March 1997. His latest nonfiction book, *Infinite Loop: How the World's Most Insanely Great Computer Company Went Insane,* about Apple Computer, was published by Doubleday in February 1999. It was named one of the top tech and business books in 1999 by the *Library Journal.*

In August 1998, Malone was named editor of *Forbes ASAP.* He is now Editor-at-Large. He also has a weekly column on ABCNews.com called "Silicon Insider."

INDEX

INDEX

Index